ARY
NOTES AND MANC

# STATE OF THE ART

## IN

# Clinical Supervision

Edited by John R. Culbreth and Lori L. Brown

# STATE OF THE ART

## IN

# Clinical Supervision

**Routledge**
Taylor & Francis Group
New York   London

Routledge
Taylor & Francis Group
270 Madison Avenue
New York, NY 10016

Routledge
Taylor & Francis Group
27 Church Road
Hove, East Sussex BN3 2FA

© 2010 by Taylor and Francis Group, LLC
Routledge is an imprint of Taylor & Francis Group, an Informa business

Printed in the United States of America on acid-free paper
10 9 8 7 6 5 4 3 2 1

International Standard Book Number: 978-0-415-99130-8 (Hardback)

For permission to photocopy or use material electronically from this work, please access www.
copyright.com (http://www.copyright.com/) or contact the Copyright Clearance Center, Inc.
(CCC), 222 Rosewood Drive, Danvers, MA 01923, 978-750-8400. CCC is a not-for-profit organization that provides licenses and registration for a variety of users. For organizations that have been
granted a photocopy license by the CCC, a separate system of payment has been arranged.

**Trademark Notice:** Product or corporate names may be trademarks or registered trademarks, and
are used only for identification and explanation without intent to infringe.

---

**Library of Congress Cataloging-in-Publication Data**

---

State of the art in clinical supervision / [edited by] John R. Culbreth and Lori L.
  Brown.
    p. cm.
  Includes bibliographical references and index.
  ISBN 978-0-415-99130-8 (hardcover : alk. paper)
  1. Counselors--Supervision of. I. Culbreth, John R. II. Brown, Lori L.
  [DNLM: 1. Counseling--organization & administration. 2. Clinical
Competence. 3. Personnel Management--methods. WM 55 S797 2009]

BF636.65.S73 2009
158'.307155--dc22                                                                                 2009012536

---

**Visit the Taylor & Francis Web site at**
**http://www.taylorandfrancis.com**

**and the Routledge Web site at**
**http://www.routledgementalhealth.com**

It seems weird to write a dedication in a book. Something that other people do, but not me. But here goes. I continue to be greatly appreciative of the support I receive from my wife, Barbara, and her patience with her husband and his "projects." My son is one of my constant, in the moment, teachers of how to keep perspective on the important things in life. Sometimes I don't pay attention enough, and he reminds in his wonderful, 12-year-old way. Thank you Alex. Let's go play some video games. And finally, I would like to dedicate my work in this book to my father, Jack Culbreth. I can't think of a better way to learn how to be than from watching you in all your snortin', spittin', carryin' on, wrestling with CHANGE, working on our relationship, and continuing to softly support me in my own personal AFGEs, especially over the past year or so with Allen, a new and wonderful relationship that has blossomed more than I ever imagined possible. I am not sure that you will ever truly know how much I appreciate you, and who you have helped me to become. Thanks Dad!

**John R. Culbreth**

This book would not have been possible without the diligence and hard work of the authors, especially that of my co-editor, Jack Culbreth. You made it happen, Jack! Also, I want to dedicate this book to my husband James Zisa, for his strength and support, and to his parents William and Viola Zisa, for doing such a wonderful job with their son.

**Lori L. Brown**

TRUST LIBRARY
CENTRAL MANCHESTER AND MANCHESTER
CHILDREN'S UNIVERSITY HOSPITALS
NHS TRUST
EDUCATION CAMPUS SOUTH, OXFORD ROAD
MANCHESTER, M13 9WL

# Contents

# Preface

We are excited about having the opportunity to help create, develop, and promote the ideas that are included in this book. There are many fascinating and creative ideas about counseling supervision that often have very small audiences. It is our intent to hopefully expand the audience for at least a few of those ideas through the pages of this book. As we have spent time conducting our own research and writing on the topic of counseling supervision through the years, it has seemed as though there was a tendency to repeat a lot of the questions or concepts, with merely a change of dressing to make them different. One could certainly argue that this is the case for many topics. And while that may be so, both of us believe there is a greater depth to the topic of counseling supervision.

This book began as an effort to help answer a simple question: "What are the topics in the field of counseling supervision that do not seem to get much exposure in the traditional professional venues?" In other words, how can we talk about the issues, ideas, methods, and theories that might be considered fringe, or, at the very least, less mainstream? By doing so, we hope to advance the professional discussion about clinical supervision issues and ideas.

As this book idea developed, we began talking about some of these topics, our conversations snowballing into discussions with others, each time picking up speed and excitement over the possibilities. The result is this book; a collection of writings expounding on a variety of topics in the growing field of clinical supervision. Some of these chapters may not interest everyone. Some of the techniques or theories may not work for everyone, either. But we anticipate that many of these ideas will give both practicing and future supervisors pause to consider learning new approaches to dealing with a current challenging supervisory situation in a different and more effective way.

We begin this book with an important topic in the counseling field, multiculturalism, and how it is applied to the supervision setting. Cultural encapsulation can be as much of a problem in the supervisory relationship as it is in the counseling relationship, potentially negatively impacting both. The chapter authors present key findings from the multicultural counseling literature and discuss findings and recommendations for the practicing supervisor and the multicultural supervision context. Specifically, the authors provide guidance for supervisors in how to work in a cross-racial and cross-cultural supervisory relationship. They also provide suggestions for supervisors to consider when working within the cross-racial and/or cross-cultural counseling triad of supervisor, supervisee, and client. It is crucial to remember that we all have a cultural and racial heritage, and that this can be as important in supervision as it is in counseling.

Chapter 2, "No Surprises: Practices in Supervisee Evaluation," is a straightforward examination of one of the most challenging aspects of conducting supervision: that of critically evaluating another practicing professional. Counseling supervisors have long struggled with this aspect of the supervisor role. In speaking with supervisors, we have heard comments about how the act of evaluation is contradictory to a stance of acceptance and unconditional regard toward colleagues. Yet, the reality of the clinical environment is that not all counselors are created equal, and not all counselors function at the same level of skill. Just as we should all be life long learners, good evaluation allows for greater professional development of supervisee and supervisor alike. Is it challenging to deliver difficult feedback? Of course. But is it necessary to maintain the quality of services provided to our clients? Absolutely. The authors of this chapter give you an overview of an evaluation plan that can make this challenging task much more manageable and productive.

The third chapter, "Triadic Supervision," is a discussion of a unique format of supervision that provides supervisors with a way to make better use of their time and energy. Most supervision is conducted either individually or in a group. Each of these settings has its own unique characteristics. The depth that can be attained in individual supervision is significant and powerful. Yet, working with only one person at a time can be both draining and labor intensive. Conducting group supervision is more time efficient for all involved; however, it can often turn into a brief review of cases, lacking sufficient depth to adequately promote counselor professional development. Triadic supervision, or working with two supervisees in a small group, allows the supervisor to increase supervision productivity while sacrificing little of the depth of more individualized supervision.

It can also have the added benefits of supervisees assisting and learning from each other.

The next two chapters provide an overview of several different ways to deliver and conduct clinical supervision. The authors of Chapter 4 examine how developments in technology provide supervisors with new and different ways to deliver counseling supervision to supervisees. Also included in this chapter are ways in which technology can assist in the training of post-masters' level and doctoral supervisors. As with all advances in the tools of our trade, there are both positives and negatives to be considered. This chapter allows you to consider a number of these new approaches as to how they might work for you in your unique supervision or training environment. As the profession of counseling continues to develop, so too does the recognition of counseling supervision as an important role in quality service delivery to clients. Supervisees are in need of quality supervision in all parts of our country. Unfortunately, many of these supervisees do not have an easily accessible, real-time supervisor or supervision environment available to them due to distance or remoteness of location. Technological advances in communication, applied to counseling supervision and supervision training, can provide options for these supervisees, supervisors, students, and trainers that have not been available in the past. We feel that this chapter will be a significant help to many of these professionals, as well as the clients they ultimately serve.

The following chapter authors take a different approach to conducting supervision. Professional counseling has long been seen as flexible and accepting of alternative ways to assist clients through their emotional work. Thus, it follows that we consider how alternative approaches to supervision might help further promote the professional development of practitioners. Chapter 5 presents four very different ways for supervisors and supervisees to interact: using puppetry, psychodrama, bibliosupervision, and sandtray. Each section of the chapter provides an overview of the approach and how it is used in supervision, a list of needed materials, a discussion of issues that may arise when using that modality, and examples from actual supervision interactions. We look forward to this chapter providing a number of opportunities for supervisors to expand beyond their existing molds and explore new worlds of supervision delivery in order to help supervisees improve their knowledge and awareness.

Chapter 6 examines the training of supervisors. The author discusses key principles that should be considered during the course of supervisor training, typically with doctoral-level students. She provides, using an extensive literature review and many years of experience in training supervisors, a series of "Best Practices" that should be considered when training supervisors. For those active in this area, these principles will provide clear guidance on the key issues and approaches to consider in order to produce well trained supervisors capable of delivering oversight to either counselor trainees or already practicing counselors.

Chapter 7, titled "Religion, Spirituality, and Counseling Supervision," is a look at the reality of all our lives, both personal and professional, and how the personal worldview of spirituality enters into the supervisory relationship for both supervisees and supervisors. Because the process of supervision involves some form of a relationship between at least two individuals, we can assume that aspects of our personal lives will become intertwined in the counseling and supervision process. We can hold very deep beliefs on this topic, which can guide our thoughts, feelings, and actions, sometimes without our direct knowledge or awareness. It is important for the supervisor to understand this reality of the counseling process and to also understand how this topic can be brought up in counseling supervision in an accepting and open manner. Discussing spirituality in a work or school setting, as part of counseling supervision, may seem like a risky and unwise direction to take as a supervisor. However, if we as counselors believe that we, as humans, are the "tool" by which our clients get better, then it is critical that we remain open to addressing how we work, and what might impact that work for good or bad. We hope that this chapter provides guidance for supervisors as they negotiate this most challenging of topics.

Clients typically come to counseling to change in some way. In order to effect the desired change, clients need to understand and accept that they will likely be different on the other side of the counseling process. This is often true for supervisees as well, even though it is much less recognized and discussed in the supervision process. Supervisees, as well as supervisors, are at risk of changing parts of themselves, both personally and professionally, as a direct result of the supervision process. Chapter 8 focuses on how to view and facilitate this change in supervisees through a theoretical perspective developed specifically for the change process. The *transtheoretical model*, also known as *stages of change*, was developed to better understand how people go about the change process, regardless of what the change entails. Originally developed to help practitioners reconceptualize the change process for addicted clients, and how they could help clients with change, this model has been adapted to a more generalized view of change regardless of the issue or problem. The authors take the position that change is an inherent part of the supervision process, primarily, but not exclusively, for supervisees. With that in mind, they provide a different way to consider working with supervisees using the template of the change process as it fits in the supervisory relationship. Included in this chapter is a description of the processes of change, the stages of change that a person will go through, and the levels or types of change that a person can make. Examples of this view of supervision are provided for a clearer understanding of how supervisees change.

The past two decades have seen the introduction of a new theory of counseling called *narrative therapy*. The foundation of this theory is that individuals, through their lived experiences, create an ongoing "story" that is their life. It is through these stories that people make sense of their world and what happens to them. Overall, this is a universal construct that applies to the supervisor and supervisee as well. Chapter 9, "Applications of Narrative Therapy in Supervision," views the supervisory experience through this lens of narrative theory. It is important to understand that supervisees are developing as people and as professionals during the course of their counseling/supervision work. As supervisees develop, the supervisor has to help supervisees integrate these experiences into a cohesive "story" that moves the supervisee forward professionally. The author provides a four step model that blends narrative theory with the supervision technique of Interpersonal Process Recall to help this developmental process. The intended result is a more intentional supervision process for both the supervisor and supervisee that promotes counselor identity development as well as counselor effectiveness with clients.

The final chapter of the book is an examination of how emotions play a part in the supervision process for both supervisors and supervisees. Working with emotions has long been the province of counseling with clients. However, there are emotional elements at work in the supervisory process as well. If one believes in the developmental concept of counseling supervision, it is hard to imagine working with supervisees without there being an emotional context. The authors of Chapter 10 provide an overview of the role of emotions in counseling and supervision, describe emotional intelligence and how it plays an important role in both environments, and outline characteristics of a supervisor who works from an emotionally intelligent perspective.

We hope that you enjoy the innovative and challenging ideas, strategies, and approaches to counseling supervision that are presented in this book. We believe that this book represents an opportunity to expand the conversation about counseling supervision. Supervision as a topic is very challenging due to the profession's lack of knowledge concerning a significant, direct impact that it has on the counseling process. Yet, as the vast majority of supervisors know and understand, without good supervision, quality service delivery would be greatly reduced. Good supervision provided by well-trained and qualified supervisors has a positive impact on the health and well-being of untold numbers of clients. And in some instances, through the intervention of the supervisor, potential harm to clients, albeit unintentional, has been avoided or greatly lessened. Also, supervision has promoted the development of the next generation of counselors, both professionally and personally. And along the way, there have been supervisors who have done a little developing themselves, no matter how reluctantly some of us may admit it. While we may not have a clear answer to exactly how supervision contributes to the process for clients yet, we do *know* that it does.

In addition to adding to the general conversation about supervision, we hope that the ideas presented in this book also provide grist for the research mill. A significant amount of research has developed over the past 30 years about supervision, including topics such as the supervisory relationship, supervisors and supervisees as participants, methods and theories of supervision, and internal and external factors that impact supervision. The topics presented in this book should provide many future a-ha moments that result not only in good research questions, but motivation for current and future supervision researchers to take up the call to continue exploring. We must not lose our energy in the search for greater understanding of this wonderful process we call supervision. It is important for all of us involved in the helping professions to understand as much as we can about how people move through the therapeutic process, even if only to understand that something is happening that we don't yet understand.

# About the Editors

**John R. Culbreth, Ph.D.**, is an Associate Professor in the Counseling Department at the University of North Carolina at Charlotte. He is a Licensed Professional Counselor, Licensed Chemical Addiction Specialist, and holds his NCC, MAC, and ACS credentials. He has been a professional counselor for 23 years, and teaching and supervising counselors for the past 13 years. Clinical supervision has been a mainstay in his research and writing. All of this work is done to support his two primary jobs of husband and father. This involves spending time with Barbara, doing stuff around the house, developing new projects that justify purchasing new tools, riding his motorcycle, and spending a lot of time with a certain Boy Scout named Alex.

**Lori L. Brown, Ph.D.**, is currently a Professional School Counselor and Licensed Professional Counselor in private practice in eastern North Carolina. She has worked as a counselor educator and clinical supervisor at several universities, and supervised practicing counselors in private supervision practice. Dr. Brown has written extensively on the topic of clinical supervision, most recently co-authoring *The New Handbook of Supervision* with Dr. L. DiAnne Borders. She is a past president of the Southern Association of Counselor Education and Supervision and the Georgia Association of Counselor Education and Supervision. Dr. Brown currently lives near Wilmington, NC with her husband attorney James Zisa, three dogs and a cat.

# About the Contributors

**Michael L. Baltimore, Ph.D.**, earned his doctorate in Counselor Education and Supervision from Auburn University and is program coordinator of community counseling at Columbus State University. He maintains a private practice for clinical supervision. He is a founding Co-Editor of the *Journal of Technology in Counseling*, is a Licensed Professional Counselor, Licensed Marriage and Family Therapist, and a Clinical Member and Approved Supervisor with the American Association for Marriage and Family Therapy.

**L. DiAnne Borders, Ph.D.**, is Burlington Industries Excellence Professor in the Department of Counseling and Educational Development at The University of North Carolina at Greensboro. She is co-author of *The New Handbook of Counseling Supervision* and over 100 other publications, including research on developmental models of supervision and supervisor training issues. She was instrumental in the development of standards for counseling supervisors, a curriculum guide for training counseling supervisors, and ethical guidelines for the practice of counseling supervision, all endorsed by the Association for Counselor Education and Supervision, and which were the foundation for the Approved Clinical Supervisor credential offered through the National Board for Certified Counselors.

**Craig S. Cashwell, Ph.D., LPC, NCC, ACS**, is a professor in the Department of Counseling and Educational Development at The University of North Carolina at Greensboro. He has authored or co-authored over 75 publications. He has served as President of the Association for Spiritual, Ethical, and Religious Values in Counseling (ASERVIC) and as Chair of the Board of Directors for the Council for Accreditation of Counseling and Related Educational Programs (CACREP).

**Catherine Y. Chang, Ph.D.**, is an associate professor at Georgia State University and program coordinator for the Counselor Education and Practice doctoral program. She is a LPC and a NCC. Her research interests include multicultural counseling and supervision, social justice issues, and Asian American and Korean American concerns.

**Joseph B. Cooper, Ph.D.**, is an assistant professor of psychology in the department of counseling at Marymount University in Arlington, VA. His research interests have focused on the use of emotions in counseling supervision and in the counseling relationship. He maintains a private practice in Washington, DC specializing in emotion-focused psychodynamic psychotherapy.

**Lea R. Flowers, Ph.D., LPC, NCC**, is an assistant professor in the Department of Counseling and Psychological Services at Georgia State University. Her research interests include culturally competent counselor training and supervision, group work, gender, and post-traumatic growth.

**Hildy G. Getz, Ph.D.**, is Associate Professor Emeritus of counselor education at Virginia Tech. As an Approved Supervisor with both NBCC and the American Association of Marriage and Family Therapy, she has taught clinical supervision and provided it for graduate students, licensure applicants, and agency professionals. She has presented many programs on clinical supervision throughout the United States and has had articles published in six of the premier counseling journals.

**S. Lenoir Gillam, Ph.D.**, is a professor in the Department of Counseling, Foundations, and Leadership at Columbus State University in Columbus, GA. She received her Ph.D. in Counseling Psychology from The University of Georgia and has worked in school, community, and university settings. She is also an LPC and licensed psychologist in Georgia and a nationally certified counselor. Her research agenda and special interests include group work, supervision and training, multicultural issues, and school counseling.

**Mary Amanda Graham, Ph.D.**, is an assistant professor in the Counseling and School Psychology Department at Seattle University. Her past and present research interests focus on the use of creativity in counselor education and supervision. She has developed, researched, and utilizes a model of bibliosupervision in her work with students.

**Charles F. Gressard, Ph.D.**, is an associate professor in the Counselor Education Program at the College of William & Mary. He has taught counselors for thirty years and has served on both the NBCC and the CACREP Board of Directors.

**Marty Jencius, Ph.D.**, is an associate professor in the Counseling and Human Development Services program at Kent State University. His scholarship includes the application of technology to counseling as listowner of CESNET-L (a listerv for counselor educators and supervisors), co-founder of the *Journal of Technology in Counseling*, column editor for *The Digital Psyway*, and producer for CounselorAudioSource.Net podcasts. Dr. Jencius is currently exploring the use of virtual worlds for counseling pedagogy.

**Brandy L. Kelly, Ph.D.**, is a full-time practitioner in Ohio. She provides, and has provided, individual and group supervision to counseling students and practitioners. Dr. Kelly's focus has been feminist supervision practices including the dynamics of the supervisor-supervisee relationship, as well as strategies for managing conflict and ruptures in the alliance.

**Kok-Mun Ng, Ph.D., LPC, NCC**, is an associate professor in the Department of Counseling at the University of North Carolina at Charlotte, North Carolina. His research and clinical interests include marriage and family, attachment, psychological assessment, well-being, emotional intelligence, counselor education and supervision, and multicultural and cross-cultural counseling issues. Dr. Ng has held state and national level leadership roles in professional counseling organizations.

**Cynthia J. Osborn, Ph.D.**, is an associate professor in the Counseling and Human Development Services program at Kent State University in Kent, OH where she has provided individual and group supervision to counseling students who undertake their practicum experience in the on-site Counseling and Human Development Center. Dr. Osborn's focus in counseling supervision includes solution-focused and other strengths-based approaches to supervision, and the use of written supervision contracts.

**Clarrice Rapisarda, Ph.D.**, is an assistant professor in the Department of Counseling at the University of North Carolina at Charlotte. Dr. Rapisarda is a Licensed Professional Counselor and has been practicing for over ten years. She incorporates the use of puppets and other creative elements into her counseling, supervision, and teaching to enhance the process of learning and increase insight and awareness.

**Mark B. Scholl, Ph.D.**, is an assistant professor in the Department of Counselor and Adult Education at East Carolina University in Greenville, NC. He is the editor of *The Journal of Humanistic Counseling, Education and Development* and the Chair of the ACA Council of Journal Editors. His research interests include college student development and career counseling.

**Sondra Smith-Adcock, Ph.D.**, is an associate professor in Counselor Education at the University of Florida in Gainesville. She teaches and advises in the school counseling and mental health counseling areas. Her research interests include using creative approaches in counselor preparation and child and adolescent mental health.

**Debbie Crawford Sturm, Ph.D.**, is a Clinical Assistant Professor at the University of South Carolina and a Licensed Professional Counselor. Her clinical experiences have primarily focused on trauma, abuse, neglect, and people/children who have been victims or witnesses of violence. Her research interests include pre-practicum clinical experiences for counselors in training, poverty as an important component to multicultural training, and understanding and treating trauma in children.

**Catherine Tucker, Ph.D.**, is an assistant professor of counseling at Indiana State University. She was an elementary school counselor for nine years, and has also worked in mental health settings. Catherine has been a play therapist for over twelve years.

**J. Scott Young, Ph.D.**, is a professor and chair of the Department of Counseling and Educational Development at the University of North Carolina at Greensboro. Most of his professional writing has related to the interface of spirituality and the practice of counseling. He is a past president of the Association for Spiritual Ethical and Religious Values in Counseling.

**Elaine Wittmann** is a Licensed Professional Counselor, an Approved Clinical Supervisor, and Registered Play Therapist-Supervisor with more than 35 years of experience working with children and families as teacher, counselor, and clinical supervisor. She has a private practice in Beech Mountain, NC and contracts, consults, and supervises with other practices and agencies. She presents locally and nationally on play therapy, sandtray therapy, supervision, and on issues around children and families.

# CHAPTER 1

# Multicultural Supervision Competence

## CATHERINE Y. CHANG and LEA R. FLOWERS

In light of the growing diversity within the United States and the emergence of the Association for Counselor Education and Supervision (ACES, 1990) supervisory competencies, it is essential for supervisors to enhance their awareness and knowledge of multicultural issues in supervision. Cross-racial and cross-cultural issues have not been addressed widely within the supervisory process. The purpose of this chapter is to identify and discuss the importance of addressing cross-racial and cross-cultural issues within the supervisory triad (i.e., supervisor, supervisee, and client). Additionally, the authors will present various models and frameworks for understanding multicultural supervision, and highlight challenges as well as recommendations related to multicultural supervision competence.

As you read this chapter, reflect on your past supervisory experiences. Which supervisors did you find to be the most helpful? Which ones did you find to be the least helpful? What aspects of the supervisory relationships were helpful and which aspects were either neutral or not helpful? How openly were cultural issues discussed in supervision? Who initiated the cultural dialogue? Did you feel that there was too much or too little attention to cultural issues in your supervision experiences?

## Importance of Multicultural Supervision

Multicultural supervision is a complex relationship involving a minimum of three individuals: a supervisor, supervisee/counselor, and client, who are engaged in a triadic relationship that involves the intermingling of diverse cultural backgrounds. Multicultural supervision involves open dialogue regarding relevant cultural issues with the goal of promoting cultural competence in both the counseling and supervisory relationships (Chang, Hays, & Shoffner, 2003; D'Andrea & Daniels, 1997). Ancis and Ladany (2001) argue that addressing multicultural issues in supervision is essential to ethical and effective practices involving clients from diverse backgrounds. There has been debate in the literature on how to define culture in the context of the supervisory and counseling relationships. Some have argued for a narrow definition of culture (e.g., Locke, 1990; Sue, Arredondo, & McDavis, 1992), that is, race and ethnicity, while others offer a more broad definition (e.g., D'Andrea & Daniels, 1997; Garrett, Borders, Crutchfield, Torres-Rivera, Brotherton, & Curtis, 2001; Stone, 1997). For the purpose of this chapter, we suggest a broader definition of culture, and argue for the term *multicultural supervision* to be inclusive of race, ethnicity, language, class or socioeconomic status, sexual identity, gender, religious or spiritual identity, ability status, and age.

By taking a more inclusive approach to multicultural supervision, we acknowledge that all individuals have multiple cultural identities that interact with each other, and these various cultural identities may become more or less salient across time and situations. In recognizing multicultural supervision, we acknowledge within-group differences, thus avoiding stereotyping and allowing supervisors and supervisees to examine how various aspects of their cultural identities may influence the supervisory and counseling relationships. The supervisor–supervisee/counselor–client triad will become more complex as our society becomes more diverse, thus increasing the need for multicultural supervision (McLeod, 2008).

Because cultural self-awareness is an important aspect of multicultural supervision, we suggest the following activity before engaging in multicultural supervision. Draw three columns on a piece of paper. In the first column, list all the cultural groups of which you are a member (e.g., Asian, female, heterosexual, able-bodied, married with children). In the second column, list all the advantages of being in that group (i.e., privileges). In the third column, list all the disadvantages of being in that group (i.e., oppressions). Now review the list and, based on your cultural group memberships, determine if are there any individuals from any cultural groups that you would have a difficult time either supervising or receiving supervision from?

The importance of addressing multicultural issues in counseling and supervision is highlighted by several documents. *Standards for Counseling Supervisors* (ACES, 1990) supports the need to recognize individual differences and their impact on the supervisory relationship. The concept of multicultural counseling competencies (MCC; Sue et al., 1992) stresses the need for professional counselors to seek awareness of their own assumptions and biases, to understand the worldviews of culturally different clients, and to develop appropriate intervention strategies for working with culturally diverse clients. The American Psychological Association's (APA's) *Guidelines on Multicultural Education, Training, Research, Practice, and Organizational Change for Psychologists* (2002) promotes addressing multiculturalism and diversity in psychological education and training. According to the American Counseling Association (ACA) *Code of Ethics*, counselor educators are responsible for infusing multicultural and diversity issues into all counseling courses and workshops, as well as addressing multicultural issues in the supervisory relationship (ACA, 2005). The Council for Accreditation for Counseling and Related Educational Programs (CACREP, 2009) standards require that counselor training programs provide counselor trainees with educational experiences that result in an understanding of the cultural context of relationships, multicultural trends and concerns, the role of the counselor in social justice and advocacy work, and an increased level of knowledge, skills, and awareness of attitudes and beliefs related to working with a culturally diverse population.

Clearly, professional organizations advocate for and recognize the importance of addressing multicultural issues in supervision. The importance of addressing cultural issues in supervision is also highlighted in the literature. When cultural variables were discussed in the supervisory relationship, supervisees reported increased multicultural awareness, knowledge, skill and confidence level for addressing cultural issues in supervision and counseling (Toporek, Ortega-Villalobos, & Pope-Davis, 2004), increased satisfaction with supervision and enhanced supervisory working alliance (Burkard et al., 2006; Inman, 2006; Silvestri, 2003; Tsong, 2005), increased supervisee self-efficacy for working with culturally diverse client populations (Fukuyama, 1994), and perceived their supervisors to be more credible (McLeod, 2008; Yang, 2005). Additionally, when cultural issues were discussed in supervision, supervisees reported that it positively impacted client outcomes (Ancis & Marshall, in press).

## Models for Multicultural Supervision

Many authors have developed models for multicultural supervision. The Systems Approach to Supervision (SAS; Martinez & Holloway, 1997) model examines the relationship between contextual factors (e.g., cultural characteristics, organizational structure of the institution), supervision functions (e.g., assessment, teaching, consulting), supervision tasks (e.g., counseling skills, case conceptualization), and the supervisory relationship. Additionally, the SAS model promotes engaging the supervisee, establishing a professional relationship, and focusing on both content and process in supervision and counseling.

González (1997) presented a postmodern approach to supervision by integrating Interpersonal Process Recall with the Discrimination Model and live supervision techniques. In this model, the supervisor establishes a collaborative environment in which the expertise of the supervisee and client is highly valued. In order to gain insight into the cultural belief system and worldviews of the supervisee and client, supervisors attend to language usage, emotional expressions of the supervisee, and the client's verbal and nonverbal statements.

The VISION model of cultural responsiveness (Garrett et al., 2001) provides a framework for exploring multicultural issues in supervision through increasing supervisor cultural awareness and cultural responsiveness. This model outlines the importance of focusing on the values and beliefs (V) of the supervisor and the supervisee, reminds the supervisor to address the supervisee's interpretation (I) of their experiences both in the supervisory and the counseling process, and encourages the supervisor to consider the needs and cultural characteristics of the supervisee in structuring (S) the supervision sessions. Additionally, the supervisor must attend to the interactional styles (I) or the preferred modes of both verbal and nonverbal communication, for both the supervisor and the supervisee, in order to reduce the chance of unintentional miscommunication. The supervisor should also give thought to the operational strategies (O), or level of intentionality in using culturally based strategies, to achieve goals for supervision. Finally, the supervisor considers both the supervisors' and the supervisees' perceived needs (mental, physical, spiritual, emotional, or environmental) related to desired outcomes (N). Unlike the SAS (Martinez & Holloway, 1997) or the González (1997) model for supervision, the VISION model presents an interactional framework for multicultural supervision by examining the impact of communication styles, behavior, perception, expectation, and belief systems within the supervisory relationship (see Chen, 2001 for an additional interactional model for supervision).

Several authors have proposed racial identity development (RID) models for multicultural supervision that consider not only the interaction between cultural characteristics but the supervisor's and the supervisee's RID (Chang, et al., 2003; Cook, 1994; D'Andrea & Daniels, 1997). These RID models for supervision are based on Helms and Carter's (1990) White RID model and Atkinson, Morten, and Sue's (1998) RID model for people of color. According to the Helms and Carter model, White racial identity development progresses through six ego statuses: contact, disintegration, reintegration, pseudoindependence, immersion-emersion, and autonomy. Similarly, Atkinson et al. posited that minorities progress through five statuses: conformity, dissonance, resistance and immersion, introspection, and integrative awareness. Applying these RID models to the supervisor and the supervisee, the supervisory relationship can be described as parallel (supervisor and supervisee are at similar levels of RID), progressive (supervisor is at a more advanced level of RID), or regressive (supervisee is at a more advanced level of RID). It has been suggested that if RID issues are not addressed in supervision, several consequences may occur, including perpetuation of stereotypes, misdiagnosis, inappropriate treatment planning, and countertransferences based on racial issues. Additionally, failure to discuss racial identity issues in supervision may have a negative impact on the supervisory relationship and the working alliance (Chang, et al., 2003; Constantine, Warren, & Miville, 2005; Ladany, Brittan-Powell, & Pannu, 1997). According to these models, parallel and progressive relationships will lead to more beneficial supervisory relationships while regressive relationships may lead to avoidance of, or inappropriate attention to, cultural issues in supervision.

Several research studies provide evidence for the efficacy of applying RID to supervision. According to the Bhat and Davis (2007) study that explored the relationship between RID and working alliance in supervision, the strongest working alliances were found in supervisory dyads in which both the supervisor and the supervisee were at advanced statuses of RID, while the lowest levels of working alliance were found in supervisory dyads with both the supervisor and supervisee at lower RID statuses.

Ladany et al. (1997) investigated the influence of supervisory racial identity interactions and racial matching on the supervisory working alliance and supervisee's multicultural counseling competence. Supervisees in parallel-high and progressive dyads reported the highest levels of supervisory working alliance, while regressive interactions predicted the weakest supervisory working alliance. Similarly, Constantine et al. (2005) found that the supervisees in more advanced White RID schemas (i.e., progressive and parallel high dyadic relationships) reported higher self-perceived multicultural counseling competence and obtained higher multicultural case conceptualization ratings than those supervisees in supervisory dyads with lower RID schemas (i.e., parallel-low dyadic relationships). These studies point to the importance of addressing RID in supervision. Interestingly, although RID of the supervisor and the supervisee are related to supervisory working alliance and multicultural counseling competence, cultural match does not significantly predict level of supervision satisfaction or working alliance (Gatmon et al., 2001).

The Heuristic Model of Nonoppressive Interpersonal Development (HMNID; Ancis & Ladany, 2001) provides one of the most comprehensive multicultural models for supervision, by not only considering RID but also cultural identity development (i.e., race, ethnicity, sexual orientation, gender, disability, and socioeconomic status). According to this model, the central task for the supervisor is to facilitate the awareness and growth of the supervisee, thus leading to a more advanced level of cultural identity development. This model acknowledges that individuals can belong to multiple cultural groups simultaneously and that these groups can be either privileged or oppressed. For example, an Asian American, able-bodied, heterosexual female maintains membership in both privileged (i.e., able-bodied, heterosexual) and oppressed (Asian American, female) groups. For each cultural identity, the individual will progress through four developmental phases based on one's thoughts and feelings about oneself, while the individual's behaviors are based on the individual's identification with a particular cultural identity. The developmental phases include: (a) adaptation (complacency, stereotypical attitudes, minimal awareness of privilege and oppression); (b) incongruence (beginning to question beliefs about cultural variables); (c) exploration (active exploration of cultural issues); and (d) integration (multicultural integrity). Based on the developmental stage of the supervisor and the supervisee, Ancis and Ladany propose four supervisor–supervisee interpersonal interactions: (a) progressive, where the supervisor is at a more advanced stage (i.e., exploration and integration); (b) parallel-advanced, where the supervisor and the supervisee are both at advanced developmental stages; (c) parallel-delayed, where the supervisor and the supervisee are at comparable delayed stages (i.e., adaptation and incongruence); and (d) regressive, where the supervisee is at a more advanced stage than the supervisor. Ancis and Ladany predict that the interpersonal interaction will have an impact on the supervisory working alliance and outcomes of the supervisory relationship.

These models for multicultural supervision point to the importance of the supervisor, supervisee, and client interaction and provide a general framework for addressing cultural issues in supervision. In addition to these models, multiculturally competent supervisors need to be aware of the various challenges associated with multicultural supervision competence.

## Challenges to Multicultural Supervision Competence

The challenges related to multicultural supervision competence include supervisor training, professional counseling culture, and supervisor multicultural competence. In a study examining the multicultural training of supervisors, Constantine (1997) reported that 70% of supervisors had never had coursework in multicultural counseling, while 70% of the supervisees reported having completed a course in multicultural counseling. Additionally, Constantine found that only 15% of supervision time was spent discussing multicultural issues. Gatmon et al. (2001) also found that although cultural issues are critical in supervision, discussions related to cultural issues occur at a low frequency. However, McLeod (2008) found that participants in her study reported a range of frequencies. Some supervisors and supervisees reported addressing cultural issues in every supervision session, while others reported very rarely or never addressing cultural issues in supervision. Duan and Roehlke (2001) found that supervisees may be more sensitive to cultural issues than their supervisors, while supervisors reported that they attempted to address cultural issues in supervision more often than was perceived by supervisees. McLeod (2008) also reported that supervisors in her study reported attending to cultural issues in supervision at a greater frequency than was perceived by their supervisees.

The lack of multicultural training of supervisors may be linked to another challenge to multicultural competent supervision. The counseling profession is largely based on White male values; thus, supervisees of color may have a difficult time integrating into this professional identity. Additionally, racial and ethnic minority supervisees may refrain from discussing their minority clients for fear of reinforcing cultural stereotypes (McNeill, Hom, & Perez, 1995).

A related challenge is the lack of multicultural competence of supervisors due either to lack of training and coursework or perpetuation of the White male value system. White supervisors were less likely to address multicultural issues in supervision compared to racial and ethnic minority supervisors, and White supervisors were more likely to discuss multicultural issues with racial and ethnic minority supervisees than with White supervisees (Hird, Tao, & Gloria, 2005). Additionally, White supervisors lacking multicultural competence may place their minority supervisees in the "expert" role, assuming that just because they are from a specific cultural background (e.g., Asian student) the supervisee is an expert in working with clients from that background (e.g., Asian; McNeill et al., 1995). Estrada, Frame, and Williams (2004) also cautioned against supervisors who may avoid racial issues completely or address racial issues at a simplistic level.

## Multicultural Supervision Competence

Clearly, there are challenges to multicultural supervision competence. To assist in facilitating multicultural supervision competence and to combat these challenges, Ancis and Ladany (2001) developed the Multicultural Supervision Competencies and McLeod (2008) developed the Continuum of Supervisor Multicultural Competence. The Multicultural Supervision Competencies focuses on five domains: personal development (supervisor-focused and trainee-focused), conceptualization, interventions/skills, process, and evaluations.

*Personal Development*

Personal development includes self-awareness on the part of both the supervisor and the supervisee. It involves self-exploration of one's values, biases, and limitations and how these impact the supervisory and counseling relationships. Examples of competencies in this dimension include the following:

- Supervisors actively explore and challenge their attitudes and biases toward diverse supervisees.
- Supervisors are knowledgeable about their own cultural background and its influence on their attitudes, values, and behaviors.
- Supervisors facilitate the exploration of supervisees' identity development.
- Supervisors help supervisees understand the impact of social structures on supervisee and client behavior, including how class, gender, and racial privilege may have benefited the counselor (Ancis & Ladany, 2001, pp. 80, 81).

*Conceptualization*

The conceptualization domain involves an understanding of both individual and contextual factors on the lives of clients. It involves acknowledging the impact stereotyping and oppression have on the presenting concern. Conceptualization competencies include the following:

- Supervisors facilitate supervisees' understanding of culture-specific norms, as well as heterogeneity within groups.
- Supervisors facilitate supervisees' understanding of the intersections of multiple dimensions of diversity, or socio-identities, in clients' lives.
- Supervisors help supervisees explore alternative explanations to traditional theoretical perspectives (Ancis & Ladany, 2001, p. 82).

*Interventions/Skills*

Multiculturally competent supervisors encourage the use of culturally relevant and appropriate counseling interventions. Interventions/skills competencies include the following:

- Supervisors model and train supervisees in a variety of verbal and nonverbal helping responses.
- Supervisors encourage supervisee flexibility with regard to traditional interventions and the use of alternative therapeutic interventions, such as those emphasizing group participation and collective action.
- Supervisors encourage supervisees to gain knowledge of community resources that may benefit clients (Ancis & Ladany, 2001, p. 82).

## Process

The process dimension relates to the relationship between the supervisor and the supervisee. A multiculturally competent supervisor encourages open and respectful communication, with the use of power being openly addressed, and works toward a safe supervisory climate in which cultural issues can be discussed openly and safely. Process competencies include the following:

- Supervisors are honest about their biases and struggles to achieve cultural competence.
- Supervisors foster a climate that will facilitate discussion of diversity issues.
- Supervisors attend to and process issues related to power dynamics between supervisor and supervisee and supervisee and client (Ancis and Ladany, 2001, p. 83).

## Evaluation

Evaluation relates to the primary goal of supervision, which is to assist the supervisee in providing ethical and appropriate counseling for clients. As such, the supervisor engages in ongoing assessment and evaluation of the supervisee in order to become aware of any personal or professional limitations of the supervisee that would hamper the supervisee's professional performance. Evaluation competencies include the following:

- Supervisors are able to identify supervisees' personal and professional strengths, as well as weaknesses, in the area of multicultural counseling.
- Supervisors provide ongoing evaluation of supervisees to ensure multicultural competence.
- Supervisors recognize their responsibility to recommend remedial assistance and screen from the training program, applied counseling setting, or state licensure those supervisees who do not demonstrate multicultural competence (Ancis & Ladany, 2001, p. 83).

Using the Ancis and Ladany (2001) model, Ancis and Marshall (in press) investigated how multicultural competencies were demonstrated in supervision. In agreement with the model, it was found that supervisees described culturally competent supervision across the five domains, while supervisees described their supervisors as proactive in addressing cultural issues and open and genuine in discussing the supervisor's cultural background, experiences, and biases. The open dialogue about cultural issues appeared to have a positive impact on the supervisory and the counseling relationships.

McLeod (2008) developed the *Continuum of Supervisor Multicultural Competence* based on her interviews with both supervisors and supervisees who were engaged in a multicultural supervisory relationship. The themes associated with supervisors who were considered to be more multiculturally competent included high frequency of attention to multicultural issues; supervisor responsible for initiating multicultural discussion; intentionality in addressing cultural issues; supervisor actively encourages multicultural discussions; and culture discussed in relation to relationships and process. The themes associated with less competence included low frequency of attention to multicultural issues; supervisee responsible for initiating multicultural discussions; cultural issues were discussed spontaneously; supervisor does not encourage, or silences, multicultural discussions; and culture discussed separately from the relationship and process.

*Activity*

Reflect on past supervision experiences, if you were the supervisee, where would you place your supervisor on the continuum? If you were the supervisor, where do you place yourself on the continuum?

Taking into consideration both the Multicultural Supervision Competencies (Ancis and Ladany, 2001) and the Continuum of Supervisor Multicultural Competence (McLeod, 2008), it appears that a multiculturally competent supervisor is one who takes on the responsibility of, and initiates, cultural dialogue in supervision and does so frequently and with intentionality. Additionally, the multiculturally competent supervisor integrates cultural discussion as it relates to personal development, case conceptualization, interventions/skills, and process.

**Recommendations**

Based on the various models for multicultural supervision, the Multicultural Supervision Competencies (Ancis & Ladany, 2001), and the Continuum of Supervisor Multicultural Competence (McLeod, 2008), we recommend the following:

1. Supervisors are multiculturally competent: that is, they are aware of their own values and biases, have knowledge of various cultural groups, and have skills to work with culturally diverse individuals (see the MCC; Sue et al., 1992). Questions to facilitate one's self-awareness include the following: Describe your cultural background. What biases do you have related to various cultural groups? How will your cultural values and biases influence your supervisory relationship? With which cultural groups do you feel most comfortable working, and with which cultural groups do you feel least comfortable?

2. Supervisors are encouraged to assist their supervisees in self-exploration related to their supervisees' cultural heritage. See earlier questions.
3. Supervisors are encouraged to consider the many possible cultural interactions between their supervisees and themselves. Additionally, if supervisors are conducting group supervision, they should consider the cultural interactions between their supervisees. One activity to assist supervisor and the supervisees consider the intricacies of multiple cultural interactions is to create a group supervision cultural genogram. We recommend that you conduct this activity early during the group supervision process. Using a whiteboard or a large flip chart, draw a genogram with the supervisor on one generation and the supervisees on the second generation. The supervisor and the supervisees list all their cultural group memberships. The supervisees are asked to create a "third" generation listing all the cultural groups of their client population. Once the genogram has been created, the supervisor facilitates a discussion related to the cultural genogram. Some processing questions can include the following: What patterns do you see in the cultural genogram? Now that you have seen what others have written, are there any cultural groups that you omitted in your own descriptions? Are there any areas for potential conflicts/misunderstanding or overidentification between group members or between you and your client population based on your cultural group memberships?
4. Supervisors are encouraged to address RID issues with their supervisees. We suggest that supervisors assess their own status of RID, assess the RID status of their supervisee, and then consider the interaction between the supervisor RID status and the supervisee RID status. We recommend the White Racial Identity Attitude Scale (WRIAS; Helms & Carter, 1990) or the People of Color Racial Identity Attitude Scale (POCRIAS; Helms & Parham, 1990) for assessing racial identity.
5. White supervisors are encouraged to acknowledge and have an open discussion related to White privilege, and supervisors working with White supervisees are encouraged to facilitate dialogue about White privilege. Hays and Chang (2003) provided some sample questions to facilitate this awareness. "What does being White mean to you? What values and traditions do you associate with your White heritage? How might your racial heritage influence your relationship with minority clients?" (p. 141).
6. Supervisors are encouraged to address the power differential in the supervisory relationship and to openly acknowledge when

they are putting on their "power hat" in supervision. For example, if there is something that you feel that your supervisee needs to do, it is helpful to recognize that you are putting on your "power hat" and giving a directive as opposed to facilitating dialogue.

7. Supervisors are responsible for addressing cultural issues in supervision, and this dialogue should occur early in the supervisory relationship.

## Activities

The following multicultural activities are effective in both individual and group supervision. The purpose is to provide the reader with quick adaptable activities that can be utilized in multicultural supervision.

### The Name Story (Edchange Multicultural Pavilion)

This activity brings the supervisee's multicultural experiences and stories to the forefront in a relaxed and fun way. It can be a written assignment whereby the supervisee writes a 1 or 2 page short story about their name, or it can be done verbally, with the supervisor asking questions and the supervisee providing a thoughtful answer. The directions and structure for this assignment should be left as broad and open to the supervisee's interpretation as possible. Supervisees are asked to discuss the following prompts: (a) Who gave you your name? Why? (b) What is the ethnic origin of your name? (c) What are your nicknames, if any? (d) Do you like your name? (e) If you could change it to a different name, what would it be and why?

Supervisees are encouraged to be thoughtful in their responses. This activity is most appropriate during the initial rapport-building stage of supervision. Initially, supervisees may display resistance in sharing personal information regarding their names and the history of how they received their names. Supervisors may want to share their name story first as a way to provide an example of how to approach the prompts as well as increase the safety and trust level with the supervisee. After the mutual sharing of name stories, the supervisor facilitates discussion regarding the importance of this activity and learning points gleaned from this activity. This is a relatively simple activity captures many multicultural themes.

Within the supervisee's name history, the supervisor gains information about his or her culture, ethnicity, family traditions, and religion. For instance, "My name is Joseph. My family is Catholic, and it is tradition within my Catholic family for all of the children to be named after a saint" or "My name is Imani. My dad has been a social activist for many years, our family made frequent trips to Africa when I was a child. I like my name because it means purpose in Swahili." Another example would be a supervisee from China who may highlight the fact that Chinese names are different from Western names such as John Smith, where the family name is last and the given name is first. Chinese names differ from Western names, in that the family name is first followed by the given name, for instance Hu Jintao (Zang, 2005). The name story activity highlights cultural differences. The Chinese greatly value and respect their origins and ancestors; hence, the family names come before their given names. This level of sharing and understanding offers a mutual opportunity to increase sensitivity to cultural differences within the supervisory relationship.

## Reflection Papers

Reflection Papers are tools that help promote an understanding of the supervisee's cultural identity and explore how this conceptualization of their identity affects their counseling clients of other cultural, racial, and socioeconomic identities. The reflection paper is a noninvasive method of stimulating the supervisee's thinking about multicultural issues in counseling and counselor–client complexity.

## Journal

Similar to the reflection papers, journaling is another activity that helps the supervisee move forward in the process of becoming culturally competent counselors. By journaling their reactions, feelings, thoughts, and "turning points" within their work with clients, the supervisor, and the overall process of the supervised experience, they increase their awareness and acknowledge their perceived assumptions in written form. By the end of the supervised experience, the journal provides a tool of reflection for the supervisee to go back and read past entries; many are amazed at how far they've grown or shocked by the issues they grappled with in the past that are no longer a source of angst. Periodically, the supervisor can instruct the supervisee to journal about a specific area that seems to present a challenge. For example, an African American female supervisor could ask her Caucasian, male supervisee to journal about his experience of what he described as "frustration" in his attempts to establish rapport with his first African American female client. This journaling experience provides a backdrop for a rich discussion regarding assumptions and biases, feedback and continued dialogue to increase self-awareness in a nonintrusive manner.

## Self and Other Exercise (Baird, 2005)

The foundation to understanding others is to maintain an awareness of self; the goal of this exercise is to provide a tool to help supervisees increase their awareness of their personal cultural background (Baird, 2005). This exercise can be completed as a written assignment, orally, or in pairs within group supervision. Discuss the following prompts thoughtfully and completely:

1. My gender is _____, and this is how it might influence my experiences and how I understand and relate to others.
2. My age is _____, and this is how it influences my experiences and how I understand and relate to others.
3. My physical appearance includes the following qualities (Describe these accurately, without oversimplification or the use of racial terms):

Skin:
Hair:
Facial features:
Body Type/Build:
Other features:

This is how those features might influence my experiences and how I understand and relate to others:

4. The nationality and cultural background of my parents and grandparents:

My father's mother:
My father's father:
My mother's mother:
My mothers' father:
My father:
My mother:

This is how the culture of my family influences my experiences and how I understand and relate to others.

5. With regard to economic resources, the family I was raised in was _____.

This is how my social and economic background influences my experiences and how I understand and relate to others.

6. The religious orientation of my mother is _____.
   The religious orientation of my father is _____.
   My religious orientation is _____.

This is how that background influences my experiences and how I understand and relate to others.

7. My physical health and abilities are _____.

This is how that background influences my experiences and how I understand and relate to others.

8. My sexual orientation is _____.

This is how that background influences my experiences and how I understand and relate to others.

9. My mother's educational background is _____.
My father's educational background is _____.
My educational background is _____.

This is how that background influences my experiences and how I understand and relate to others.

10. Other characteristics that have influenced my experiences and how I understand and relate to others are _____.

*Knowing What You Know and Don't Know About Others (Baird, 2005)*

Provide this list of characteristics that distinguish individuals and groups from one another. Instruct supervisees to be thoughtful in their attempt to identify how their own personal knowledge, understanding, or experiences would enable them to accurately understand and relate to the specified groups' experiences, thoughts, concerns, emotions, or needs in a therapeutic, empathic, and culturally competent way. For each group that supervisees feel they have a level of competence to work effectively with, ask them to provide reasons that explain why they feel such competence. For example, the supervisor may want to ask, what experience, training, or personal knowledge do you have relation to this group? (Baird, 2005). This exercise is also useful in highlighting the supervisee's awareness and knowledge regarding within-group differences.

Age groups:
Genders:
Appearance (e.g., skin, color, facial features):
Ethnic or cultural background:
Generations lived in this country:
Economic status:
Education level:
Religion:
Sexual orientation:
Physical abilities and disabilities:

## Summary

In this chapter, the authors discussed the importance of multicultural supervision competence. Various models and frameworks for understanding multicultural supervision were presented. Additionally, the authors discussed the challenges to and provided some recommendations and suggested activities for providing supervision that is culturally competent.

## References

ACA (American Counseling Association) (2005). *Code of ethics and standards of practice*. Alexandria, VA: Author.

ACES (Association for Counselor Education and Supervision) (1990). Standards for counseling supervisors. *Journal of Counseling and Development, 69,* 30–32.

American Psychological Association (2002). Guidelines on multicultural education, training, research, practice, and organizational change for psychologists. *American Psychologist, 58 (5),* 377–402.

Ancis, J. R., & Ladany, N. (2001). A multicultural framework for counselor supervision. In L. J. Bradley and N. Ladany (Eds.), *Counselor Supervision: Principles, process, and practice* (pp. 63–89). Philadelphia: Taylor & Francis.

Ancis, J. R., & Marshall, D. S. (in press). Using a multicultural framework to assess supervisees' perceptions of culturally competent supervision. *Journal of Counseling and Development*.

Atkinson, D. R., Morten, G., & Sue, D. W. (1998). *Counseling American minorities (5th ed.)*. Boston: McGraw Hill.

Baird, B. (2005). *The internship, practicum, and field placement handbook: A guide for the helping professions (4th ed.)*, Upper Saddle River, NJ: Pearson Education, Inc.

Bhat, C. S., & Davis, T. E. (2007). Counseling supervisors' assessment of race, racial identity, and working alliance in supervisory dyads. *Journal of Multicultural Counseling and Development, 35 (2),* 80–91.

Burkard, A. W., Johnson, A. J., Madson, M. B., Pruitt, N. T., Contreras-Tadych, D. A., Kozlowski, J. M., Knox, S., & Hess, S. A. (2006). Supervisor cultural responsiveness and unresponsiveness in cross-cultural supervision. *Journal of Counseling Psychology, 53 (3),* 288–301.

CACREP (Council for the Accreditation of Counseling and Related Educational Programs) (2009). *CACREP standards*. Alexandria, VA: Author.

Chang, C. Y., Hays, D. G., & Shoffner, M. F. (2003). Cross-racial supervision: A developmental approach for white supervisors working with supervisees of color. *The Clinical Supervisor, 22 (2),* 121–138.

Chen, E. (2001). Multicultural counseling supervision: An interactional approach. In J. G. Ponterotto, J. M., Cross, L. A. Suzuki, and C. M. Alexander (Eds.), *Handbook of multicultural counseling (2nd ed.)*, Thousand Oaks, CA: Sage.

Constantine, M. G. (1997). Facilitating multicultural competency in counseling supervision: Operationalizing a practical framework. In D. B. Pope-Davis and H. L. K. Coleman (Eds.), *Multicultural counseling competencies: Assessment, education and training, and supervision* (pp. 310–324). Thousand Oaks, CA: Sage.

Constantine, M. G., Warren, A. K., & Miville, M. L. (2005). White racial identity dyadic interactions in supervision: Implications for supervisee's multicultural counseling competence. *Journal of Counseling Psychology, 54 (4),* 490–496.

Cook, D. (1994). Racial identity in supervision. *Counselor Education ad Supervision, 34 (2),* 132–141.

D'Andrea, M., & Daniels, J. (1997). Multicultural counseling supervision: Central issues, theoretical considerations, and practical strategies. In D. B. Pope-Davis and H. L. K. Coleman (Eds.), *Multicultural counseling competencies: Assessment, education and training, and supervision* (pp. 290–309). Thousand Oaks, CA: Sage.

Duan, C., & Roehlke, H. (2001). A descriptive snapshot of cross-racial supervision in university counseling center internships. *Journal of Multicultural Counseling and Development, 29,* 131–146.

Edchange Multicultural Pavilion (n.d.). Awareness Activities. Retrieved September 4, 2008 from www.edchange.org/multicultural/activities/name.html.

Estrada, D., Frame, M. W., Williams, & C. B. (2004). Cross-cultural supervision; Guiding the conversation toward race and ethnicity. *Journal of Multicultural Counseling and Development, 32,* 307–319.

Garrett, M. T., Borders, L. D., Crutchfield, L. B., Torres-Rivera, E., Brotherton, D., & Curtis, R. (2001). Multicultural supervision: A paradigm of cultural responsiveness for supervisors. *Journal of Multicultural Counseling and Development, 29,* 147–158.

Gatmon, D., Jackson, D., Koshkarian, L., Martos-Perry, N., Molina, A., Patel, N., & Rodolfa, E. (2001). Exploring ethnic, gender, and sexual orientation variables in supervision: Do they really matter? *Journal of Multicultural Counseling and Development, 29,* 102–113.

Fukuyama, M. (1994). Critical incidents in multicultural counseling supervision: A phenomenological approach to supervision research. *Counselor Education and Supervision, 34 (2),* 142–151.

González, R. C. (1997). Postmodern supervision: A multicultural perspective. In D. B. Pope-Davis and H. L. K. Coleman (Eds.), *Multicultural counseling competencies: Assessment, education and training, and supervision* (pp. 350–386). Thousand Oaks, CA: Sage.

Hays, D. G., & Chang, C. Y. (2003). White privilege, oppression, and racial identity development: Implications for supervision. *Counselor Education and Supervision, 43,* 134–145.

Helms, J. E., & Carter, R. T. (1990). White Racial Identity Attitude Scale (form WRIAS). In J. E. Helms (Ed.). *Black and White racial identity: Theory, research, and practice* (pp. 145–163). New York: Greenwood.

Helms, J. E., & Parham, T. A. (1990). Black Racial Identity Attitude Scaled (form RIAS-B). In J.E. Helms (Ed.). *Black and White racial identity: Theory, research, and practice* (pp. 145–163). New York: Greenwood.

Hird, J. S., Tao, K. W., & Gloria, A. M. (2005). Examining supervisor's multicultural competence in racially similar and different supervision dyads. *The Clinical Supervisor, 23 (2),* 107–122.

Inman, A. G. (2006). Supervisor multicultural competence and its relation to supervisory process and outcome. *Journal of Marriage and Family Therapy, 32 (1),* 73–85.

Ladany, N., Brittan-Powell, C., & Pannu, R. (1997). The influence of supervisory racial identity interaction and racial matching on the supervisory working alliance and supervisee multicultural competence. *Counselor Education & Supervision, 36 (4),* 284–304.

Locke, D. C. (1990). A not so provincial view of multicultural counseling. *Counselor Education and Supervision, 30 (1)*, 18–25.

Martinez, R. P., & Holloway, E. L. (1997). The supervision relationship in multicultural training. In D.B. Pope-Davis and H. L. K. Coleman (Eds.), *Multicultural counseling competencies: Assessment, education and training, and supervision* (pp. 325–349). Thousand Oaks, CA: Sage.

McLeod, A. L. (2008). A phenomenological investigation of supervisors' and supervisees' experiences with attention to cultural issues in multicultural supervision. Unpublished doctoral dissertation, Georgia State University.

McNeill, B., Hom, K., & Perez, J. (1995). The training and supervisory needs of racial and ethnic minority students. *Journal of Multicultural Counseling and Development, 23 (4)*, 246–258.

Silvestri, T. J. (2003). The temporal effect of supervisor focus, the supervisor working alliance, and the graduate training environment upon supervisee multicultural competence (Doctoral dissertation, Leheigh University, 2003). *Dissertation Abstracts International, 63*, 6108.

Stone, G. L. (1997). Multiculturalism as a context for supervision: Perspectives, limitations, and implications. In D. B. Pope-Davis and H. L. K. Coleman (Eds.), *Multicultural counseling competencies: Assessment, education and training, and supervision* (pp. 263–289). Thousand Oaks, CA: Sage.

Sue, D. W., Arredondo, P., & McDavis, R. J. (1992). Multicultural counseling competencies and standards: A call to the profession. *Journal of Counseling and Development, 70*, 477–486.

Tsong, Y. V. (2005). The role of supervisee attachment styles and perception of supervisors' general and multicultural supervision in supervisory working alliance, supervisee omissions in supervision, and supervision outcome (Doctoral dissertation, University of Southern California, Los Angeles, 2005). *Dissertation Abstracts International, 65*, 3291.

Toporek, R. L., Ortega-Villalobos, L., & Pope-Davis, D. B. (2004). Critical incidents in multicultural supervision: Exploring supervisees' and supervisors' experiences. *Journal of Multicultural Counseling and Development, 32*, 66–83.

Yang, P. H. (2005). The effects of supervisor cultural responsiveness and ethnic group similarity on Asian American supervisee's perception of supervisor credibility and multicultural competence (Doctoral dissertation. University of California, Santa Barbara, 2004). *Dissertation Abstracts International, 65*, 6681.

Zang, Y. (2005). Basics about Chinese names. Retrieved September 3, 2008, from http://www.lexicool.com/article-chinese-names-yi-zhang.asp.

# CHAPTER 2

# No Surprises

*Practices for Conducting Supervisee Evaluations*

CYNTHIA J. OSBORN and BRANDY L. KELLY

"I will be evaluating your work as a counselor" may not only be difficult words for a new supervisee to hear; they may be difficult words for a supervisor (novice or seasoned) to say. The impression supervisees have of "being under" their supervisor's "microscope" is understandable, and their anxiety about what their supervisor will "find" is to be expected. Supervisors may also struggle with conducting evaluations (see Gould & Bradley, 2001) and experience what Nelson, Barnes, Evans, and Triggiano (2008) referred to as "supervisor gatekeeping anxiety." One explanation for this is that as counselors, supervisors may be more accustomed to and more comfortable with providing encouragement to other people (e.g., clients) and less familiar or comfortable with what they may construe as the authoritarian and dictatorial role of evaluator. Both supervisees and supervisors may therefore enter the evaluation process with trepidation because of unclear role expectations: the supervisee may not know the specific counselor behaviors that will be acceptable or regarded as favorable, and the supervisor may not know exactly how to deliver the constructive feedback supervisees need and often expect.

Watkins (1997b) described evaluation as "one of the key definitional features of clinical supervision" (p. 611), and Bernard and Goodyear (2004) further prioritized it by characterizing it as "the nucleus of clinical supervision" (p. 19). Indeed, they emphasized that "there is an evaluative message in all supervision ... [and] evaluation is a constant variable in supervision .... Because we are always communicating, an evaluative message can always be inferred" (p. 20). They listed "evaluative" as the first of three characteristics of the supervisory relationship, and Holloway (1995) listed "monitoring/evaluating" as the first of five functions of the supervisor. Evaluation can therefore be regarded as a default feature of supervision and a function of the counselor supervisor that cannot be avoided. This is expressed best by Watkins (1997a):

> If supervisees are to receive feedback about their performance; are to be told about their therapeutic strengths and weaknesses; are to be informed about their skills or areas of functioning that need to be developed, further enhanced, or improved; and if patient care is to be monitored and protected, then supervision must be evaluative. (p. 4)

Despite its centrality to counselor supervision, evaluation remains "the conundrum of supervision" (Gould & Bradley, 2001, p. 271). Questions persist about how the process of evaluation should be conducted and what criteria should be used in evaluating supervisees. Lehrman-Waterman and Ladany (2001) developed the 21-item *Evaluation Process within Supervision Inventory* (*EPSI*) to assess supervisees' experiences with the process of evaluation, specifically with goal-setting and feedback. Fall and Sutton (2004) constructed their 102-item *Supervisee Performance Assessment Instrument* according to five dimensions of evaluation: intervention skills, conceptualization skills, personalization skills, professional behavior, and supervision skills for the supervisee. These and other measures provide some guidance about the process and content of evaluation. Definitive evaluation practices, however, remain elusive, and supervisors must rely on their best judgment, which is hopefully informed by their direct observation of supervisee skills, interactions with the supervisee, supervisory training, ethical inclination, and consultation with other professionals.

Our intention in this chapter is to provide further guidance to counselor supervisors about the nature and process of evaluation. We do not enumerate decisive prescriptions. Rather, we offer a guiding principle that has assisted us in our own practice of supervisee evaluation: *no surprises*. By this we mean that the supervisee should not be surprised by either the content of his or her evaluation or how the evaluation was conducted on the occasion of formal evaluation (which may be at the close of a supervision working relationship). As Kaiser (1997) indicated, "supervisees should know all along what is expected of them and whether they are meeting those expectations" (p. 93). Supervisor–supervisee collaboration, mutual understanding about the purpose and practice of supervision, and supervisor consistency are therefore paramount. We describe six specific practices to help prevent supervisee surprise with his or her evaluation and also enhance supervisee professional development. We provide examples from our own supervisory practice.

## The Formative–Summative Link

There are two primary types of evaluation conducted in supervision: formative and summative. *Formative evaluation* is considered the ongoing provision of direct feedback during the course of the supervision process. It is typically provided in oral form (i.e., not formally recorded) during each supervision session and represents a here-and-now assessment, thus constituting clear and timely feedback. In medical training, the purpose of formative feedback is to improve the learning process so as "to help students develop under conditions that are non-judgmental and non-threatening" (Rolfe & McPherson, 1995, p. 837; see also Chur-Hansen & McLean, 2006; Benson & Holloway, 2005). Because formative evaluation is a continuous process, it "represents the bulk of the supervisor's work with the supervisee" (Bernard & Goodyear, 2009, p. 21). According to participants in Benson and Holloway's (2005) study, formative evaluation provides supervisors with the opportunity to deliver ongoing feedback that may include "teaching a new skill," "providing a trainee support and encouragement," and "clarifying expectations." It can serve as a form of remedial guidance (see Rolfe & McPherson, 1995) and is an opportunity for supervisees to engage in self-evaluation.

*Summative evaluation* is conducted at specific intervals (e.g., mid-semester, end of training experience or probationary period), is more comprehensive than formative evaluation, and represents a summation of the supervisee's clinical work for a specified period of time. Summative evaluation is therefore a culminating activity that may represent the final process of evaluation in which the supervisor reviews the supervisee's areas of strength, as well as areas requiring continued or greater attention. As a formal type of evaluation, summative evaluation is typically provided in written form and the "results" placed in the supervisee's file (academic, personnel, and/or licensure file). Chur-Hansen and McLean (2006) described summative evaluation as "passing judgment" on whether the supervisee will "pass or fail" (p. 67). Their definition of summative evaluation is thus a prime example of what is referred to as "gatekeeping": determining whether the supervisee should pass a practicum or internship course, graduate from a counselor preparation program, or even be licensed or certified as a counselor.

Feedback is often used to refer to formative evaluation, and evaluation is often used to refer to summative evaluation. However, we believe that the terms are interchangeable: feedback *is* evaluation, and evaluation *is* feedback. We also believe that they are inextricably linked, and that supervisors should not practice either one independent of the other. That is, formative evaluation is conducted for the purpose of constructing and rendering a formal and final evaluation. Put in another way, formative evaluation leads to summative evaluation, and summative evaluation builds on, and is the product of, a series of formative evaluations. Both constitute "the supervisor's response to the supervisee's counseling performance" (Gould & Bradley, 2001, p. 281). Chur-Hansen and McLean (2006) concurred, stating that both formative and summative evaluations should be based on behaviors that the supervisor has directly observed as opposed to simply relying on supervisee self-report. In this way, supervisors are able to conduct accurate and comprehensive evaluations, provide supervisees with specific examples to substantiate their evaluative comments, and offer specific and concrete recommendations.

Rolfe and McPherson (1995) described formative evaluation as the supervisor's response to the supervisee's question, "How am I doing?" and summative evaluation as the supervisor's response to the supervisee's question, "How did I do?" Formative evaluation is therefore an ongoing supervisory activity, assessing the supervisee's current performance and providing feedback that describes the supervisee's work as being in progress. With this in mind, Chur-Hansen and McLean (2006) recommended that supervisees not view formative evaluation as having pass–fail consequences. We agree. Such consequences would be contrary to and, in effect, undercut the very purpose of formative evaluation, that being to facilitate supervisee remediation and promote his or her continuous learning and development. We do not agree, however, with Chur-Hansen and McLean's reasoning that because formative evaluation does not pass judgment on whether a supervisee passes or fails, it "is quite separate from any summative assessment" (p. 70). As stated earlier, we view both types of evaluation as interchangeable and conducted in the service of the other; neither should be practiced independently. Imagine continuous feedback that has no point, a series of "whereas" statements without an eventual "therefore" statement, or a graduate counseling course in which the weekly assignments reviewed by the instructor and returned to students do not result in a final grade (whether a letter grade or pass/fail grade). Formative evaluation and summative evaluation are therefore inextricably linked and cannot be practiced separately. Formative evaluation *informs* summative evaluation, and summative evaluation *summarizes* the supervisory conversations up until the formal and possibly final evaluation.

The challenge for supervisors is to skillfully connect formative evaluation (or feedback) and summative evaluation so that (a) the latter is informed and shaped by the former, (b) supervisees receive ongoing feedback about their performance, (c) supervisors are practicing the skill of clinical assessment and providing constant evaluation in preparation for summative evaluation, (d) supervisors are not overwhelmed or intimidated by the task of summative evaluation, and (e) supervisees are not surprised by the outcome of the summative evaluation. Connecting these two types of evaluation seems to be mutually beneficial for supervisors and supervisees. Bernard and Goodyear (2004) described the investment of time and care in the formative evaluation process as the "chief antidote to summative disdain" (p. 21). Supervisors may thus ease their discomfort with summative evaluation by consistently providing their supervisees with oral feedback in every supervision session and documenting in writing the feedback supplied. This practice also seems to be what supervisees prefer.

From her pilot study of supervisee preferences for supervision, Heckman-Stone (2003) reported that one of the primary concerns about supervision that supervisees described had to do with the context of feedback (i.e., immediacy and frequency). Specifically, the 40 participants (graduate students in three different training programs at one university) were not satisfied with receiving feedback only at the end of the academic term and receiving written feedback without being able to discuss it orally with their supervisor. From their experiences in supervision, however, and their responses to one item on the questionnaire ("There were inconsistencies between my supervisor's feedback to me in session and written evaluations"), participants indicated a high consistency between the content of the oral feedback they received in session and the content of the written, formal, and summative feedback they received at the end of the semester. These supervisee comments suggest to us that supervisees view formative and summative feedback as intertwined and that satisfaction with supervision is based in part on whether the oral feedback agrees with the written evaluation. Practicing the principle of no surprises is therefore beneficial to supervisors and preferred by supervisees. Ensuring that weekly supervision conversations are summarized in the summative evaluation is, however, the supervisor's responsibility.

### Supervisor and Supervisee Impressions of Evaluation

Although supervisors tend to agree that evaluation is an important function of supervision, they may not identify their role as being primarily that of "evaluator." Freeman and McHenry (1996) reported that 78% of the 329 faculty supervisors they surveyed from counseling programs accredited by the Council for Accreditation of Counseling and Related Educational Programs (CACREP) ranked "evaluation of student" as one of five very important functions of supervision. Only 2.8% ($n = 8$), however, described their supervisory style/approach as "screening/evaluator" ("director/teacher" was the most frequently listed, by 18%). Providing feedback and conducting evaluations, therefore, may not necessarily equate with being an evaluator, or at least identifying primarily as an evaluator. And one role may not sufficiently capture the many functions of a supervisor.

The experience of "supervisor gatekeeping anxiety" (Nelson et al., 2008) might suggest a disconnection between function and role or between expectations and actual practice. Supervisors may understand that they need to evaluate, but may not know how. This is suggested in Ladany, Ellis, and Friedlander's (1999) survey of 151 psychologists in training in various practice settings. The most frequent ethical violation reported by these supervisees (by 33.1% of respondents) of their supervisors was that of "performance evaluation and monitoring of supervisee activities." Specific supervisor evaluation practices regarded as unethical included "gives me little feedback" and "never listened to my audio tapes." One supervisee in Ladany et al.'s study reported, "At the end of the semester I was very surprised to find that she was unsatisfied with my work ... I had never been evaluated or critiqued."

Failure to provide supervisees with regular feedback may be associated with supervisor anxiety about conducting evaluations, and this in turn may describe a supervisor who has not been able to fully appreciate the connection between formative evaluation and summative evaluation. Participants in Nelson et al.'s (2008) qualitative study reported learning from past conflicts with supervisees the importance of clarifying expectations from the beginning and providing more feedback early on. Intentionally and consistently practicing formative evaluation, beginning even in the first supervision session, and summarizing this feedback in the summative evaluation may therefore reduce supervisee surprise as well as supervisor gatekeeping anxiety. Such practice is also consistent with a strong supervisory working alliance. Lehrman-Waterman and Ladany (2001) found that clinical and counseling psychology student supervisees whose supervisors conducted effective evaluation (based on supervisee *EPSI* scores) were satisfied with supervision, reported a strong supervisory working alliance, and tended to view their supervisor as influencing their (i.e., the supervisees') self-efficacy.

## Recommended Practices for Conducting Evaluation in Counseling Supervision

Freeman (1985) identified nine characteristics of effective evaluation or supervisee feedback (whether formative or summative): timely, frequent, objective (based on behaviorally defined criteria), consistent, clear, specific, credible (based on direct observation, supervisor credentials), balanced (positive and negative), and reciprocal. These criteria are incorporated into the six practices for conducting supervisee evaluations described in this section.

*Use of a Written Supervision Contract*

Due to the hierarchical nature of the supervisory relationship, the supervisor has the responsibility to ensure that the supervisee is clearly informed about the evaluative structure, expectations and goals, and limits to confidentiality in supervision (Nelson & Friedlander, 2001). One way to ensure supervisee clarity on these matters is to construct with the supervisee a written supervision agreement or contract. Contracting in supervision has been described as possibly "the most important task engaged in by supervisor and supervisee" (Hewson, 1999, p. 81), and Storm (1997) referred to the contract as the "blueprint" for the supervision relationship.

We recommend that a written supervision contract be introduced in the first supervision session to alert the supervisee to the function of supervision and to how evaluation will be conducted. Osborn and Davis (1996; see also Osborn, 2005) described the purpose of a written supervision contract as (a) clarifying the methods, goals, and expectations of supervision; (b) encouraging professional collaboration between the supervisor and supervisee; (c) ensuring that ethical principles are upheld; (d) documenting services to be provided; and (e) aligning supervision with counseling and consultation, two services that utilize a written contract with clients. Nelson and Friedlander (2001) reported that most conflict occurs due to opposing expectations between supervisor and supervisee about what should occur in the supervision relationship (e.g., confusion over who was in charge, who would be evaluating). Because of this, we agree with Thomas (2007) that the use of a written supervision contract can serve to prevent misunderstandings or at least lessen the extent or intensity of conflict between the supervisor and supervisee.

Although several examples of written supervision agreements exist (e.g., Haynes, Corey, & Mouton, 2003; Sutter, McPherson, & Geeseman, 2002), the contracts we have devised when we work with individual supervisees have followed the structure recommended by Osborn and Davis (1996). There are six content areas or sections (see Appendix A at the end of this chapter for a sample of a written supervision contract). First, the purpose, goals, and objectives of supervision are listed, including the need to fulfill academic and licensure requirements. Second, the context of supervision services is described. This refers in part to when and how often supervision will take place, and the method the supervisor will use to monitor the supervisee's performance (e.g., live supervision). The third section of the written supervision contract clarifies how the supervisee will be evaluated and refers to both formative and summative evaluations. We recommend that when the supervisor reviews the initial contract with supervisees in the first supervision session, each supervisee receive a copy of the actual evaluation form that the supervisor will use when conducting summative evaluations. This allows the supervisee to become familiar with the criteria on which he or she will be formally evaluated, which should also correspond to the type of oral feedback the supervisee will get in each supervision session. The remaining three sections of the written supervision contract are separate listings of the supervisor's and supervisee's duties and responsibilities (including three or four supervisee learning objectives), procedural considerations (e.g., emergency procedures and contact, record keeping, process for addressing supervisor–supervisee disagreement), and the supervisor's competencies or scope of practice.

Reviewing with a new supervisee the draft of a written supervision contract in the first supervision session establishes the structure of supervision (including roles, responsibilities, and expectations; see Appendix B for guidelines for constructing a written supervision contract and introducing it to supervisees in the first supervision session). It thus serves as a role induction exercise, which Bahrick, Russell, and Salmi (1991) found contributed to supervisee clarity about the nature of supervision and also helped supervisees to recognize and express their needs to their supervisor. Reviewing the contract with a new supervisee also establishes a collaborative working relationship in supervision, which we believe facilitates the supervisor's practice of formative evaluation. Indeed, Johnson (2007) proposed that "when a supervisor establishes a strong and collegial relationship of trust with a trainee, he or she will be in a stronger position to competently fulfill an evaluative role" (p. 265).

Not only has the written supervision contract allowed us to set the tone for a collaborative supervisory working relationship, it has also served as a "check" or an assessment of our work with supervisees once supervision is under way. In the academic setting where we practice, the midsemester summative evaluation is an occasion to revisit the written supervision contract with supervisees. "How are we doing?" is the question we ask our supervisees. Additional questions include: "Is our work together so far addressing your learning objectives?" and "What revisions do we need to make in our contract for the remainder of the semester to be beneficial for you?" Even if midsemester corrections are not needed, questions such as these promote joint reflection and signal to the supervisee the supervisor's concern for clarity, consistency, and collaboration.

*Delivering Oral Feedback in Session*

The evaluation section of the written supervision contracts we construct with our supervisees mentions that feedback will be provided in every supervision session. This might even begin in the very first supervision session, alluding to in-session supervisee behavior. For a brand-new counselor trainee (e.g., practicum student), an example of supervisory feedback in the first session might be: "You have a ready and natural smile. I think we'll have conversations here in supervision about how you can minimize how often you smile when you're in session with clients." A supervisor comment such as this can have the effect of encouraging early supervisee self-assessment or self-monitoring; alert the supervisee to the evaluative nature of supervision; and prepare the supervisee for routine, specific, and relevant feedback. This type of specific and timely feedback appears to be what many supervisees prefer. Anderson, Schlossberg, and Rigazio-DiGilio (2000) reported that 90.5% of the 158 marriage and family therapy students surveyed endorsed the statement "Supervisor's feedback was direct and straightforward" as a characteristic of their best supervision. Other highly endorsed statements characterizing their best supervision were "Mistakes were welcome as learning experiences," "Time was set aside exclusively for supervision," and "Supervisor provided useful conceptual frameworks for understanding clients."

For supervisees not to be surprised by the nature and content of the final or summative evaluation and for the summative evaluation to represent a summary of supervisory conversations, we recommend that supervisors be generous with and explicit about their provision of feedback in every supervision session. Feedback should become routine, an integral part of each session, and offered as part of the standard supervision conversation. In other words, supervisors should become accustomed to offering direct and specific feedback about their supervisees' performance in every session; and supervisees should become accustomed to receiving such feedback from their supervisors. This includes feedback about supervisees' in-session behavior or presentation in supervision. Indeed, Dohrenbusch and Lipka (2006) found that the 12 supervisors in their study evaluated their supervisees primarily on their behavior in supervision rather than their behavior in sessions with clients. Although we recommend that oral feedback be based on both counseling session behavior and supervision session behavior, the latter may be more difficult for some supervisors to provide. That is, supervisors may be less comfortable assessing and commenting on issues of immediacy, or how their supervisees conduct themselves in-the-moment of supervision. These issues, however, may parallel supervisee behaviors in counseling. An illustration may be helpful.

A beginning counselor trainee one of us worked with lamented in supervision the number of clients who elected not to return for counseling following their initial session with him. This supervisee naturally nods his head repeatedly when listening to other people (e.g., classmates, clients, supervisor), a behavior the supervisor had observed in practicum class, in his video-recorded initial counseling sessions, and in individual supervision. The supervisor's theory had been that this supervisee's frequent (although slight) head nodding inadvertently conveyed to the speaker (e.g., client) premature understanding and agreement; this was the supervisor's experience when talking to the supervisee in individual sessions (i.e., "He's nodding his head, but I'm not sure he really knows or understands what I mean"). The supervisee's lament about clients not returning was used as an occasion to provide the supervisee with this feedback: "You know, I've noticed that you often nod your head when you're listening to someone, like you're doing right now as I talk. This seems like a very natural thing for you to do, and something I've observed you doing when you meet with clients. I wonder, though, if your head nodding might be communicating agreement, say with a client, when you really don't have enough information yet to form a judgment or an opinion. I've thought this myself in supervision, whether what I say is actually as clear to you as your head nodding suggests to me. I don't know, but I wonder how clients have interpreted your head nodding." This supervisor's observation led to an extended conversation about nonverbal communication and how the supervisee could be more attentive to his body language. Nonverbal communication was a topic in subsequent supervision sessions and was addressed in the midsemester summative evaluation in terms of supervisee progress (less frequent head nodding in counseling sessions, more frequent empathic reflections offered to his clients).

*Soliciting Supervisee Feedback in Session*

Not only is it important in each supervision session for supervisors to provide supervisees with oral feedback, it is equally important for supervisees to offer their supervisors feedback. We believe it is essential in each supervision session for the supervisor to invite supervisees to assess their counseling knowledge and skills, and also assess supervisory procedures and dynamics. This practice is likened to formative evaluation, although in this instance it is the supervisee who provides feedback to the supervisor about the process of supervision. Psychotherapy research suggests that clients whose therapists actively solicit client perspectives about therapy (e.g., preferences, opinions) are more likely to assess the therapeutic relationship as collaborative (Bachelor, 1995; Lilliengren & Werbart, 2005) and feel empowered and satisfied with therapy (Timulak & Elliott, 2003). Supervisees might respond in a similar fashion when routinely asked by their supervisors for their perspectives and ideas about the process of supervision and their progress as counselor trainees. Indeed, Fernando and Hulse-Killacky (2005) recommended that supervisors should formally and informally evaluate how aspects of their style are helping or hampering supervisee development, which we believe engages our supervisees in self-assessment and professional collaboration. This practice also models for supervisees a style of genuine inquisitiveness and collaboration to use in session with their clients and may also influence their practice as future supervisors.

The open-ended and constructive questions we ask our supervisees in order to garner their impressions of their counseling performance and their supervision involvement are consistent with a solution-focused approach to supervision (see Juhnke, 1996). "How do you think you did in this fourth session with this client?" and "What did you have planned for this particular counseling session?" encourage supervisee self-assessment and also allow the supervisor to gauge supervisee skills. Questions about the supervisory process include "What do you think about my recommendation?" and "What is one thing that you and I have discussed in today's session that (a) stood out for you, (b) was helpful, or (c) you will take with you today and apply to your next session with this client?" This latter question is one we typically ask at the conclusion of each supervision session and because of its focus and specificity (i.e., "one thing"), can be asked even when only one or two minutes remain in the session and as we and our supervisees gather our materials before one of us exits the room. Supervisee responses are included in our supervision notes to assist with constructing the summative evaluation.

*Maintaining Supervision Notes*

Falvey (2002) and her colleagues (Falvey, Caldwell, & Cohen, 2002; Falvey & Cohen, 2003) have reinforced the importance of documentation in supervision. Their primary motive for maintaining clear, specific, and timely written supervision notes is to prevent supervisor legal or ethical misconduct. The forms they have developed to encourage supervisor documentation are referred to as *The Focused Risk Management Supervision System* (*FoRMSS*; Falvey et al., 2002). The forms include a log of all client cases assigned to the supervisee and reviewed in supervision; an overview of each client case (including a list of all services provided to each client, client treatment plan); and a list of services provided in each supervision session (including supervisor's treatment recommendations). The prominent theme throughout the *FoRMSS* appears to be that clients, supervisees, and supervisors are all at risk: clients are at risk of receiving too few counseling sessions due to managed care restrictions; supervisees are at risk of not being fully prepared for assessing and treating complex and severe client issues; and supervisors may be at risk for inadequate client oversight by not reviewing specific aspects of each client case with the supervisee.

We appreciate Falvey et al.'s (2002) provision of a detailed and thorough format to track supervisee activities (interventions and concerns) and supervisor activities (treatment and training recommendations) in the interest of ethical and legal standards. However, our emphasis or theme in maintaining supervision notes is not risk prevention; it is enhancement. That is, our focus is on supervisee skill development, and we document our observations of the supervisee's intervention, conceptualization, and personalization skills (according to Bernard's 1997, supervisor focus areas), skills performed adequately and exceptionally, as well as skills that have yet to be demonstrated adequately. Although we record important client information in our supervision notes (e.g., demographics, presenting and current concerns, dates of services) and track the supervisee's work with each of his or her clients (e.g., written observations from tape review) as Falvey et al. recommend, our emphasis in documentation is on the supervisee's growth or enhancement as a professional counselor.

We write notes when we review supervisee video recordings of counseling sessions outside of scheduled supervision times, during each supervision session, and immediately following each supervision session. We do not use a specific form for this (we go through a lot of legal pads!), but our format generally follows documenting client information, supervisee skills, and supervisor recommendations. Often we make a copy of the notes we took while reviewing a video-recorded counseling session outside of supervision, and we provide this copy to our supervisee after reviewing it with him or her. We also take notes during supervision to capture information exchanged in the session and model for the supervisee conscientious and disciplined practice. We encourage our supervisees to maintain their own notes during supervision, a practice that Dohrenbusch and Lipka (2006) found contributed to favorable supervisee evaluations. Notes we take immediately following a supervision session are for the purpose of highlighting specific supervisee skills observed and lacking, specific feedback we offered to the supervisee in session, and further actions we should take as supervisors prior to the next scheduled supervision session.

Each supervision note represents a summary of our observations, formative feedback, and recommendations. Our intent is to capture in writing the highlights of our conversations with our supervisees, and this includes notes taken as we watch the video recordings of our supervisees meeting with their clients (because we provide supervisees with a copy of these notes, these notes can be considered notes *to* our supervisees). As much as possible, we try to document specifics: specific skills observed, specific feedback offered, and specific recommendations provided. In this way, we have a running list of examples to help us construct the eventual formal or summative evaluation. It also means that the summative evaluation is indeed a summary of the conversations we have had with our supervisees: conversations about their growth and enhancement. During the review of the formal evaluation, this allows us to make references to earlier conversations, such as "As we talked about after your second session with client Cassandra ..." and "This is something that I emphasized when you started meeting with client Jamie and we talked about the difficulty you had knowing how to handle her disclosure." Referring to earlier supervisory conversations (made possible by maintaining detailed notes of each supervision session) suggests that the supervisee has been kept apprised of his or her performance throughout supervision and should therefore not be surprised with the content of his or her formal or summative evaluation.

*Constructing Narrative Reviews*

Consistent with our philosophy that the summative evaluation reflects a summary of supervisory conversations is our practice of appending a narrative review to each standard numerical rating form often used by counselor preparation programs, community agencies and schools, and credentialing bodies (e.g., state licensure boards) to evaluate a supervisee's work. We write a one- to two-paragraph narrative for the purpose of expounding on the numerical ratings. The narrative can be written in the third person or addressed directly to the supervisee as a letter. We often structure our narrative reviews according to "What you did well" and "What you need to continue to work on." Because it accompanies the standard numerical rating form, the narrative should be consistent with and explain the supervisee's quantitative evaluation.

Examples of narrative reviews we have constructed (pseudonyms are used) are as follows:

- "Tony is current about the status of his clients and prepared to discuss their issues and goals as needed to conceptualize their cases. He intentionally infuses directives and suggestions into client sessions, and he has offered thoughtful commentary on the utilization of feedback in conversations with his supervisor."
- "Alexia is encouraged to continue building upon her skills and abilities in looking for meaning behind the content that is presented in client sessions (e.g., decrease emphasis placed on verbalized words) ... . Alexia is advised to continue working to decrease her perceived sense of responsibility for clients (e.g., increasing comfort with client termination and recognition of client's work that is needed to achieve goals)."
- "Mark, you have been able to demonstrate a more direct style, replete with observations and reflective statements. In one session, you were able to inquire about the client's alcohol use in an inquisitive and nonthreatening manner, posing specific questions that elicited detailed information. The client later remarked that your expression of concern was what stood out for him in this session, indicating that your feedback was interpreted as helpful and nonjudgmental."
- "Specific improvements I have witnessed in Jennifer this semester include her provision of more reflective statements/empathic reflections, particularly statements that are 'truncated' or concise (e.g., 'Almost painful' and 'Got some order back'). I would encourage Jennifer to consider how she can reflect *more* than client verbalizations (i.e., not just client *content* or *what* the client has actually said) and reflect client *nonverbals* and what client is *not* saying (i.e., what client is not yet able to verbalize but feels or is experiencing)."

The narrative review is intended to explain the numerical ratings, provide specific examples to support the supervisee's quantitative assessment, and personalize or customize the evaluation to each supervisee. Supervisees have commented that the narrative reviews help them understand their ratings and clarify for them what they need to continue to work on in ongoing counseling and supervision.

### Evaluative Exchange

There is evidence to suggest that supervisees and supervisors seem to agree on important topics discussed in supervision (Henry, Hart, & Nance, 2004), specifically (a) skills and techniques and (b) personal issues. There is further evidence to suggest that supervisees and supervisors agree on characteristics of supervisees who use supervision well (Vespia, Heckman-Stone, & Delworth, 2002). These characteristics include the following: (a) demonstrates respect and appreciation for individual differences, (b) actively participates in supervision sessions, (c) gives supervisor feedback regarding needs and wants, (d) takes responsibility for consequences of own behavior, and (e) implements supervisor's directives when client welfare is of concern to supervisor. Supervisees are therefore able to be actively engaged in the evaluation process and we encourage supervisors to solicit their participation.

Gould and Bradley (2001) described evaluation as "a two-way street" (p. 276) and Freeman (1985) referred to reciprocal feedback wherein the supervisee is able to clarify feedback, provide alternative perspectives, and offer feedback to the supervisor. We direct our supervisees to complete a supervisor evaluation at midsemester and at the end of the semester, and we provide them with the supervisor evaluation form in the very first supervision session. We then dedicate a significant portion of a supervision session to what we refer to as the exchange of evaluations: the supervisor first reviews his or her evaluation of the supervisee with the supervisee, and the supervisee then reviews his or her evaluation of the supervisor with the supervisor. We model straightforward communication by reviewing each numerically rated item with the supervisee and then reading aloud the narrative review to the supervisee. Our intent is to reinforce that evaluation has been a constant focus and activity throughout supervision and that conversation during the formal or summative evaluation session is consistent with and a summary of prior supervisory conversations.

## Evaluation as Mentoring and Preparing Future Colleagues

Evaluation is a necessary and integral part of supervision. It "goes with the territory" of being a professional. Indeed, continuous review or evaluation of trainees and colleagues is an important characteristic of scholarship

(Shulman, 1998). Not only does supervisory evaluation serve preventive and remedial functions (e.g., hindering the advancement of trainees or colleagues who demonstrate inadequate skills or who are impaired; see Rapisarda & Britton, 2007, for a discussion of *sanctioned supervision*), it is also intended to promote or enhance professional development. In order to accomplish this purpose and reflect a collaborative process, we recommend that evaluation be the product of open and straightforward communication between the supervisee and supervisor. The intent of such dialogue is that the supervisee not be surprised by the nature or content of his or her final evaluation because the summative evaluation is indeed a summary of supervisory conversations that have occurred throughout the supervision period. This has been a guiding principle of our own supervisory practice.

Research suggests that supervisees want to be kept apprised of their performance (see Heckman-Stone, 2003; Ladany et al., 1999; Lehrman-Waterman & Ladany, 2001). This reinforces for us the importance of formative evaluation or continuous feedback. Supervisors can be intentional about this by constructing with their supervisees a written supervision contract that includes the understanding that feedback will be provided (perhaps even in writing) in every supervision session. Supervisors can then be sure that formative feedback (in)*forms* and leads to summative evaluation by maintaining supervision notes with specific examples of supervisee performance to include in the formal evaluation. Throughout the process, supervisee feedback is also solicited and processed in every supervision session, something that can be accomplished with only a few minutes remaining in the session.

Le Maistre, Boudreau, and Paré (2006) referred to "situated evaluation" or the manner in which veteran helping professionals "track a newcomer's growing ability to take part in professional practice—and to see this as a complex relationship between old-timer and neophyte" (pp. 345–346). The manner in which evaluation—and supervision in general—is conducted is a model for supervisees: a model for conducting assessments and other forms of evaluation with clients; and a model for conducting evaluations with their own supervisees when they assume the role of counselor supervisor. The supervisor is therefore very much of a mentor, as Johnson (2007) suggested, and one who has the potential to significantly impact the supervisee's development and practice as a counselor. The *no surprises* principle of supervisee evaluation implies that the supervisor understands his or her role as a role model, mentor, and future colleague to the supervisee and thus maintains open lines of communication, fosters collaboration, and links and intertwines formative and summative evaluation.

## Appendix A
## Counseling Supervision Contract*

(Based on Osborn & Davis, 1996)

This contract serves as verification and a description of the counseling supervision provided by Brandy Kelly, Ph.D., LPCC-S ("University Supervisor"), to Alexia Jones, ("Supervisee"), Counselor Trainee enrolled in Practicum I in the Community Counseling Program at Pursuit of Excellence University (PEU) for the fall 2008 semester.

   I. Purpose, Goals, and Objectives:
      a. Monitor and ensure welfare of clients seen by supervisee.
      b. Promote development of supervisee's professional counselor identity and competence.
      c. Fulfill academic requirement for supervisee's practicum.
      d. Fulfill requirements in preparation for supervisee's pursuit of counselor licensure.
   II. Context of Services:
      a. One (1) clock hour of individual supervision weekly.
      b. Individual supervision will be conducted in the supervisor's office (100 Education Hall), Pursuit of Excellence University, on Tuesdays, from 1:00 p.m. to 2:00 p.m., where monitor/VCR is available to review videotapes.
      c. Cognitive-behavioral methods, interpersonal process recall, and role plays will be used in supervision.
      d. Regular review of counseling videotapes in weekly individual supervision.
   III Method of Evaluation:
      a. Feedback will be provided by the supervisor during each session, and a formal evaluation, using the PEU Counseling Program standard evaluation of student clinical skills, will be conducted at midsemester and at the conclusion of the fall semester. A narrative evaluation will also be provided at midsemester and at the conclusion of the semester as an addendum to the objective evaluations completed.
      b. Specific feedback provided by supervisor will focus on supervisee's demonstrated counseling skills and clinical documentation, which will be based on supervisor's regular observation of supervisee's counseling sessions (via videotape and live), as well as review of clinical documentation.
      c. Supervisee will evaluate supervisor at midsemester and at the close of Fall semester, using the PEU Counseling Program standard evaluation form for evaluating supervisors. A

narrative evaluation will also accompany the objective evaluations.

    d. Supervision notes will be shared with supervisee at supervisor's discretion and at the request of the supervisee.

IV. Duties and Responsibilities of Supervisor and Supervisee:

    a. Supervisor:

        a. Examine client presenting complaints and treatment plans.

        b. Review on a regular basis supervisee's videotaped counseling sessions.

        c. Sign off on all client documentation.

        d. Challenge supervisee to justify approach and techniques used.

        e. Monitor supervisee's basic attending skills.

        f. Present and model appropriate directives.

        g. Intervene when client welfare is at risk.

        h. Ensure American Counseling Association (ACA; 2005) *Code of Ethics* is upheld.

        i. Maintain professional liability insurance coverage.

        j. Maintain weekly supervision notes

        k. Assist supervisee in reviewing various counseling theories, with the goal of gaining an appreciation for an integrative practice approach.

        l. Assist supervisee in gaining greater self-awareness during counseling and supervision sessions.

    b. Supervisee:

        a. Uphold ACA (2005) *Code of Ethics.*

        b. Maintain professional liability insurance coverage.

        c. View counseling session videotapes in preparation for weekly supervision.

        d. Complete "Counselor Trainee Self-Critique and Reflection Form" as a result of having viewed counseling session videotapes and have these ready to discuss in supervision.

        e. Be prepared to discuss all client cases: have client files, current and completed client case notes, and counseling session videotapes ready to review in weekly supervision sessions.

        f. Justify client case conceptualizations made and approach and techniques used.

        g. Complete client case notes and supervision notes in a timely fashion and place in appropriate client files.

        h. Consult with counseling center staff and supervisor in cases of emergency.

        i. Implement supervisory directives in subsequent sessions.

       j. Practice working from a variety of and appropriate counseling theories.

   c. Supervisee's Expressed Learning Objectives for Practicum I:

       a. Refine personal counseling approach/style. This includes the implementation and integration of the following theories of personal interest to me: existential, cognitive-behavioral, and person-centered.

       b. To increase my ability to build trust and rapport with clients, especially with resistant and involuntary clients. This includes the effective implementation of relationship building and attending skills and basic micro-skills (e.g., paraphrasing, asking open-ended questions).

       c. Becoming more comfortable counseling diverse populations (e.g., age, gender, race, socioeconomic status). This includes gaining exposure to diverse populations, becoming aware of my personal biases, adhering to nonjudgmentalism, and establishing appropriate boundaries.

       d. To increase my ability to conduct lethality assessments. This also includes recognizing the limits of my competence and seeking immediate consultation/supervision when necessary.

 V. Procedural Considerations:

   a. Supervisee's written case notes, treatment plans, and videotapes will be reviewed and evaluated in each session.

   b. Issues related to supervisee's professional development will be discussed in each supervision session.

   c. Sessions will be used to discuss issues of conflict and failure of either party to abide by directives outlined here in contract. If concerns of either party are not resolved in supervision, Dr. John Smith, PEU Community Counseling program coordinator, will be consulted.

   d. In event of emergency, supervisee is to contact supervisor at the office, (999) 999-9999, or at home, (222) 222-2222, or on her cell phone, (555) 555-5555.

VI. Supervisor's Scope of Competence:

Dr. Kelly successfully earned her Ph.D. in counselor education and supervision from Kent State University in 2008. She is licensed as a Professional Clinical Counselor, with supervisory endorsement (PCC-S; #E8072) by the state of Ohio, and is a Nationally Certified Counselor (NCC). She is currently a Professional Clinical Counselor at Turning Point Counseling Services and an adjunct faculty member at Pursuit of Excellence University. She has received formal academic training in clinical supervision and has supervised master's degree students at two local universities. She has received training and has practiced as a PCC-S in the areas of individual, group, family, and couples counseling with children, adolescents, and adults in multiple settings (i.e., outpatient, inpatient, residential, and crisis) and utilizes primarily a cognitive-behavioral counseling approach.

VII. Terms of the Contract:

This contract is subject to revision at any time, upon the request of either the supervisor or supervisee. A formal review of the contract will be made at the midterm of fall semester 2008, and revisions will be made only with the consent of the supervisee and the approval of the supervisor.

We agree, to the best of our ability, to uphold the directives specified in this supervision contract and to conduct our professional behavior according to the ethical principles of our professional association.

_____    _____
Supervisor                     Date

_____    _____
Supervisee                     Date

Pursuit of Excellence University
100 Education Hall
City, State 44444
(777) 777-7777

This contract is effective from _____ to _____.

Date of contract revision or termination _____.

*Names of the supervisee, university, and program coordinator are fictitious.

## Appendix B
## Guidelines for Constructing a Written Supervision Contract

### Introducing the Supervision Contract

1. Discuss with supervisee the twofold purpose of supervision: (a) to protect welfare of clients seen by supervisee, and (b) to assist in the professional development of the supervisee.
2. Introduce concept of contract with supervisee in first supervision session.
3. Explain and discuss the rationale and purpose of the contract.
4. Provide supervisee with copy of draft contract.

### Rationale for the Use of a Supervision Contract

1. Clarifies the methods, goals, and expectations of supervision:
   - Roles and responsibilities of both supervisor and supervisee are clarified right from the start, a means of minimizing any "surprises."
   - Minimizes ambiguity and confusion for the supervisee, particularly at the beginning of supervision, when the process is new and questions abound.
   - Helps prevent communication gaps and misunderstanding on the part of both parties.
2. Encourages professional collaboration:
   - Allows both supervisor and supervisee to establish a collaborative working relationship.
   - Means of promoting supervisee's contribution to the supervisory process.
   - Cultivates professional cooperation and a positive working alliance.
3. Upholds ethical principles:
   - Contract exemplifies some of the principles of ethical practice:
     a. Autonomy
        - Supervisee given freedom to participate in the supervisory process.
     b. Justice or Fairness
        - Having things spelled out in writing addresses supervisee's right to know what to expect in supervision.
        - Contract also a means of ensuring that supervision process is fair.

    c. Fidelity
- Contract encourages supervisor and supervisee to remain faithful to the supervision process.
- "We're going to do what we say we're going to do."
- Clarifies components of ethical practice, such as:
  - Helps to further explain the nature of and limits to confidentiality.
  - Ensures client has been informed that supervisee is receiving supervision on a regular basis.
  - Contract clearly describes nature of supervisory relationship and thus minimizes conflicts related to dual relationships.
4. Documents services to be provided:
- Supervisor is ultimately legally responsible for welfare of clients seen by supervisee.
- Contract verifies the intent, nature, and occurrence of supervision; clarifies names of supervisor and supervisee, and duration of supervision.
  - "What was not recorded didn't happen."
- Clarifies expectations and duties of both parties:
  - Contract is a means of holding both parties accountable for their actions.
5. Aligns supervision with counseling and consultation, two services that currently utilize a written contract with clients:
- Supervision contract similar to informed consent used in counseling.
- Supervision contract similar to written contract used in mental health consultation.
- Supervision contract similar to syllabus used in academic course work.
- Supervision contract exemplifies professional courtesy and respect for supervisee.

## Example of Introducing the Contract

"We've talked so far about the purpose of supervision and some of the specific responsibilities and tasks both you and I have in this working relationship. So that both of us are clear about what's going to take place when you and I meet, and to ensure that both of us agree, or are on the same page, so to speak, about our obligations in supervision, I suggest that you and I put together a written supervision contract. My thinking is that having such things in writing, and having our signatures to attest to an agreement, will help us stay on track and remain clear and focused as we work together. Think of the contract as a type of syllabus, but one that you get to contribute to at the outset!"

## Reviewing the Six Elements of Supervision Contract

The sample contract provided uses each of these six elements as a section heading. Supervisors are encouraged, however, to tailor or customize the contract to their specific supervision context and to encompass distinctive aspects or needs represented in each supervisory relationship of which they are a part.

1. Purpose, Goals, and Objectives of Supervision:
   - Explanation of, rationale for clinical supervision.
   - Mention dual purpose of supervision (i.e., ensure client welfare and promote professional development of supervisee).
   - Also mention training or legal requirements (e.g., to fulfill accreditation standards and/or state licensure eligibility).
2. Context of Services:
   - Amount and length of supervision (specify regular meeting day and time).
   - Setting and format (e.g., group or individual, on- or off-site).
   - Educational and monitoring activities implemented (e.g., live supervision, viewing of audio- and/or videotaped counseling sessions outside of scheduled supervisory sessions, or the audio- and/or videotaping of supervision sessions).
   - Model of supervision used by the supervisor (e.g., developmental, cognitive-behavioral, experiential).
3. Method of Evaluation:
   - Supervisees should be told the amount, type (formal or informal, written or verbal), timing, and frequency of evaluation procedures to be used.
   - Explain how such information will be recorded by the supervisor (e.g., specific evaluation form, narrative, etc.).
   - Explain where evaluative information will be stored (e.g., placed in practicum/internship or personnel file).
   - Explain with whom evaluative information will be shared (e.g., faculty supervisor, clinical director).
4. Duties and Responsibilities of the Supervisor and Supervisee:
   - "Job descriptions" of supervisor and supervisee.
   - Clarifies what both supervisor and supervisee's obligations are to clients being seen by the supervisee.
   - Allows each party to clearly understand not only his or her particular obligations, but the parameters of the supervisory relationship as well.

5. Procedural Considerations:
   - Include type of information supervisee will be expected to discuss in supervisory sessions (e.g., therapeutic skills used, client diagnosis and treatment plan, countertransference issues).
   - Clarify how that information is to be presented (i.e., case notes, audio or video recordings, assessment results).
   - Mention types of record keeping supervisee will be required to conduct.
   - Specify procedures to follow in instance of conflicts between supervisor and supervisee, as well as in the event of client and/or supervisee emergency (specifically, names and telephone numbers of contact persons should be listed on contract).
6. Supervisor's Scope of Competence:
   - Include formal clinical and other professional (e.g., in clinical supervision) training, and areas of expertise.

**Additional Items to Include in the Contract**

- Contract should be identified as such.
- Names of both the supervisor and supervisee should be clearly marked and their signatures included.
- Places of employment, business addresses, and telephone numbers of both parties should be noted.
- Date on which contract was drafted and approved, day supervision was terminated, and dates of any revisions of contract are important to include.
- Insert statement such as "Subject to Revision" (allows contract to be regarded as a working document, as opposed to an intractable and "set in stone" document).

**Reviewing Draft Contract with Supervisee**

- Provide a copy of the draft contract to your supervisee in first supervision session.
- Review each of the six sections with the supervisee during your first supervision session.
- Solicit questions from supervisee as you review the contract together.
- Have supervisee take copy of draft contract home to review; encourage supervisee to write questions or comments he or she might have about the contract directly on the draft contract; have supervisee bring draft contract in for the next supervision session.

- Review any questions or comments supervisee has about draft contract in second supervision session.

## Constructing Written Contract

- It will be the supervisor's responsibility to construct the final version of contract (typed out, ready for signatures) to present to supervisee in third supervision session.
- If there are no additions to contract or questions about it, both supervisee and supervisor sign contract in third supervision session; provide supervisee with copy of signed contract.
- Supervisor retain original contract and inform supervisee where this will be kept.
- Inform supervisee that contract will be reviewed together periodically (e.g., at midterm), as well as at the conclusion of your supervision work together.

## References

Anderson, S. A., Schlossberg, M., & Rigazio-DiGilio, S. (2000). Family therapy trainees' evaluations of their best and worst supervision experiences. *Journal of Marital and Family Therapy, 26,* 79–91.

Bachelor, A. (1995). Clients' perception of the therapeutic alliance: A qualitative analysis. *Journal of Counseling Psychology, 42,* 323–337.

Bahrick, A. S., Russell, R. K., & Salmi, S. W. (1991). The effects of role induction on trainees' perceptions of supervision. *Journal of Counseling & Development, 69,* 434–438.

Benson, K. P., & Holloway, E. L. (2005). Achieving influence: A grounded theory of how clinical supervisors evaluate trainees. *Qualitative Research in Psychology, 2,* 117–140.

Bernard, J. M. (1997). The Discrimination Model. In C. E. Watkins (Ed.), *Handbook of psychotherapy supervision* (pp. 310–327). New York: Wiley.

Bernard, J. M., & Goodyear, R. K. (2009). *Fundamentals of clinical supervision* (4th ed.). Boston: Allyn and Bacon.

Chur-Hansen, A., & McLean, S. (2006). On being a supervisor: The importance of feedback and how to give it. *Australasian Psychiatry, 14,* 67–71.

Dohrenbusch, R., & Lipka, S. (2006). Assessing and predicting supervisors' evaluations of psychotherapists—An empirical study. *Counselling Psychology Quarterly, 19,* 395–414.

Fall, M., & Sutton, Jr., J. M. (2004). *Clinical supervision: A handbook for practitioners.* Boston: Pearson Education.

Falvey, J. E. (2002). *Managing clinical supervision: Ethical practice and legal risk management.* Pacific Grove, CA: Brooks/Cole.

Falvey, J. E., Caldwell, C. F., & Cohen, C. R. (2002). *Documentation in supervision: The Focused Fisk Management supervision System.* Pacific Grove, CA: Brooks/Cole.

Falvey, J. E., & Cohen, C. R. (2003). The buck stops here: Documenting clinical supervision. *The Clinical Supervisor, 22*(2), 63–80.

Fernando, D. M., & Hulse-Killacky, D. (2005). The relationship of supervisory styles to satisfaction with supervision and the perceived self-efficacy of master's-level counseling students. *Counselor Education and Supervision, 44,* 293–305.

Freeman, E. M. (1985). The importance of feedback in clinical supervision: Implications for direct practice. *The Clinical Supervisor, 3 (1),* 5–26.

Freeman, B., & McHenry, S. (1996). Clinical supervision of counselors-in-training: A nationwide survey of ideal delivery, goals, and theoretical influences. *Counselor Education and Supervision, 36,* 144–158.

Gould, L. J., & Bradley, L. J. (2001). Evaluation in supervision. In L. J. Bradley & N. Ladany (Eds.), *Counselor supervision: Principles, process, and practice* (3rd ed.; pp. 271–303). Philadelphia, PA: Brunner-Routledge.

Haynes, R., Corey, G., & Moulton, P. (2003). *Clinical supervision in the helping professions: A practical guide.* Pacific Grove, CA: Brooks/Cole-Thomson Learning.

Heckman-Stone, C. (2003). Trainee preferences for feedback and evaluation in clinical supervision. *The Clinical Supervisor, 22*(1), 21–33.

Henry, P. J., Hart, G. M., & Nance, D. W. (2004). Supervision topics as perceived by supervisors and supervisees. *The Clinical Supervisor, 23*(2), 139–152.

Hewson, J. (1999). Training supervisors to contract in supervision. In E. Holloway & M. Carroll (Eds.), *Training counselling supervisors: Strategies, methods and techniques* (pp. 67–91). London: SAGE.

Holloway, E. (1995). *Clinical supervision: A systems approach.* Thousand Oaks, CA: Sage.

Johnson, W. B. (2007). Transformational supervision: When supervisors mentor. *Professional Psychology: Research and Practice, 38,* 259–267.

Juhnke, G. A. (1996). Solution-focused supervision: Promoting supervisee skills and confidence through successful solutions. *Counselor Education and Supervision, 36,* 48–57.

Kaiser, T. L. (1997). *Supervisory relationships: Exploring the human element.* Pacific Grove, CA: Brooks/Cole.

Ladany, N., Ellis, M. V., & Friedlander, M. L. (1999). The supervisory working alliance, trainee self-efficacy, and satisfaction. *Journal of Counseling & Development, 77,* 447–455.

Le Maistre, C., Boudreau, S., & Paré, A. (2006). Mentor or evaluator? Assisting and assessing newcomers to the professions. *Journal of Workplace Learning, 18,* 344–354.

Lehrman-Waterman, D., & Ladany, N. (2001). Development and validation of the Evaluation Process Within Supervision Inventory. *Journal of Counseling Psychology, 48,* 168–177.

Lilliengren, P., & Werbart, A. (2005). A model of therapeutic action grounded in the patients' view of curative and hindering factors in psychoanalytic psychotherapy. *Psychotherapy: Theory, Research, Practice, Training, 42,* 324–339.

Nelson, M. L., Barnes, K. L., Evans, A. L., & Triggiano, P. J. (2008). Working with conflict in clinical supervision: Wise supervisors' perspectives. *Journal of Counseling Psychology, 55,* 172–184.

Nelson, M. L., & Friedlander, M. L. (2001). A close look at conflictual supervisory relationships: The trainee's perspectives. *Journal of Counseling Psychology, 48,* 384–395.

Osborn, C. J. (Producer). (2005). *The written supervision contract: Documenting ethics in action.* DVD recording of TeleProductions Program at Kent State University. (Available from the American Counseling Association, 5999 Stevenson Ave., Alexandria, VA 22304, www.counseling.org, or by calling 1-800-422-2648 x222.)

Osborn, C. J., & Davis, T. E. (1996). The supervision contract: Making it perfectly clear. *The Clinical Supervisor, 14*(2), 121–134.

Rapisarda, C. A., & Britton, P. J. (2007). Sanctioned supervision: Voices from the experts. *Journal of Mental Health Counseling, 29,* 81–92.

Rolfe, I., & McPherson, J. (1995). Formative assessment: How am I doing? *Lancet, 345,* 837–839.

Shulman, L. S. (1998). Course anatomy: The dissection and analysis of knowledge through teaching. In P. H. Hutchings (Ed.), *The course portfolio: How faculty can examine their teaching to advance practice and improve student learning* (pp. 5–12). Washington, DC: American Association for Higher Education.

Storm, C. L. (1997). The blueprint for supervision relationships: Contracts. In T. C. Todd & C. L. Storm (Eds.), *The complete systemic supervisor: Context, philosophy, and pragmatics* (pp. 272–282). Boston: Allyn and Bacon.

Sutter, E., McPherson, R. H., & Geeseman, R. (2002). Contracting for supervision. *Professional Psychology: Research and Practice, 33,* 495–498.

Thomas, J. T. (2007). Informed consent through contracting for supervision: Minimizing risks, enhancing benefits. *Professional Psychology: Research and Practice, 38,* 221–231.

Timulak, L., & Elliott, R. (2003). Empowerment events in process-experiential psychotherapy of depression: An exploratory qualitative analysis. *Psychotherapy Research, 13,* 443–460.

Vespia, K. M., Heckman-Stone, C., & Delworth, U. (2002). Describing and facilitating effective supervision behavior in counseling trainees. *Psychotherapy Theory/Research/Practice/Training, 39,* 56–65.

Watkins, C. E. (1997a). Defining psychotherapy supervision and understanding supervisor functioning. In C. E. Watkins (Ed.), *Handbook of psychotherapy supervision* (pp. 3–10). New York: John Wiley.

Watkins, C. E. (1997b). Some concluding thoughts about psychotherapy supervision. In C. E. Watkins (Ed.), *Handbook of psychotherapy supervision* (pp. 603–616). New York: John Wiley.

# CHAPTER 3

# Triadic Supervision

## S. LENOIR GILLAM and MICHAEL L. BALTIMORE

Clinical supervision is an essential component in preparing competent clinical mental health and school practitioners as it provides the function of promoting the welfare, autonomy, and best interests of families and individuals in counseling. The form of clinical supervision has varied depending on a number of factors inherent in the training process. Mainly, the two most common modalities have been individual (i.e., one supervisor and one supervisee) and small-group supervision with more than two supervisees. In recent years, triadic supervision, a type of clinical supervision, was approved for counselor education programs in order to lessen the course load of counselor educators in large institutions. This form of supervision, according to CACREP, the Council for Accreditation of Counseling and Related Educational Programs (2001), could be used as an alternative to individual one-to-one supervision. Thus, this alternative became equated with individual more so than group supervision and distinguished as a form of individual supervision. However, a closer examination of the dynamics and process issues related to triadic supervision may show that it more resembles the group supervision already put in place by the national accreditation body.

Triadic supervision has lacked critical research support prior to, and even after, implementation among counselor education training programs through the accreditation standards. Implementation within counselor education programs of triadic supervision may, in some cases, be chosen in place of individual supervision of counselors-in-training. With a lack of acknowledged distinction between individual and triadic supervision, administrative and clinical issues connected to the practice of triadic supervision become an important area of research. A closer examination of this approach is needed, and practice guidelines can only help provide a more sound approach to the delivery of clinical supervision.

## History and Review

Generally, best practice approaches for clinical supervision, especially individual supervision, are well established (see, for example, Bernard & Goodyear, 2009). Bernard and Goodyear (2009) state:

> Supervision is an intervention provided by a more senior member of a profession to a more junior member or members of that same profession. This relationship
> - is evaluative and hierarchical,
> - extends over time, and
> - has the simultaneous purposes of enhancing the professional functioning of the more junior person(s); monitoring the quality of professional services offered to the clients that she, he, or they see; and serving as a gatekeeper for those who are to enter the particular profession. (p. 7)

Thus, a supervisor's role clearly is to enhance the professional development of the supervisee. The interaction between supervisor and supervisees provides a learning environment that includes evaluation, self-awareness and reflection, and adherence to goals leading to competence in the field and the enhancement of functioning as a professional.

Providing clinical supervision with one supervisor and two supervisees, while not new to the field, was first established as a choice under the CACREP standards of 2001 (CACREP, 2001) for counselor education programs. The standards state the requirement for practicum students:

"weekly interaction with an average of one (1) hour per week of individual and/or triadic supervision which occurs regularly over a minimum of one academic term by a program faculty member or a supervisor working under the supervision of a program faculty member;..." (CACREP, 2001, Clinical Supervision section)

and for internship students:

"weekly interaction with an average of one (1) hour per week of individual and/or triadic supervision, throughout the internship, (usually performed by the on-site supervisor;) (CACREP, 2001, Clinical Supervision section)

Supervisors, including site supervisors, must have earned a master's degree and have "at least two (2) years of pertinent professional experience in the program area in which the student is completing clinical instruction;" (CACREP, 2001, Clinical Supervision section)

According to these standards for training programs in counselor education, an average of 1 hr of supervision, either triadic or individual, must be provided weekly for the student. With limited interactions, clinical supervisors must work to establish a positive working relationship with counselors-in-training that meet their needs and the standards of training.

## The Supervisory Relationship and Its Elements

The creation of a good supervisory relationship that allows for professional growth, assesses client–counselor interaction, and improves the functioning of the counselor-in-training is essential. Both supervisor and supervisee have to prepare, engage, and communicate within a process-oriented context of learning. The platform for this learning should be based on honest and open communication and the giving and receiving of critical feedback with a clear structure. Thus, the structure of clinical supervision becomes a foundation for these processes to take place.

In general, the essential elements of the supervisory relationship contain the building of a working alliance that sets the stage for supervision to begin. As supervisor and supervisee begin a "joining" process in the establishment of a supervisory relationship, the first session or sessions will cover elements such as theoretical backgrounds, formative and summative feedback processes, and what the supervisee can expect from the supervisor. Goals and a working contract are also established. After the initial overview, supervisor and supervisee begin the process, including discussion of client cases and other relevant training issues associated with professional goals and program outcomes.

In the course of supervision, many factors affect the process. Differences among supervisor training, background, and experience may vary widely (Fitch, Gillam, & Baltimore, 2004). Supervisors may also vary on factors such as theoretical orientation, previous supervision experiences, and cultural background. The same is true of supervisees. For counselors-in-training, background and experience in the helping role, as well as ability to effectively use counseling content with clients, become part of the supervision process.

Individual and triadic supervision both contain these elements. Yet, when the structure of supervision is changed, the process and practice of supervision become different as well. In triadic supervision, the definition of supervision does not change, but the process becomes more challenging for all concerned. Guidelines are yet to be established that will assist counselor education programs, supervisors, or supervisees in the practice of triadic supervision. Numerous considerations in the examination of triadic supervision will be addressed in this chapter.

## Triadic Supervision: Setting the Stage

The accreditation standards do not touch upon instructions regarding how to conduct or participate in triadic supervision sessions. This is left to the programs and individual supervisors to create and provide. The research offers one conceptual model called "the reflective model of triadic supervision" (Kleist & Hill, as cited in Stinchfield, Hill, & Kleist, 2007, p. 173), while other studies address perceptions related to the use of triadic supervision (Hein & Lawson, 2008; Newgent, Davis Jr., & Farley, 2004). However, little is found regarding the importance of considering group process and practice in providing this modality of supervision. In fact, Newgent et al. (2004) report that "trainees tended to view the individual and triadic models more similarly" (p. 76).

Knowledgeable supervisors who have experienced this model, either as a supervisee or a supervisor, may have an advantage over those without such experience. It certainly demands a set of skills that are not only associated with individual supervision, but importantly, skills in group supervision and leadership. Process and practice issues, including administrative and clinical, come into play in the triadic model.

## Theoretical and Management Issues

In establishing triadic supervision with two supervisees, thought must be given to the effect of theory upon the process. Supervision theory, those models such as social role development, and counseling-oriented approaches will directly impact supervision. Supervisors trained in the developmental models, for example, will consider the supervisee's readiness and abilities for counseling. One counselor development model (Stoltenberg, McNeil, & Delworth, 1998) proposes a three-level classification where level-one trainees may be anxious, lack accuracy in perception of clients, and need additional support. This may be especially true with practicum students beginning their first cases.

In Skovholt and Ronnestad's (1992) stage model of counselor development and themes that affect supervision, a supervisor must consider perspectives and issues that are particularly relevant to the supervision of both the beginning and the advanced supervisee. Anxiety may play a part, especially early on in supervision for beginning supervisees. Triadic supervisors, considering such factors as anxiety on the part of the supervisees and a need for tolerance and support—more so at the outset of supervision—can effectively manage these needs while promoting competence. Differences between supervisees on these factors compels the clinical supervisor to establish a supportive environment that is conducive to supervisees' growth.

With the development of the supervisee in mind, the supervisor intending to begin triadic supervision might look at both supervisees to decide whether to mismatch more advanced and less experienced supervisees, or to evenly match supervisees based on similar developmental standings. Homogenous triadic pairings may provide support with factors such as experience level or developmental stage in training, yet heterogeneous matching may provide for a wider range of exposure for supervisees. The Association for Specialists in Group Work's Best Practice Guidelines (ASGW, 2007) state that group selection should include "group members whose needs and goals are compatible with the goals of the group" (Group and Member Preparation section, para. 1).But what criteria should a supervisor establishing triadic supervision consider?

Theoretical approaches such as counseling-based supervision provide important interpersonal data that affect the supervision process. For example, using a psychodynamic supervision model, the notion of transference, and even parallel process, occurring in supervision, will be altered by the presence of a third party. It is up to the supervisor to adapt counseling-based models, based on individual paradigms, to the triadic scenario. Systemic counseling models, such as the family therapy approaches, might be easier for adaptation due to the incorporation of multiple members with the treatment process, for example. In any case, the supervisor using a counseling-based approach to triadic supervision must become aware that there are obstacles to such application.

## Management

A supervisor's advanced decision-making regarding triadic supervision can assist supervisees in having a positive professional growth experience. One such decision is directly related to time management within sessions. Given a limited amount of contact with supervisees, particularly in training programs, consideration of how to conduct the process is important. Supervisees as well as the supervisor must share time; training concepts that must be covered in supervision, client caseloads, crisis management response and personal and professional issues may all evolve. An equity-based approach allows for time to be apportioned between the two supervisees. Scheduling one supervisee to take a larger portion of the time in supervision and then reversing that the next week is one example. Allowing for crisis cases to go first, in a "triage" model, is another approach. Regardless of how time is allotted, careful consideration must be given in order for both supervisees to have adequate time to discuss cases and professional concerns and the supervisor to provide feedback.

Supervisees must develop good communication skills with their peer in triadic supervision. It may be the case that a supervisee wishes more time to discuss an issue during supervision. During these moments, drawing on good basic counseling skills, the participants can be aware of this need and support each other. It will be necessary for the supervisor to monitor these situations in order for both voices to be heard. In addition, it is certainly the case that peers learn from each other (directly related to group supervision process) and that this process adds to the experience in a positive way. In sharing cases, interventions, and responses within the triadic model, supervisees benefit from the learning environment. Acting as peer-supervisors, participants may also learn the beginnings of supervisory skill from the interactions.

Given the aforementioned time restraints, being fully prepared for supervision is crucial. Many supervisors require their supervisees to bring in questions related to cases and/or their professional issues. If audio- and videotapes of counseling sessions are used, then they should be cued and ready for play. Being ready to use the clinical supervision session as efficiently as possible will aid in a successful outcome.

Time constraints affect the number and type of cases chosen by supervisees for supervision. A complex case may take the entire session, yet supervisors are responsible for a counselor's entire caseload. It is necessary for supervisor and supervisees to discuss the issues of caseload and the decisions regarding how time will be spent in session. While this may be associated with all forms of supervision, it becomes even more crucial as triadic is substituted for individual supervision.

There are numerous issues related to the process and practice of triadic supervision. The authors will attempt to address important considerations that speak to the differences and similarities between individual, group, and triadic supervision as guidelines for triadic supervision are outlined.

## Administrative, Clinical, and Program Considerations

Whether by program faculty or individual supervisor, informed decisions regarding the structure and management of clinical supervision issues related to triadic supervision are necessary for positive outcomes. The decision to implement triadic supervision must involve more than the convenience of scheduling. It must be based on providing a quality supervision experience for the supervisee that meets the highest standards of supervision practice. These issues are also relevant for practitioners in nonuniversity settings, as there will be someone assigned administratively to organize the supervision process and provide oversight.

## Administrative Supervision Issues

According to Bernard and Goodyear (2009), "the administrative supervisor, while obviously concerned about service delivery and staff development, must also focus on matters such as communication protocol, personnel concerns, and fiscal issues, to name just a few" (p. 193), though Bernard and Goodyear use the terms "*managerial* and *organizational*" (p. 194) to refer to these administrative organizational interventions that lend support to the supervision process. Clinical supervisors must attend to these managerial tasks, but practitioners or counseling program personnel other than those professionals providing clinical services may have a role in the management of clinical supervision, as well.

*Program considerations.* The organization of clinical supervision experiences may, in many cases, be handled by a professional responsible for the oversight of all program field experiences (e.g., a program coordinator, director of clinical services). Before clinical supervisors even have supervisees assigned to them for supervision, managerial functions will be taking place. Some of these functions include practicum or internship placement, identification of faculty or part-time instructors to handle the supervision load for the program, and assignment of students to practicum or internship sections (or parallel process for practitioners such as assignment of senior, licensed staff to supervise nonlicensed staff). The management of these tasks is critical to the overall success of the clinical field experiences. Decisions about which supervisees should be assigned to various groups ought to include considerations such as developmental issues (e.g., practicum versus internship), personnel matters (e.g., avoiding potential role conflicts), and group composition (e.g., relationship issues). In many cases, the clinical supervisors may not be making decisions about which participants are assigned to their groups, but they are likely to have a role in determining which supervisees will partner for triadic supervision and how triadic supervision will be employed.

*Supervisor considerations.* CACREP (2001) guidelines provide direction for counselor training programs in determining the supervisor/supervisee ratio and the number of hours required for group and individual/triadic supervision. Within those guidelines, clinical supervisors make decisions about the structure of supervision sessions and how to meet the requirements. Given that triadic and one-to-one supervision are both considered individual supervision, supervisors can meet the individual supervision requirement in one of several ways: (1) they can meet with one supervisee at a time; (2) they can meet with two supervisees at a time; (3) they may employ a combination of one-to-one and triadic supervision; or (4) they may supervise others with relevant training experience in the supervision of practicum students/interns. In addition, CACREP enables the individual supervision requirement for internship to be met though on-site supervision. It is possible, therefore, that the program may not provide individual supervision for internship. Program faculty ought to be aware of the quality of supervision that supervisees receive on-site. Whatever the choice, regardless of whether supervision occurs within a counselor training program or a clinical setting, the decision requires appropriate planning and clinical judgment in order to ensure a satisfactory supervision experience and to address the features unique to triadic supervision. For example, how do supervisors match partners for triadic supervision when supervising an odd number of supervisees? With a number of supervisees not divisible by two, someone is going to be left out, or there may be a tendency to change partners over the course of the supervision term, an action that will have its own implications on the dynamics of the supervisory relationship. That is, group dynamics are impacted by membership changes. Furthermore, if supervisors assign the matches for supervision, then they may not be aware of interpersonal or other factors that could derail the effectiveness of supervision. Conversely, allowing supervisees to choose their own partners may result in ineffective matches for other reasons (e.g., allowing best friends to work together or allowing decisions to be made solely based on schedules might not lead to optimal matches). Though the benefits of triadic supervision are clear, one-to-one supervision provides less risk in terms of the possibility of one supervisee negatively impacting the individual supervision of another supervisee.

*Contextual and ethical issues.* Among the composition issues noted earlier, supervisors responsible for placing supervisees in groups should be aware that triadic partners may experience role conflicts that could impact the supervision process (e.g., one partner is the supervisor of the other partner in a work setting outside of counselor training). These kinds of conflicts need to be avoided when assigning supervisees to groups or triadic supervision due to the potential for harm for either party or for negatively impacting the training experience.

Where counselor education is concerned, a coordinated effort at the program level to enhance consistency across field experiences is important. Though allowing for flexibility in the process and practice of supervision, congruence across sections in practicum and internship syllabi provides general guidelines to insure that the use of triadic supervision is in compliance with professional standards (e.g., accreditation).

*Clinical Supervision Issues*

The clinical supervisor's responsibility is to facilitate supervisee development through a process that promotes and protects client welfare.

*Supervisee development.* Although triadic supervision offers benefits as a training modality, it is important to provide a supervisory experience that will help supervisees meet individual goals for professional growth and to explore personal issues that emerge within the context of professional development and/or impact work with clients. According to the Discrimination Model (Bernard, as cited in Bernard & Goodyear, 2009), the *personalization* piece is an important and appropriate part of clinical supervision. Even in developmentally homogeneous pairings, supervisees are likely to have variance in terms of individual needs for supervision. The context of triadic supervision challenges the supervisor to structure a process that will help both parties meet individual needs while providing an environment that promotes supervisee participation and growth. Participation that feels safe to one supervisee may feel high-risk to the other supervisee. The supervisor roles identified by the Discrimination Model (Bernard, as cited in Bernard & Goodyear, 2009) will vary based on the focus of supervision (e.g., *conceptualization skills*) and the supervisee's needs in that area. At any point in triadic supervision, the supervisor's role with one supervisee might be incompatible with the developmental needs of the other supervisee. For example, if Supervisee A has experience in working with clients with suicidal ideation, and Supervisee B has never worked with clients at risk for self-harm, then Supervisee A may need the supervisor to serve more as a consultant in focusing on case conceptualization of a suicidal client, whereas Supervisee B may need the more concrete explanations of a supervisor serving in the teaching role. Consequently, supervisors may struggle with the delivery of interventions that can keep both parties involved in a way that is appropriate to their different levels of development. The challenge is to avoid providing disjointed supervision to one student at a time while the other becomes simply an observer. Though there is benefit in being an observational learner, supervisees traditionally get this benefit in group supervision. In triadic supervision, where the focus is supposed to be on the individual, observational learning may not occur if the intervention is pitched above the developmental level of the observing supervisee. Structuring insight-oriented supervision interventions with trainees who can deal with this level of complexity may make trainees who have a more concrete approach feel lost.

*Relational/process issues.* Social interaction is one characteristic that defines what constitutes a group (Forsyth, 2006). Similar to group supervision, triadic supervision is impacted by the nature of interaction among members, including the supervisor. The nature of triadic supervision offers supervisees the opportunity to not only learn about themselves and their work with clients but also gain insight about themselves, relationships, and group process through the interactions with one another. A skilled supervisor who understands group dynamics and can facilitate groups effectively is critical to realizing the benefits provided by this modality of supervision. Without this expertise in group work, the triadic supervision process may resemble a one-to-one supervision session with an audience consisting of the other participant. The challenge is to find an appropriate balance of process and content in triadic supervision that enables supervisees to create individualized goals, receive formative and summative evaluation, and participate in an environment that provides necessary support and challenge within a growth experience intended to serve the needs of both parties. Compared with one-to-one supervision, relationships between the supervisor and supervisees are established within the context of the triadic relationship. It is necessary at the outset for the supervisor to remember that relationships between the supervisees need to be facilitated, regardless of the existence of prior relationships between them. The development of the new triad, supervisor included, reflects the emergence of a new group. Despite any history among all three parties, this experience is likely to be the first time that this group has been together to address the professional development of these particular supervisees. Therefore, attention ought to be paid to the *Forming* stage (Tuckman, 1965) of this triadic supervision process.

Within this *Forming* stage (Tuckman, 1965), supervisors have the additional role of educating supervisees about issues such as the process of supervision and the responsibilities of the supervisor and supervisees. It is critical that supervisors provide aspects of informed consent regarding supervisee expectations and client welfare, and having this information can help participants become better consumers of supervision (i.e., knowing what to expect can assist them in articulating their needs).

Supervisees also have the right to understand the role of formative and summative evaluation processes. The triadic supervision process is likely to complicate the delivery of feedback. How do supervisors give feedback, and how do participants receive it in this triadic context? It is important that the quality of feedback not suffer due to the presence of more than one supervisee in the room. When discrepancies exist in the performance of two supervisees, or when one supervisee's performance is unsatisfactory, supervisors may withhold or put off providing feedback because the environment may not allow for candid feedback. Inadequate feedback about evaluation can create ethical conflicts regarding client care, impede supervisee growth, or potentially create a violation of the supervisee's due process (e.g., if in a university setting the trainee ultimately fails the field experience or gets dismissed from the program). When giving verbal feedback to one supervisee within the context of triadic supervision, the supervisor needs to be aware that an audience is always present, which can impact how feedback is received. Interventions that provide opportunities for individual supervisees to engage in self-reflection (e.g., goal setting, narratives, logs) or receive feedback that is not shared with others (e.g., written evaluation) may help to combat this problem.

Aside from evaluation challenges, supervisors must be purposeful in structuring sessions so that equal attention is paid to both supervisees' professional development or client issues. For example, if one supervisee has several clients with difficult issues, then there may be a tendency to focus the session on case conceptualization with that person's clients, thus missing opportunities to provide needed supervision to the other party. Although supervisees can benefit from vicarious learning through their partner's experiences, too much of an imbalance can detract from the effectiveness of triadic supervision. In addition, the supervisee with less experience may be hard to draw out, believing that she/he has little to add to the triad. Supervisees who appear to be reluctant or resistant may respond differently in one-to-one versus triadic environments.

Logistical issues need to be addressed as well. Scheduling problems, absences, and emergencies are examples of factors that need to be considered in structuring triadic supervision. These issues may make it necessary to provide supervision sessions to only one party of the triad. Supervisors are then faced with the decision of how these individual sessions relate (or not) to the work of the triad. Even if none of the aforementioned concerns arise, supervisors should have a planned format for running triadic supervision and communicate those procedures to supervisees (e.g., check in, agenda, prioritizing, case presentation, and so forth).

*Supervisee considerations.* Supervisees who are trained in supervision process and practice and have an understanding of the unique factors related to triadic supervision may be better able to advocate for getting their needs met in supervision. Group work offers members opportunities to learn to give and receive feedback appropriately, and triadic supervision provides this same benefit. In this modality of supervision, each supervisee is able to serve in the role of peer supervisor to the other, as opposed to the supervisor being the sole provider of feedback.

Another benefit of triadic supervision, as noted earlier, is that supervisees can learn vicariously through the experiences of their partner. While this benefit may assist participants in gaining new insights and skills without experiencing issues directly, supervisors should be aware that some supervisees may react positively (e.g., feel relief) or negatively (e.g., experience agitation and anger) to having the other person's work as the focus of supervision. Again, finding an appropriate balance of focus on both parties is important.

Although triadic supervision offers benefits of group supervision while also allowing for more individual time than is generally experienced, trainees need opportunities to set and work toward individual goals for their professional development. It is important that supervision goals be developed within the context of the specific modality.

*Contextual and ethical issues.* A number of ethical considerations that pertain to individual or group supervision also relate to triadic supervision. First, supervisors should possess relevant training and experience to provide supervision. A competent supervisor of triadic supervision should be an experienced supervisor who is also skilled as a group worker in order to deal with the complexities of promoting counselor development, safeguarding client welfare, and facilitating group dynamics.

Informed consent is also a cornerstone of ethical practices in supervision. Although some issues pertaining to informed consent have already been addressed, when orienting supervisees to individual and group supervision, supervisors should help them understand how issues such as theoretical orientation, structure of supervision, and evaluation processes apply across one-to-one, triadic, and group supervision. For example, it would be important to address how an ethical violation would be handled in the different modalities.

The issue of confidentiality needs to be addressed as a unique feature of triadic supervision, as well. Although supervisees are expected to adhere to the professional counseling codes, participants may learn personal information about each other as it pertains to their work with clients, and the expectation that this information be held confidential should be discussed. Supervisees may feel more comfortable sharing in the triadic context than in the group setting; their concerns that information might be disclosed outside of supervision may limit their willingness to explore issues that are relevant to their professional development as counselors. Furthermore, supervisees may be aware to some degree of evaluative feedback provided to each other, and this information should be also protected.

Although orientating supervisees to the process of triadic supervision is necessary, planning for termination is equally important. Planning for and dealing with the end of the triadic supervision relationship is as important as addressing termination in individual and group supervision. Acknowledging termination not only provides an opportunity for all parties to reflect on what has been learned through the supervision experience and to say goodbye but also serves as a model for supervisees in dealing with future termination processes.

Regardless of the ethical consideration under question, supervisors should be as transparent as is appropriate in dealing with ethical issues as they arise in triadic supervision (there may be times when situations are best addressed individually). These ethical decision-making processes may provide excellent opportunities for learning when addressed in the context of supervision.

## Best Practices in Triadic Supervision

Planning for triadic supervision must incorporate considerations of group process and practice. Both administrative and clinical issues are important to address in providing a purposeful and reflective approach to triadic supervision. Further, administrative and clinical issues often overlap. That is, administrative functions may be closely related to clinical, ethical, and legal concerns during supervision. In the university setting, programs can establish the overall structure of clinical instruction, with individual supervisors deciding how administrative issues within the supervision sessions are managed. It should be noted that both administrative and clinical considerations differ for individual and triadic supervision.

*Administrative practices.* Supervisors in university training programs using triadic supervision should be purposeful in employing this modality. Using triadic supervision for the sake of convenience does not mean that the supervisor will be effective. The skilled supervisor is one who has a strong understanding of both supervision as well as group process and practice. Several suggestions for training programs and program faculty addressing administrative aspects of triadic supervision within the context of group work follow in this section (these issues are relevant also in clinical settings where triadic supervision is used):

- *Recognize the similarities and differences among one-on-one, triadic, and group supervision and use that information in planning program field experiences.* Although the supervisor–supervisee ratio is smaller in triadic supervision than in group supervision, the process of triadic supervision more closely resembles group supervision than one-on-one supervision. Designing syllabi that not only address accreditation requirements but also include exercises for reflecting on individual goals (e.g., log entries, personal narratives), providing opportunities for individual evaluation, and noting logistics of scheduling are ways to address some of the shortcomings of triadic supervision. In short, if one-on-one time is lost altogether, then programs should implement plans for addressing trainees' needs when an alternative to triadic supervision is necessary (e.g., in an emergency situation).

- *Consider group composition when assigning supervisees to practicum or internship sections, and be careful about matching individuals to be partnered for triadic supervision.* Although partnerships for triadic supervision are likely to be made in group sections and not by a program faculty member responsible for administrative aspects of all field experiences, the person assigning trainees to sections can consider that pairings will be generated from among those trainees in each group. Attention to composition can help to minimize potential conflicts that may emerge. Allowing students to choose their own supervisors and group supervision sections negates attention to group composition. Furthermore, if partners are formed out of sections with an odd number of trainees, then a plan needs to be in place for addressing this issue. Simply switching partners regularly for the sake of convenience alters dynamics of the triadic relationships. In a sense, this configuration becomes an *open* group, which can generate problems with group development, cohesion, and trust.
- *If a part-time faculty member is providing triadic supervision, then consider how oversight of effectiveness will be monitored.* In addition, university programs can provide training or orientation sessions about training program expectations and clinical issues pertaining to the use of triadic supervision.
- *Consult with colleagues when necessary in order to enhance supervision effectiveness.* The nature of triadic supervision may be more complex than individual supervision due to the dynamics of a three-person group, and unexpected issues may arise that warrant consultation.
- *Consider providing training and open discussions among clinical program faculty and providers.* As the impact of reducing or stopping individual supervision and substituting triadic supervision has not been fully researched, informed faculty can consider, monitor, and revise their practice of providing clinical supervision to students and practitioners.

*Clinical practices.* Clinical supervisors need to put extra thought into how they structure supervision sessions. It is important to remember that having three parties in the supervision process adds complexity to the dynamics of the supervision relationship. In addition, the use of supervision theories and interventions, goal development, evaluation procedures, and eventual outcomes may be affected. Process issues in clinical supervision become shared, much as in group supervision, and the supervisor must carefully consider the impact of the overall experience. This section addresses considerations for clinical practices in triadic supervision.

- *Be purposeful about structuring supervision sessions, and demystify the process of triadic supervision.* Supervisees will look to supervisors for direction, especially in the early stages of the supervision relationship. If the structure of triadic supervision is vague, or if the expectations are unclear, then supervisees may not understand their roles in the process. If supervisors are unclear about the structure, then triadic supervision is likely to be limited in effectiveness.
- *Share information about your theoretical orientation to supervision and offer insight about how that orientation might be expressed differently depending on the type of supervision intervention employed (e.g., one-on-one supervision versus triadic supervision).* Addressing these issues can help clarify the expectations for supervisees' participation.
- *Provide informed consent about other aspects related to the process and practice of triadic supervision.* Supervisees have the right to understand how issues such as evaluation and confidentiality factor into this supervisory experience and how the application of these issues in triadic supervision is similar to and different from the application in individual or group supervision.
- *Consider that supervisees may have varying needs for supervision and anticipate how to intervene when individual needs conflict with the needs of the triad.* Employing structure up front (e.g., having participants check in and identify agenda items for that session) may help avoid this problem because they can work together to prioritize issues to address in session that day.
- *Consider also developmental differences between supervisees and how those differences may impact the supervision process.* Too great of a mismatch between supervisees may lead to interventions that fit one person but are developmentally inappropriate for the other. Counselor development theories can provide a framework for understanding possible differences and responses.
- *Be prepared to be an effective time manager.* Serving two supervisees at a time while attending to the dynamics of the triad may make it difficult to accomplish session goals. Again, prioritizing agenda items and/or increasing the length of sessions (e.g., 90-min versus 60-min sessions) may help alleviate this problem. As there are several commonly used approaches to the management of time within supervision sessions, adjusting a schedule may be in the best interest of supervisees and supervisor. Additionally, open discussion and formative feedback support good time management in triadic supervision.
- *Consider how to address sensitive issues that arise in supervision.* Focusing on one supervisee's issues while having an "audience"

present may impact the dynamics of the supervision process and the supervisee's receptivity to the intervention. Providing opportunities for individualized feedback or attention is important to structure. It may be that adjunct individual sessions are necessary to completely address some sensitive issues. Good group and supervisory skills on the part of the supervisor are important, as well as an open and supportive environment from the outset of supervision. Finally, consultation and supervision of supervision can aid in the management of the impact of these issues.

- *Notice patterns that develop in the supervision relationship (e.g., consistently going into greater depth with one supervisee than with the other or withholding/tailoring feedback that you would be reluctant to offer in front of another supervisee).* Triadic supervision is about much more than the content of what is addressed in supervision; attending to the process is important, too. Helping supervisees explore process issues can model attention to important process issues in the therapeutic relationship, as well.

- *Seek feedback from supervisees regarding the benefits and limitations of triadic supervision.* Specifically request input about how individual needs are met or not met through this modality in preparation for future use of triadic supervision. Formative and summative feedback regarding the process of supervision becomes central in evaluating triadic supervision. These experiences may differ between individuals in the same supervision triad.

- *Help supervisees structure individual goals and goals that are conducive to the process of triadic supervision.* That is, partners should explore together how they can benefit best from that modality of supervision, in addition to developing individual learning goals for the semester.

- *Be aware of how supervisee defenses can impact the dynamics of the supervision sessions.* As indicated previously, conceptualization of those defenses should be considered within the context of triadic supervision. It may become apparent that a supervisee's defensive reaction to a peer, or even a supervisor's presentation, indicates a greater need for intervention or counseling outside of the triad.

- *If requiring case presentations, consider a format that is conducive to the structure of the supervision sessions so that one person's case does not monopolize the entire session.* Once again, time management includes assisting supervisees in the case conceptualization and presentation of cases. The skill of presenting cases in a succinct and clear manner is an essential skill of good clinicians.

- *Anticipate occasional scheduling problems and have a procedure in place for dealing with them.* Consider your policy for offering one-on-one or special sessions when needed and make sure that trainees are fully informed about these policies. Individualized sessions can impact the dynamics of the triadic relationship.

- *Recognize that the evaluation process can be challenging in triadic supervision, particularly if one supervisee is not performing effectively and requires critical feedback that might not be appropriate to share in triadic supervision.* As the evaluative process in supervision is often stress-producing, offering an adjunct individual session may relieve some of the stress. However, providing critical feedback is an essential process within supervision and counseling and can provide a modeling experience for supervisees.
- *Anticipate ethical concerns that may arise by using this format (e.g., one supervisee having a dual or multiple role relationship with the other supervisee's client).* Again, a clear policy up front for handling issues requiring individualized attention is important.

## Conclusion

Triadic supervision is a training intervention that can satisfy CACREP (2001) individual supervision requirements. Though there are benefits associated with triadic supervision, this modality more closely resembles group supervision than individual (i.e., one-to-one) supervision. If triadic supervision is used simply for the sake of efficiency, then supervisors are likely to be unaware of the impact of group dynamics on the supervision process. Competent supervisors of triadic supervision ought to be knowledgeable, experienced supervisors who are also skilled group workers. By attending not only to clinical issues that are impacted by group process and practice but also to administrative considerations related to preparing university training programs, supervisors, and supervisees for triadic supervision can help ensure effective delivery of this modality of supervision.

## References

ASGW (Association for Specialists in Group Work) (2007). *Association for Specialists in Group Work best practice guidelines.* Retrieved December 14, 2008 from http://www.asgw.org/PDF/Best_Practices.pdf
Bernard, J. M., & Goodyear, R. K. (2009). *Fundamentals of clinical supervision* (4th ed.). Upper Saddle River, NJ: Merrill/Pearson Education.
CACREP. (2001). The Council for Accreditation of Counseling and Related Educational Programs, *Accreditation standards and procedures manual.* Alexandria, VA: American Counseling Association.
Fitch, T., Gillam, S. L, & Baltimore, M. L. (2004). Consistency of clinical skills assessment among supervisors. *Clinical Supervisor, 23*, 71–81.

Forsyth, D. R. (2006). *Group dynamics* (4th ed.). Belmont, CA: Thomson.

Hein, S., & Lawson, G. (2008). Triadic supervision and its impact on the role of the supervisor: A qualitative examination of supervisors' perspectives. *Counselor Education and Supervision, 48,* 16–31.

Newgent, R. A., Davis, Jr., H., & Farley, R. C. (2004). Perceptions of individual, triadic, and group models of supervision: A pilot study. *The Clinical Supervisor, 23,* 65–79.

Skovholt, T. M., & Ronnestad, M. H. (1992). Themes in therapist and counselor development. *Journal of Counseling & Development, 70,* 505–515.

Stinchfield, T. A., Hill, N. R., & Kleist, D. M. (2007). The reflective model of triadic supervision: Defining an emerging modality. *Counselor Education and Supervision, 46,* 172–183.

Stoltenberg, C. D., McNeil, B., & Delworth, U. (1998). *IDM Supervision: An integrated developmental model for supervising counselors and therapists.* San Francisco: Jossey-Bass.

Tuckman, B. W. (1965). Developmental sequence in small groups. *Psychological Bulletin, 63,* 384–399.

# CHAPTER 4

# Innovative Uses of Technology in Clinical Supervision

MARTY JENCIUS, MICHAEL L. BALTIMORE, and HILDY G. GETZ

The onset of technology use in counseling and supervision dates back over 60 years when Carl Rogers demonstrated the values of audiotape recordings of clinical session (Rogers, 1942). The audiotape remains the standard technology tool used in time-delayed supervision to this day. What has emerged in 60 years is other formats, including text and video (in real time and time-delayed options), that give the supervisor greater access to the supervisee's experience.

Use of video for supervision and training began in the 1960s as universities and professional training programs had access to video recording technology. The leap from celluloid film to magnetic videotape eliminated the need and cost for processing film. With videotape, the session could be recorded 1 hr and watched in the next. Gelso (1974) noted that videotaping sessions for supervision became the preferred method as the supervisor could hear and see the interaction between client and supervisee. Videotape remains a valued technology tool for supervision, providing a means of exchanging information between supervisor and supervisee, a method of self-reflection and change in supervisees, and a way for supervisees and supervisors to reexperience the session for supervisor evaluation (Huhra, Yamokoski-Maynhart, and Prieto, 2008).

In addition to these time-delayed methods of supervision, other real-time technologies developed in the 1970s and 1980s were incorporated into the supervision process. Phone calls into sessions from behind the one-way mirror brought the supervisee directly into the room with counselor and client. Less obtrusive than a telephone ring, "bug-in-the-ear" and then "bug-in-the eye" supervision, where audio or text prompts are sent to the supervisee in real-time, were incorporated with the development of small radio transceivers and computer monitors. Live, real-time video became publicly available with two technological advances: the development of portable miniaturized video cameras (eliminating the need for large production studios) and the public availability of high-speed Internet transmission to share the video.

With Internet-based technologies developing in the mid-1980s, a whole new opportunity to incorporate technology into the supervision process opened up. Initially we saw the inclusion of time-delayed platforms such as e-mail and LISTSERV (Myrick & Sabella, 1995), but as software and supportive hardware became available, more real-time opportunities developed, such as chat rooms (Coker, Jones, Staples, & Harbach, 2002), desktop videoconferencing (Berger, 2004), and online group meetings (Page, Jencius, Rehfuss, Foss, Den, & Petruzzi, 2003). Other digital products such as CD-ROM and DVD technology can be used as a time-delayed method for distributed education for supervisees and supervisors (Manzanares, O'Haloran, McCartney, Filer, Varhley, & Calhoun, 2004).

This chapter will introduce the reader to a variety of technologies and how they are incorporated into the supervision process. First, we define the typology of current technologies and highlight their use, advantages, and limitations. Second, we provide two examples from two supervision programs, of how these technologies are being implemented in the training of supervisors and continuing education of practicing supervisors. We then look at recommendations for adopting technology in your supervision practice followed by guidelines that may have meaning for supervisors using technology. Finally, we take a look at what the future may hold regarding technology and supervision.

## Typology

When organizing technology supervision tools, consider whether they are synchronous or asynchronous (Manhal-Baugus, 2001). Synchronous tools are real-time technology that works in the moment. Examples of synchronous supervision technology are bug-in the-ear receivers, phone-in supervision, bug-in-the-eye methods, and videoconferencing. Tools that are asynchronous are ones that are used to capture the experience of counseling or supervision with the captured information used at another time (i.e., time-delayed) while you are supervising the supervisee. Examples of asynchronous supervision technology include e-mail, Web sites or courseware, and digital audio and video recording.

*Live Supervision Using Synchronous Technology*

Live supervision with synchronous technology combines direct observation of the therapy session with some technology-based method that enables the supervisor to communicate with, and therefore influence, the work of the supervisee. The combination of live supervision and synchronous technology permits the immediate involvement of the supervisor in the supervision process; without technology, the supervisor would have to do in-session supervision to have that kind of immediacy with a supervisee.

*Bug-in-the-ear (BITE).* This method consists of a wireless earphone worn by the supervisee through which the supervisor can speak to the supervisee. Borders and Brown (2005) suggest that BITE is best used for coaching because the supervisor can communicate immediate suggestions and reinforcements. This premise is supported by recent work looking at teacher trainees' supervision by Goodman, Brady, Duffy, Scott, and Pollard (2008), where they found that the rate and accuracy of effective teaching behaviors increased when live feedback was delivered via BITE. This method has the advantage of not interrupting the class or session but can problematically be overused. One potential concern suggested by Byng-Hall (1982) is the danger of "echo therapy," where the supervisee just repeats the words of the supervisor and does not understand their implication.

*Phone-ins.* This method has been used when the supervisor is watching a therapy session and phones in to the supervisee using an intercom system. It has an advantage over the bug-in-the-ear method or the computer method because it stops the therapy session while the supervisee listens to the supervisor's directive. Also, the client realizes that there may be a change in the direction of the therapy session. The consensus about using phone-ins is that they should be used infrequently, that they should be brief and concise, and that the directive should be action-oriented (Haley, 1987). Another suggestion is that the supervisor should begin a phone-in with some type of positive support. If the therapy session is more complex or the supervisee needs more clarification, phone-ins are not advised. Instead, the supervisor and supervisee should consider a consultation break.

*Monitor text.* This method uses a computer monitor in the therapy room so that supervisors can send written messages across the screen to supervisees in session (Neukrug, 1991; Miller, Miller & Evans, 2002). It was termed bug-in-the-eye by Klitze and Lombardo (1991) and is similar to the teleprompter used in journalism. One advantage of this method is that the supervisee can decide when to read the messages. However, a disadvantage is that it can overwhelm the supervisee if overused. The advent of new text technology in smartphones and PDAs means that the size of the display unit on these devices could be less of a distraction to the supervision process (McGlothlin, Jencius, & Page, 2008).

*Supervision Using Asynchronous Digital Audio Recording*

Another transition that we have seen in the last 60 years is the transition of audio recording from large reel-to-reel analog magnetic tape to small digital recorders with flash memory. While tape recording sessions allowed for supervisors to review sessions with supervisees, tapes exchanged between supervisors and supervisees always could potentially be lost or damaged in the process. First the actual recording medium (magnetic tape) remained the same, but the housing became more portable (reel-to-reel, then cassette, and then microcassette). In the last decade, digital recorders have advanced in technology and lessened in cost to where digital audio recording is an available, reliable option. Supervision done with audio recordings is essentially asynchronous; the supervisor listens to the session at some time after the session and then meets and reviews it with the supervisee.

Digital audio recording allows for the supervisee to capture the session with the recorder, transfer it to his/her computer, and e-mail the session to his/her supervisor. The convenience of a digital recording is that one can easily move back or ahead using a digital audio player or computer software. One can also time-stamp a section in the session to revisit during the review with the supervisee. The convenience of transferring and playing audio recordings this way does not come without the caveat of concern for confidentiality and unauthorized access to the audio file. A recommendation is that both the sender and receiver of the file use an encryption/decryption program that password-protects the audio file, rendering it useless if it is lost, copied, or sent to an unintended person.

*Supervision Using Asynchronous Videotape*
*or Digital Video Recording*

With the advent of digital technology, analog recording is beginning to give way to recordings made to disk and portable storage devices. This change in format means that recording technology can reach a wider audience of users, and it has become easier for the consumer to use and manipulate. For video recording, this transition is very similar to that of audio recording. The advent of new software and hardware that records and stores video to hard disk or burns to DVD or CD-ROM creates a new paradigm that has many applications.

Recordings on analog tape, while still the method of choice, continue to have limitations that are overcome by the use of digital recordings. Camcorders, which are prevalent in our society, mostly use videotape to capture, store, and play back recorded events. Most use smaller, more compact video recording tape. Yet this tape must be played using the recorder itself or connected by cable to a player or other device. Using this method, tape must be rewound and searched through to find a specific instance for viewing. Digital video recording using a DVD disc, for example, can be configured for "chapter points" or markers (found on most DVD recordings) for instant playback and search capability.

There are numerous ways in which digital video recordings can be made from analog or digital tape. Direct input into a computer through the use of cabling and a video capture card allows for the taped input to be converted into a format for playback on a computer. Once a tape is converted to a digital file, this file may be used for DVD creation. Another instance of digital recording becoming readily available is recording directly to disc. This method involves using cameras directly connected to disc drives that capture digitally in real time. The "disk" can be a rewritable and removable DVD with the video feed going directly into a DVD recorder, or the "disk" can be a computer hard drive where the video is archived and stored in digital format. Either method—recording directly to a removable DVD or to stationary hard drive—is fast becoming the standard approach.

For those capturing material from tape into computers, software for the creation of DVD production is available on most computers. More advanced versions of software that allow for menus, titles, and graphics to be added, multi-track editing, and added production value can be acquired. Here, additional training and expertise is necessary.

Digital recording options of recordable DVDs or hard drive storage provides multiple advantages over older analog or even digital tape recordings. Videotape, whether analog or digital tape, must be captured and brought into a computer for conversion into a deliverable medium that can be used by supervisor and supervisee. Another problem with the use of analog videotape players and recorders is that manufacturers no longer support the hardware. For example, it is difficult to order and replace VHS tape recorders, the standard in recent supervision settings. Connectors to computer for capturing recordings from videotape machines require separate converter boxes or special capture cards, adding to expense and setup. Although there is great availability of digital cameras in the form of mini-DVD and recordable mini-DVD cameras, the medium does not lend itself to easy use in supervision without conversion to a portable format such as recordable DVD.

In clinical supervision, the use of digital video recordings means that supervisors and supervisees can target specific instances of a counseling or supervision session for examination. This eliminates the valuable supervision time lost searching for a particular moment in the analog method. Counseling labs equipped with digital recorders and disc recorders can create a DVD of a session for the supervisee and supervisor to review immediately after a session.

One currently marketed digital recording and coding system is the Landro Play Analyzer (www.landro.com). The Landro Play Analyzer was adapted for use in counseling from its already popular function in analyzing athlete performance during athletic practice and competition. The system allows the user to review a time-stamped video of events and tag information directly into the video for later analysis. Desmond, Dandeneau, and Guth (2007) have used the system successfully with training counselors. Sessions can be recorded, analyzed, and coded by trainees and supervisors for later playback and review. If a series of trainees are working on a technique, such as confrontation, a supervisor can call up the coded video across sessions and show multiple examples of confrontation with clients. Being able to find quickly coded clinical examples within and across client sessions is one of the great advantages of this type of system. Landro Play Analyzer system has both a Personal Edition (for laptops and individual use) and an Enterprise Edition (for larger institutional training). The Enterprise edition includes storage hardware as a part of the system and an established network for recording and playback. New to the athletic play analysis market is XOS Coaching Solutions from XOS Technology (www.xostech.com). Similar to the Landro Play Analyzer, the XOS Coaching Solutions is beginning to cross over for counseling clinic use.

Finally, counseling labs may also transmit live recordings using the intranet or LAN connection directly to a supervisor's office. In some training centers, clinical supervisors can view from their office various counseling rooms while in session and record segments of live counseling for use in supervision sessions. Transmitted over a secure LAN computer network, the video stream remains secure.

Digital video recording is becoming the standard for new counseling labs and is similar to the advent of desktop publishing for writers. Video is becoming easier to create and use. It has widespread potential for training and skill development for counseling. For clinical supervisors, the use of digital recordings instead of analog tape will be a welcome technology transition.

## Using Technology in Teaching and Practice of Supervision

It is no longer a case of whether or not technology is being employed in the teaching and practice of clinical supervision, but in what form and focus. Technology that supports clinical supervision, as well as the extent to which that technology is infused in the teaching and delivery of clinical supervision, is an area in definite need of further examination. The use of technology is naturally dependent on a number of factors, including faculty familiarity and resource availability. So far, the question of how to deploy technology has been largely left to the instructor of record.

Depending on factors such as one's interest, willingness to put in the extra work that is involved, willingness to solicit assistance from outside sources, availability of equipment and one's level of expertise, technology may be used to a greater or lesser degree. For clinical supervision, particularly for the review of supervisee skills, technology presents a means for supervisors to monitor supervisors-in-training in meeting requirements and ensuring competent treatment of clients through session review. In this regard, supervisors typically depend on recordings of counseling sessions and supervision sessions, whether audiotape or videotape, handed in by the supervisee.

In the practice of clinical supervision, quality review of counseling sessions remains an essential component. A supervision private practice presents more difficulty in the implementation of technology and requires a supervisor to construct a paradigm where technology is beneficial. For example, a clinical supervisor must put in place all the necessary policies and procedures to gain permissions, set up a recording approach (including cameras and other recording devices), and determine the purpose of recording when using technology to record sessions. While the clinical practice of supervision can be enhanced using technology, especially video recording technology, additional resources are required whether in a group or solo practice. Observing degree-granting programs' approach to technology use in supervision training will help determine how a practitioner may wish to develop a practice in this regard.

The teaching of clinical supervision is often carried out in an experiential practicum or internship in supervision, under the direction of a faculty member or advanced instructor. A course may include classroom instruction, clinical group training, and individual supervision of supervision. Each of these methods may have a technology component. In particular, recorded supervision sessions are an indispensable feature for quality review. This section will examine two universities' (Columbus State University and Virginia Tech) use of e-mail, Web sites, courseware, videoconferencing, and analog/digital recordings in the teaching of clinical supervision.

### Teaching Clinical Supervision: Digital Video Production (Columbus State University)

The counseling programs in the College of Education at Columbus State University have advanced their use of technology in the counseling curriculum. Along with the *Journal of Technology in Counseling*, founded within the department, a new video production laboratory was created for faculty teaching and professional development. This focus on technology has led to the creation of video products that are used in the classroom and on the Web. With instructor interest and support from the administration, hardware and software products have been organized in a video production studio so that faculty can supplement their classroom teaching online, in the classroom and with supplemental materials for students.

While the adaptation and integration of video for teaching purposes remains challenging, more instructors are taking advantage of the studio setting for lectures, interviews, podcasts, panel discussions, and other professional productions. In particular, for counseling-related course content, recording role plays in counseling practice scenarios allows both instructor and student to review their work from a professional production venue. In addition, a faculty member can design specific scenarios tailored to a training objective. Students, having prior exposure and experience in past courses, readily adapt to video recording in the classroom, in the production studio, and on clinical sites.

For example, video recording technology and production was used in the Counseling Supervision course, which was limited to those students with a master's degree who were continuing their education and training in clinical supervision. This course introduced prospective supervisors to the research, theory, and literature in clinical methods of effective supervision. While the course was designed to survey theoretical and applied concepts appropriate to counseling supervision, an experiential approach was used. In addition, the course was designed to motivate students of supervision to formulate their own personal and professional model of supervision. Finally, this course was heavily infused with video recording and playback. This technology allowed for the practice, review, and improvement of clinical supervision effectiveness.

The didactic portion of the course focused on three textbooks: Bernard and Goodyear's *Fundamentals of Clinical Supervision* (2004); *Clinical Supervisor Training* (CST), Baltimore and Crutchfield (2002); and the *New Handbook of Counseling Supervision*, Borders and Brown (2005). Experiential activities for supervisors were suggested in part from these three texts. Course requirements for the supervisors-in-training included supervising master's level interns, video recording of individual supervision sessions with the interns for playback within the supervision class, and a major writing assignment designed to elicit their personal philosophy of clinical supervision. In addition to course requirements, the supervision class itself was recorded and used in instruction throughout the academic term. Written permission was obtained from all involved prior to beginning any recordings.

The instructor created several Web sites to support the clinical supervision course, which included training materials and student role plays demonstrating ethical dilemmas and "stuck points" in the clinical supervision process. Students were also encouraged to create their own role-play scenarios that could be used on the Web sites.

*Technology in the supervision course.* This counseling supervision course included modules on the following topics: assessment of counselor needs; defining supervision and creating a working contract; taking a supervisor's perspective; supervision models and their application; experiential moments; ethics in clinical supervision; and evaluation and feedback. Within each of these modules, video recording technology was used. In the first module (assessment of counselor needs), students reviewed videos of counseling sessions and focused on counselor training needs. Students used a rubric for evaluating counselor effectiveness and use of basic counseling skills, and then presented their evaluations. By using a linear embedded "time code," that is, a digital counter on the video (starting at zero and progressing through the videos in increments of minutes, seconds, and frames), students could mark the exact moment within the video to present to the rest of the group. This technique of using a time code to illustrate a counseling process example for use in supervision supports the supervisor-in-training's clinical decision and/or recommendation. That is, students appeared to increase their skills at finding moments in the counseling session when a supervisory intervention might be used. Also, students reported that this exercise was helpful and that they received reinforcement of their findings when shown to the group.

Students in the course were given the assignment of reviewing chapters from the CST interactive CD-ROM on defining supervision and completing exercises, including viewing a video role play of a four-part counseling session and choosing an appropriate supervisory response. This video CD-ROM can be viewed on a Windows-compatible computer. Students were encouraged to begin thinking of their own cases in terms of role-play scenarios that could be demonstrated in class and for possible recording later in the term.

As students progressed to taking a supervisor's point of view and learning to think like a supervisor, a video presentation from Borders and Benshoff, *Learning to Think Like a Supervisor* (2000), was used. This video also introduces the students to Bernard's Discrimination Model of supervision and the next module for the course, supervision theories. As part of the assignment in this section of the course, students begin to use the theories from the developmental, social role, and counseling theories' models with their supervisees. During video presentation of the individual supervision session, students applied one model from each of the categories to their supervision work. Developmental models, such as Stoltenberg and Delworth (1987), Skovholt and Ronnestad (1992), Bernard's Discrimination Model, and various counseling theories' approaches were used to familiarize the student with working from a supervision theoretical approach.

An important aspect of this course was training aimed at giving and receiving critical feedback. The modeling of appropriate feedback was demonstrated in three different ways throughout the course. First, video demonstrations of supervision were provided. There was a combination of supervision sessions recorded previously from the production lab and from the CD-ROM training text. Live demonstrations from the instructor accompanied the supervision sessions presented in the class. Finally, ongoing feedback interactions among the supervisors-in-training occurred throughout the course. Process comments made by the instructor regarding the students' feedback to each other were additive. Moreover, Interpersonal Process Recall (Kagan, 1980) was a valuable method in getting at issues below the surface level presentation. These experiential moments in supervisor training helped the participants to evaluate the impact of critical feedback.

During this portion of the course, video cameras were set up to record most if not the entire 3-hr course. Two video camcorders on tripods were used, one with a wide-angle lens and the other arranged so that close-up shots were easily made. Videotape recorded for 1 hr, so that for the entire class six videotapes were needed. The camcorder closest to the student conference table used an external microphone for improving sound quality. Prior to editing in the video production lab, the camcorders were started at the same moment using an audio marker so that the two videos could be matched and edited using one soundtrack. The postediting process took place on a video editing computer and used a video and audio timeline method that allowed for an innovative approach similar to those used in larger video production facilities.

Obviously, the recording of a classroom can be used in follow-up sessions to review material and presentations and to further discussion regarding the topic at hand. After an initial review, the faculty member chose to present various segments of the recording to the students in a later class. In addition, the same recording method was used in other ways, including professional development purposes for faculty.

To familiarize the supervisors-in-training with the ethical standards for supervisors, the CST training CD-ROM's chapter on ethics in supervision (including ethical dilemmas for supervisors) was reviewed. Short video vignettes of ethical dilemmas that arise in clinical supervision were examined, ethics codes were reviewed and assigned to the dilemma, and finally, the supervisor-in-training outlined a response.

*Student learning.* Students throughout the course had opportunities to review their own work on video, review the work of others, and to view professionally produced videos and locally created videos that were targeted to particular content for the clinical supervision course. Feedback from students regarding the heavy use of video recording of their work, both in and out of class, indicated that after an initial level of anxiety they became more comfortable with the process.

Student feedback about the course indicated that students spent more time in preparing for video presentation with their own outside recordings of their supervision session and in the preparation for classroom presentation and discussion. Interestingly, the course evaluation was recorded during class. In addition, the traditional anonymous class evaluation forms were used as well. Both forms of feedback indicated that students spend additional time with the material and worked toward a more professional presentation. Also, feedback regarding the course indicated that students felt that the technology used during the course was helpful in their training and understanding of the material.

*Instructor learning.* The use of video recording during the class and the preparation for video materials to be used in a course requires additional time and effort on the part of the instructor. Video recording in the classroom is a highly interactive process which demands that all involved be part of the learning experience. The instructor and student are both recorded and viewed. The instructor will be provided with feedback on teaching as the student receives feedback about his or her performance. Openness to learning plays an important part in the success of this method. Using this parallel process, videotaping of teaching then has multiple uses both for the improvement of teaching as well as improving supervisor-in-training skill. In the future, classrooms will have video recording capabilities built in, making this much easier for instructor and student. Just as many classrooms at a number of universities and colleges now have podcast recording capabilities, so video capability in a classroom seems like the next step.

*Multimedia production laboratory.* In recent years at Columbus State University, a classroom within the College of Education was converted to a multimedia lab for faculty. The lab was set up to assist faculty in creating video to enhance teaching and learning. The lab, designated "Studio 212," was designed to create, record, and produce video for use in teaching and learning in classrooms, conferences, Web streaming, CD-ROM, and DVD. This lab has video camcorders, wireless microphones, stage lighting, a teleprompter, backgrounds, including chromakey capability, with sets designed to fit a wide range of production needs. Any segment, event, or complete DVD production can be captured and produced in the various formats in a short amount of time compared to outsourcing video production. Planning and producing video products in-house can save time and money. In fact, recent figures collected in the region show an average of $1000 per finished minute of video charged by video production companies.

Interest in capturing events and enhancing classroom teaching and Web-based instruction has gained momentum. From this small lab alone, 24 DVDs were created in 2008. From this experience, universities and training facilities are encouraged to plan, find resources, and implement a production laboratory aimed at creating faculty-led video to enhance teaching, particularly in training counselors and supervisors. Creating specific video to support teaching clinical skills has been underutilized. The experiential activities necessary for quality training in clinical supervision are naturally suited for video production.

*Consideration in using video in clinical supervision.* The use of video and the video development process must be planned well in advance. Resources, including hardware and software for postproduction, if used, must be considered. Video recordings can be played back in most classrooms and can be produced in DVD format, CD-ROM format, and for Web streaming, as well as standard videotape. The successful use of video technology in the classroom results in more focused discussion and demands much of the instructor and student. The following is a list of tips to develop and deliver a course using video technology:

- Plan your use of video. This includes how video will be recorded and how often. In addition, you must determine your target audience. Will this be a demonstration of a technique? Then it must be clearly presented. Is it a piece that stimulates discussion? How is this achieved? Further, any video shown in class should engage the students and be closely evaluated in terms of impact on the learning process.

- Determine your purpose. Will this video recording be only for your supervision students? What will this video accomplish? Another important factor is how the video will be evaluated.

- Consider timing, budgeting, and scheduling. A syllabus that includes a production schedule can be helpful.

- Have all the hardware necessary for recording available. Making quality recordings depends on more than the recording device. This includes having quality lighting and sound. Recording rehearsals will lessen technical difficulties.

- Spend time orienting students to the project. Students who have more experience with video technology can assist your efforts. Assisting students who are unfamiliar with video recording early in the process will be helpful.

- Become familiar with simple-to-follow videography techniques such as shot composition and arrangement. Camera angle and scene composition should be considered beforehand.

- Outsource video editing and production, if possible. In order to use your video beyond the classroom, production value includes titling and graphics with other elements such as voice-over and commentary.

- If editing video yourself, make use of software that allows for transition and titling and ease of use.
- Use summative and formative evaluation techniques that include the use of technology combined with traditional methods throughout the course.
- Become acquainted with technology support at your facility.
- When using a video you have created, have others review your work. Receiving feedback prior to showing your video can help greatly.

*Teaching Clinical Supervision: Videoconferencing (Virginia Tech)*

Since its inception in 1993, the Virginia Tech Faculty Development Institute (FDI) has been the most visible component of the four-part, university-wide Instructional Development Initiative (IDI). IDI provides a systematic approach to the effective integration of current trends and technologies into teaching, learning, and research at Virginia Tech. The FDI component centers on teaching faculty how to effectively and efficiently integrate technology into their teaching and research activities. This integration includes the following approaches: rethinking faculty teaching methods and goals, exploring the potential of specific instructional technology and research applications, and investigating strategies to improve the effectiveness of current teaching and research practices. Although FDI provides a great deal of skills training for critical computer hardware and software, the FDI program is not designed to be a mastery-based teaching model. Rather, it is designed to be a program that provides general and targeted information to let faculty members decide which specific training will meet their individual needs. Support is readily available for faculty to move beyond the basic levels whenever appropriate.

As a faculty member in the Counselor Education program at Virginia Tech, the third author was able to receive training and support in using new technology tools for a Clinical Supervision class. Because the Counselor Education program had two locations, training of all the doctoral-level students in the Clinical Supervision class required the use of several technologies.

*Videoconferencing.* The first of these technologies was videoconferencing, a process in which compressed video is transmitted through digital phone lines to provide real-time, interactive audio and visual communication between sites that are geographically separated. Using this video technology, the local site was the classroom where the instructor was located. The remote site had only students and, sometimes, a facilitator who assisted with the startup of the class. Two television monitors viewed the local and remote site. Microphones were placed on the table in front of the students, and they had to press a button to speak. The instructor had a desk arrangement with both a computer and a graphics camera for presenting didactic material. A control tablet was placed on the desk for the instructor. When the instructor sat there, the students at the remote site saw the instructor on one monitor and their class on the other monitor. Sometimes the instructor asked a student to sit at the desk to learn how to use the system. The camera then showed the instructor sitting with the students and that seemed to facilitate good discussion. The system also had a videotape player. Support personnel were available at both sites if there were technical problems. Videoconferencing, the key element in cyber supervision, is more secure than e-mail or chat room transcripts, which are considered public record, and is used extensively in counselor supervision.

Many of the counselor education doctoral students were not new to videoconferencing because they had taken several videoconferencing courses, but to teach a clinical course like supervision this way presented some unique challenges. It was decided that the course would have both a didactic component and the experiential component of supervising master's students in their internships. Thus, the supervisors-in-training in both locations were required to videotape the supervision sessions with their supervisees. Informed consents were gathered from all involved. The Bernard and Goodyear book *Fundamentals of Clinical Supervision* (2004) provided most of the didactic material for discussion. The instructor supplemented with some presentations and had several guest speakers. The main focus was on the supervision processes of class members. They took turns presenting descriptions of supervision sessions and then showed video segments from those sessions. The professor and the students provided feedback so that the process became supervision-of-supervision. The professor facilitated a variety of feedback methods to the supervisee. For example, role plays were conducted sometimes with one student at one location and one at the other. A live supervision session was conducted at one site when a supervisor brought the supervisee into the class during the videoconference. Peer supervision methods were very appropriate for the instructor to facilitate. Several of these group methods such as the Structured Peer Group Format (Borders, 1991) and the Structured Group Supervision Model (Wilbur, Roberts-Wilbur, Hart, Morris & Betz, 1994) facilitated interaction between the two sites. The class syllabus, forms for the supervisors and supervisees to use in structuring the supervision sessions, examples of supervision learning contracts, and evaluation instruments were all placed on Blackboard, which provides the university's online course delivery system. The instructor developed a LISTSERV of students to support e-mail interaction among them.

Building a learning community between two sites required not just spanning physical distance but psychological distance as well. Group dynamics and the role of the instructor became very important aspects to consider. Each year the instructor has gone to the remote site to conduct class from there and to meet with individual students if desired. The students appreciated that effort, as their site was 4 hr away. Several said that the course really "began" once they met the instructor face-to-face. The instructor also decided that a meeting of the entire group was very important. So a meeting place at a midway geographical location was arranged for a Saturday. The students emphasized the benefits of a face-to-face component. Being counselors, they appreciated seeing one another "up close and personal." Most students have said that they would prefer face-to-face meetings. Showing one's clinical supervision sessions on tape produces vulnerability and anxiety, so the instructor expended a great deal of effort to make the class feel safe. In contrast though, students did see the advantages of learning about distance education technology and recognized that it was necessary to the counselor education program to use it.

Although the technical problems of connecting or reconnecting to the two sites have decreased greatly over time, there are still technical issues. Audio from the students' videotapes of supervision sessions that were being played in class was sometimes difficult to understand. Unless the videoconferencing camera is zoomed in on a speaker during class, it is hard to read facial expressions. The microphones had to be activated by the students when speaking and at times they forgot to do that.

Advantages for the instructor were several. Videoconferencing technology more closely approximates the traditional face-to-face classroom than other distance modalities such as online courses. Videoconferencing gave the professor an opportunity to teach students in different localities, which added diversity and greater perspective to the class. Classroom videoconferencing was excellent preparation for desktop videoconferencing, which may be the next significant distance education modality.

According to the recent American Counseling Association guidelines (2005), ethical issues and confidentiality apply to teachers, students, and broadcast technicians involved with distance technology. One of the features of videoconferencing is the ability to record class sessions. Faculty members, as well as students who miss class, can use the recording for review. It is vital that the recordings not be made available to anyone but the instructor and be viewed privately so that confidentiality can be honored.

The use of videoconferencing will continue to increase because of its time and cost efficiency. As the quality of the technology improves, there will be fewer technological glitches. The following is a list of tips to develop and deliver a course in videoconferencing so that it truly becomes a learning community:

- Vary instructional methods: videos, overhead, role plays, or other experiential methods, lectures, discussions.
- Limit class size to no more and preferably less than eight students at each site.

- Prepare students for technical distractions or difficulties.
- Present the instructor's view of the strengths and challenges of videoconferencing.
- Establish norms for class conduct on the first night. For example, discourage students from talking among themselves at one site because it can create misperceptions of bad manners at the other site.
- Arrange the class so that members at the remote class can see both the instructor and classmates at the same time. This means sitting with the class instead of at the instructor's desk all the time.
- Spend time on an icebreaker at the beginning of the course and team-building activities throughout.
- Pay attention to nonverbal behavior of students at both sites.
- Maintain eye contact with the camera.
- Try to have a site facilitator present at the remote site for the first several class meetings.

Albrecht and Jones (2001) give more good ideas on providing interaction in their book *High Tech/High Touch: Distance Learning in Counselor Preparation*.

*Electronic mail.* E-mail (or e-supervision) was another technology used as a supplemental training tool in the Clinical Supervision class. Myrick and Sabella (1995) developed a LISTSERV (a list of counselors and their e-mail addresses) so that when situations arose, counselors could post e-mail messages about counseling or client questions and receive feedback and suggestions from others on the list. E-mail was used in the Clinical Supervision class in several ways. For supervision sessions that were not viewed in class, the students had to e-mail their instructor a report of their supervision. The written e-mail material about a supervision session was organized so that the supervisor could read about the client and the counseling goals, about progress or lack of it, about the supervisee's reaction to the client and the process and about future direction (Getz, 1999). It provided an opportunity for supervisees to ask for and obtain written feedback in between class meetings. They could also pose any particular questions to their colleagues in the class. Written assignments about the chapters in the textbook were e-mailed to the LISTSERV of all the students in addition to the instructor.

E-supervision has aspects that supervisees and supervisors find beneficial and also challenging. In a study about e-supervision by Graf and Stebnicki (2002), they found that supervisees reported it to be very beneficial. They especially liked having ongoing access to their supervisors, and they reported it to be more relaxed and informal. For the supervisor there is an advantage in that supervisee's development can be tracked over time by analyzing the written documentation.

The biggest concern about e-supervision is confidentiality. A drawback to the use of computers for transmitting information is that there is no guarantee as to the identity of the receiver. When sent, e-mail is stored on an individual's server until it is read, responded to, saved, or deleted. E-mail messages may also be sent by mistake to the wrong recipients. If an individual is using an unsecure server, or is on a computer accessed by a group of people, confidentiality may be compromised. Protecting confidentiality is of utmost concern. The names of clients and significant others must never be used, nor should there be any identifying data about geographical location.

*Centra.* Centra courseware is a powerful tool for online multiple-user interaction and course organization that includes real-time two-way audio, application sharing, Web browsing, whiteboarding, and text chatting. Once an instructor is familiar with the Centra environment, he or she will be able to design and deliver materials for synchronous and asynchronous use by the students, as well as lead interactive sessions at a distance. The professor and students download the software for Centra and then view a tutorial that explains its use. With headsets plugged into their computers, the instructor and a student can have an individual supervision session. The instructor controls the interaction though icons viewed on the computer. The students can put brief, simple agendas on PowerPoint presentations that would be uploaded. Centra helps facilitate one-to-one audio chat so that a student can express concerns, raise questions, or request help. The one-to-one chats allow some students to share more than they would if they were reluctant to share in a larger group. Students can use the Centra system to present a short clip of a supervision session. This process has the possibility of increasing rapport between the instructor and the student that would otherwise be lost by physical distance.

*Web-based training for clinical supervisors.* Another example of the use of technology to train clinical supervisors is the development of a Web site to be used for training on-site clinical supervisors. CACREP now requires that on-site supervisors receive clinical supervision training before supervising counseling interns. One significant challenge in meeting that requirement is that some cannot attend the training provided by the university because of geographical separation or schedule conflicts. Although it is preferable to have faculty trainers and on-site supervisors come together for interaction and the development of professional alliances, a supervisor training Web site offers some unique benefits as well. Supervisor training Web sites can provide more extensive information than that provided in a one-time live training. Information about clinical supervision can be accessed at any time.

The supervisor training Web site (Getz & Schnurman, 2001) is organized around the clinical supervision competencies that are now required by NBCC for the approved supervisor credential and by many states that require these competencies of those who provide supervision for postmaster's counselors working toward state licensure. There is information about supervision models, the supervisory relationship, counselor development, supervision techniques and interventions, evaluation, and ethics. There is a resource list of valuable books and articles on clinical supervision. The Web site presents a variety of training points complete with examples and video clip demonstrations. Also, hyperlinks are included to expand the readers' connection to professional materials. The same Web site can be adapted for use in continuing education in supervision, satisfying the state's requirements that those who supervise have training or retraining.

Some researchers have suggested that developing an online learning community requires deliberate and skilled instructor facilitation to succeed (Rovai, 2001; Wikeley & Muschamp, 2004). Rovai (2001) found that instructors needed to establish group identity, foster trust between students and between the instructor and students, encourage both social and task interactions, and create opportunities for the construction of shared knowledge through virtual dialog. The technologies presented here can be used to help facilitate such development. Engagement with e-mail, videoconferencing, video production, courseware, and Web site instruction, even in a simple exercise for a short time, can produce results that aid in the teaching and learning process. The clinical supervision training process can be enhanced through the use of technology as counselor trainees and instructors gain valuable insight into their work.

## Adopting Technology in Supervision

The best strategy in considering technology adoption is to take a point of view that considers each potential user. Who will be involved with the technology you adopt? Immediately, you think of the supervisor and supervisee, but if you are working in a clinical setting, then the technology adoption may include support staff, management and information services people, and clinic administrators. A multiple user point-of-view suggests that you do a 360° analysis for each of the potential stakeholders in the technology. Put yourself in the place of each potential stakeholder and consider the issues he or she may have to address with the new technology. From this you can draw a list of questions or concerns that stakeholders might have with the adoption. The advantage of a 360° analysis is that you can emerge from the process with anticipated issues that you would not get by taking your point of view alone.

In considering and adopting a technology framework to provide supervision, careful planning and execution will lead to the most satisfying outcomes for the supervisor and supervisee. We are suggesting the 4 P's;

*Prepare, Purchase, Practice,* and *Preserve,* as a strategy for technology adoption in the supervisory experience.

## Prepare

Good preparation will make all the other steps in the process run smoothly. To achieve good preparation, one needs to take time in making decisions about the use of technology for supervision. Preparation means exploring what technology platforms for supervision may serve your needs. Research each of the technologies further and contact those colleagues who have incorporated them into their supervision process, asking for consultation with them regarding their experiences with the technology. Most tech-savvy professionals are more than happy to share their experiences, and the benefits and challenges of adopting technology in their practice. If possible, see if they will provide you a demonstration of the technology you want to adopt. Talk with your immediate colleagues, staff, and supervisees about adding a technology layer to the supervision process. Collect articles on technology-based supervision and share your ideas with instructional technologists. Consider confidentiality, safety, and security issues when using a new technology.

## Purchase

Consider the cost of equipment, software, and expenses associated with staff use and training before implementing any new technology as it applies to supervision relationships. Think about the additional cost to your program or practice. Perhaps this new technology is replacing some other costly technology or process. In this case, factor in any potential cost savings. Provide a budget to administrators or responsible parties with best estimates of the initial cost of the technology and what cost will be involved in maintenance.

## Practice

As part of your preparation for the new supervision technology, consider staff training. Establish a training program for supervisors that will allow them plenty of opportunity to learn and to practice. We suggest that you have a series of training sessions with all staff who will use the new technology. If you are considering a new videoconferencing system, supervisors and supervisees should be made aware of the process for using the equipment and training involved when the videoconferencing system is operational at the site. Pairing learners can be helpful, as they can become resources for each other. Once training is complete, you need to give counselors and supervisors opportunities to practice on the system and develop self-confidence in using the equipment, software, and supervision process.

*Preserve*

It is important that you keep any new technology in good running condition. Any software should be backed up and updated regularly. Some designate should be responsible for regular maintenance and checking the equipment and software. A designate should also periodically review and scrub computers of files that could be potential risks to confidentiality. E-mails, chat logs, and digital audio and video should be removed to reduce the likelihood that the data will fall into unauthorized hands.

## Ethics of Technology-Based Supervision

Since the provision of technology-assisted supervision is not standardized, there is no standard set of ethical guidelines for its practice. Many practitioners engaged in technology-based supervision use a combination of technology platforms that suit their pedagogical needs. The examples of Columbus State University and Virginia Tech presented in this chapter show the diverse and creative ways in which two institutions have responded to their programs' educational needs. Without specific ethical guidelines for cybersupervision, we need to turn to existing parallel ethical codes to ensure ethical and best practice.

The best first solution is to check with your professional association's general Code of Ethics and/or Standards of Practice. If your action would be considered unethical in the standard face-to-face practice, it would certainly be troublesome in cyberpractice. We would encourage you to check with state licensure laws where you practice to ensure that certain forms of technology-based supervision are considered acceptable by state licensure standards. It would also be helpful to look at the Association for Counselor Education and Supervision (ACES, 2007) *Technical Competencies for Counselor Education* as it covers ethical use of technology and issues with security of material on the Internet. The National Board of Certified Counselors (NBCC, n.d.) has a document titled *The Practice of Internet Counseling* that is a good overview of considerations one should take into account when doing online counseling. These ideas also extend to safe and ethical online supervision.

## Future Trends

What does the future hold for technology inclusion in the supervision process? If the process we see with past adoption continues likewise in the future, to predict the future in supervision we should be looking at current technology issues in allied fields that have not yet made their way into counseling and supervision.

We are just beginning to see the use of Web 2.0 tools in other fields. Web 2.0 is advancement from the first generation of Web tools that were primarily static. First-generation Web tools such as e-mail, Web pages, and discussion boards relied on one person to make a contribution and that information remained in place with little interaction from the user. Web 2.0 tools are developed so multiple users can contribute, edit, and co-construct the narrative. These next-generation tools such as blogging, microblogging, wikis, social networking sites (such as Facebook), video-sharing sites, and virtual worlds (such as Second Life) allow for more user interaction with other users. Supervision requires a higher level of interactivity between supervisor and supervisee, and Web 2.0 tools permit this interactivity.

One idea being discussed and researched in reference to human communication through technology is the idea of virtual presence. Virtual presence is the experience that users can have with technology that allows them to have an emotive connection with someone else (Patrick, 2002). In the process the user "forgets" that this relationship is being mediated through technology. The use of technology to have the experience becomes a non-issue. As we see a new generation of students making personal connections through social networks such as Facebook and MySpace, surely supervision using new media will not lag far behind.

## References

ACES (2007). *Technical Competencies for Counselor Education*. Retrieved January 5, 2009 from http://files.changemywebsite.com/774116/doc/ACES_Technology_Competencies_2007.pdf

Albrecht, A. C., & Jones, D. G. (2001). *High tech/high touch: Distance learning in counselor preparation*. Alexandria, Virginia: Association for Counselor Education and Supervision.

American Counseling Association. (2005). *ACA code of ethics*. Alexandria, VA: Author.

Baltimore, M. L. (2003). Creating multimedia for use in the counselor education classroom, in *Encore edition of Cybercounseling and Cyberlearning* published jointly by the American Counseling Association and the ERIC Counseling and Student Services Clearinghouse.

Baltimore, M. L., & Crutchfield, L. B. (2002). *Clinical supervisor training: A CD-ROM based training program for the helping professions*. Allyn & Bacon: Boston.

Berger, T. (2004). Computer-based technological applications in psychotherapy training. *Journal of Clinical Psychology, 60*(3), 301–315.

Bernard, J., & Goodyear, R. (2004). *Fundamentals of clinical supervision* (3rd ed.). Boston: Allyn & Bacon.

Borders, D., & Benshoff, J. (2000). *Learning to think like a supervisor*. Association for Counselor Education and Supervision: Greensboro, NC.

Borders, L. D. (1991). A systematic approach to peer group supervision. *Journal of Counseling and Development, 69*, 248–252.

Borders, L. D., & Brown, L. L. (2005). *The new handbook of counseling supervision.* Mahwah, N. J.: Lawrence Erlbaum Associates.

Byng-Hall, J. (1982). The use of the earphone in supervision. In R. Whitffen and J. Byng-Hall (Eds.) *Family therapy supervision: Recent developments in practice* (pp. 47–56). London: Academic Press.

Coker, J. K., Jones, W. P., Staples, P. A., & Harbach, R. L. (2002). Cybersupervision in the first practicum: Implications for research and practice. *Guidance & Counseling, 18*(1), 33–38.

Desmond, K., Dandeneau, C. J., & Guth, L. J. Non-linear supervision using innovative technology. CounselorAudioSource.Net—Podcast CAS055—Airdate 1/18/2007.

Gelso, C. J. (1974). Effects of recording on counselors and clients. *Counselor Education and Supervision, 13*(1), 5–12.

Getz, H. G. (1999). Assessment of clinical supervisor competencies. *Journal of Counseling and Development, 77,* 491–497.

Getz, H. G., & Schnurman-Crook, A. (2001). Utilization of on-line training for on-site clinical supervisors: One university's approach. *Journal of Technology in Counseling,* 2.1. Retrieved from Goodman, J. I., Brady, M. P., Duffy, M. L., Scott, J., and Pollard, N. E. (2008). The effects of "bug-in-ear" supervision on special education teachers' delivery of learn units. *Focus on Autism and Other Developmental Disabilities, 23*(4), 207–216.

Haley, M. (1987). *Problem solving therapy.* (2nd ed). San Francisco: Jossey-Bass.

Huhra, R. L., Yamokoski-Maynhart, C. A., & Prieto, L. R. (2008). Reviewing videotape in supervision: A developmental approach. *Journal of Counseling and Development, 86,* 412–418.

Jencius, M. (2008). Editor's voice: New technologies for the counseling field. *Journal of Technology in Counseling.* 5(1). Retrieved from http://jtc.colstate.edu/Vol5_1/editor.htm

Kagan, N. (1980). Influencing human interaction—Eighteen years with IPR. In A. K. Hess (Ed.), Psychotherapy supervision: Theory, research, and practice (pp. 262–283). New York: Wiley.

Klitzke, M. J., & Lombardo, T. W. (1991). A "bug-in-the-eye" can be better than a "bug-in-the-ear": A teleprompter technique for on-line therapy skills training. *Behavior Modification, 15,* 113–117.

Lewis, W., & Rohrbaugh, M. (1989). Live supervision by family therapists: A Virginia survey. *Journal of Marital and Family Therapy, 15,* 323–326.

Manhal-Baugus, M. (2001). E-therapy: Practical, ethical, and legal issues. *CyberPsychology & Behavior, 4*(5), 551–563.

Manzanares, M. G., O'Haloran, T. M., McCartney, T. J., Filer, R. D., Varhley, S. C., & Calhoun, K. (2004). CD-ROM technology for education and support of site supervisors. *Counselor Education and Supervision, 43*(3), 220–230.

McGlothlin, J., Jencius, M., & Page, B. J. (2008). Self-produced counseling applications for handheld computers. *Journal of Technology in Counseling, 5*(1). Retrieved from http://jtc.colstate.edu/Vol5_1/McGlothlin.htm

Miller, K. L., Miller, S. M., & Evans, W. J. (2002). Computer-assisted live supervision in college counseling centers. *Journal of College Counseling, 5*(3), 187–192.

Montalvo, B. (1973). Aspects of live supervision. *Family Process, 12,* 343–359.

Myrick, R. D., & Sabella, R. A. (1995). Cyberspace: New place for counselor supervision. *Elementary School Guidance & Counseling, 30,* 35–44.

NBCC (n.d.). *The practice of Internet counseling.* Retrieved January 6, 2009 from http://nbcc.org/AssetManagerFiles/ethics/internetCounseling.pdf

Neukrug, E. S. (1991). Computer-assisted live supervision in counselor skills training. *Counselor Education and Supervision, 31*(2), 132–138.

Page, B. J., Jencius, M. J., Rehfuss, M. C., Foss, L. L., Dean, E. P., & Petruzzi, M. L. (2003). PalTalk online groups: Process and reflections on students' experience. *Journal for Specialists in Group Work, 28,* 35–41.

Patrick, A. (2002, January 24). The psychology of virtual presence: Research ideas. Retrieved January 4, 2009 from http://www.andrewpatrick.ca/virtual-presence/presence-ideas.html

Rogers, C. R. (1942). The use of electrically recorded interviews in improving psychotherapeutic techniques. *American Journal of Orthopsychiatry, 12,* 429–434.

Skovholt, T. M., & Ronnestad, M. H. (1992). *The evolving professional self: Stages and themes in therapist and counselor development.* Chichester, England: Wiley.

Stebnick, M. A. (2002). Using e-mail for clinical supervision in practicum: A qualitative analysis. *The Journal of Rehabilitation, 68,* 41–49.

Stoltenberg, C. D., & Delworth, U. (1987) *Supervising Counselors and Therapists.* San Francisco, CA: Jossey-Bass.

Wikeley, F., & Muschamp, Y. (2004). Pedagogical implications of working with doctoral students at a distance. *Distance Education, 25*(1), 125–142.

Wilbur, M. P., Roberts-Wilbur, J. M., Hart, G., Morris J. R., & Betz, R. L. (1994). Structured group supervision (SGS): A pilot study. *Counselor Education & Supervision, 33,* 262–279.

TRUST LIBRARY
CENTRAL MANCHESTER AND MANCHESTER
CHILDREN'S UNIVERSITY HOSPITALS
NHS TRUST
EDUCATION CAMPUS SOUTH, OXFORD ROAD
MANCHESTER, M13 9WL

CHAPTER **5**

# Using Expressive Arts in Counseling Supervision

SONDRA SMITH-ADCOCK, MARK B. SCHOLL, ELAINE
WITTMANN, CATHERINE TUCKER, CLARRICE
RAPISARDA, and MARY AMANDA GRAHAM*

Since the development of clinical supervision to address the preparation of counselors, supervisors have created ways to effectively facilitate the process. Since the early 1990s, authors have proposed using expressive arts to help supervisors and supervisees meet personal, professional, and clinical goals. Drawing, music, movement, and writing are the most traditional forms of expressive arts that have been proposed for use in clinical supervision (Wilkins, 1995).

The overarching aim of using expressive arts in counseling supervision is to foster a creative process that promotes more in-depth learning. Expressive arts also help to facilitate the counseling supervisor's knowledge and awareness of the supervisee's learning process. Authors have associated a number of positive outcomes with using expressive arts in counseling supervision. Expressive arts have been recommended as a way to enhance students' identity development (Neswald-McCalip, Sather, Strati, & Dineen, 2003; Neswald-Potter, 2005; Newsome, Henderson, & Veach, 2005; Pearson, 2003; Scholl & Smith-Adcock, 2007; Wilkins, 1995; Young & Borders, 1998, 1999), promote learning goals, and yield positive

---

* *Note*: The authors, except for the first and second authors, have made equivalent contributions to this chapter and authorship order has been determined at random.

views of supervision by supervisees (Neswald-McCalip, et al., 2003; Young & Borders, 1998, 1999).

Using creative approaches in supervision allows students to advance their learning through approaches that are designed to liberate conscious and unconscious information and promote change. These approaches emphasize use of expressive techniques that promote more spontaneous, livelier engagement with the supervision process. In addition to encouraging spontaneity, these methods also facilitate the objectification or a disidentification with regard to aspects of oneself. This distancing or loosening of identification renders aspects of the self more amenable to creative change. In this chapter, we review the foundations, methods, and implications of four emerging creative approaches to supervision that meet these criteria.

Authors of each of the expressive arts approaches included the following in their description: (1) how to use the technique in supervision, including the proper setting, materials needed, modality (e.g., individual or group); (2) examples of how to use the approach during and across sessions, and ways to process; (3) discussion of issues related to using the approach in supervision, such as supervisees' developmental stages; and (4) anecdotes, dialogue, photos, or drawings for many of the approaches also will be included to illustrate counselor awareness and development. And finally, when appropriate, authors have included recommendations for training supervisors to use the approach.

In this chapter, we present four approaches to using expressive arts in counseling supervision. The first approach presented is the art of using puppetry in supervision, authored by Clarrice Rapisarda. The second approach, authored by Sondra Smith-Adcock and Mark Scholl, involves the use of psychodrama-related techniques in supervision. Third, Mary Amanda Graham presents her approach, called *Bibliosupervision,* which involves the incorporation of bibliotherapy into supervision. Lastly, Elaine Wittmann and Catherine Tucker present a supervision approach involving the use of Sandtray/Worldplay.

## Using Puppetry In Counseling Supervision

*Clarrice Rapisarda*

I (Rapisarda) have been working with puppets in counseling and supervision for 9 years, and during that time they have moved from being a convenient resource to a core tool. In this section, basic information about working with puppets and a general process that guides supervision work with puppets is presented. An example with photos will be discussed to help illustrate the process. Lastly, issues related to working with puppets in supervision will be examined.

*Using Puppetry in Supervision: The Basic Elements and Terminology*

*The Proper Setting*   There are no specific setting requirements for working with puppets in supervision. The key requirement for the setting is to make sure that the puppets are within reach so that they can be placed and manipulated as needed. Puppets are extremely portable and versatile for adapting to any environmental constraints, whether in a school (James & Myer, 1987), or in a community setting. During a typical academic semester, my puppets frequently make trips from my counseling office to the classroom.

*Materials Needed*   Time and puppets are the key materials needed for this technique. Due to the nature of the work with the puppets and the amount of processing that occurs when following the outlined procedure, it is important that the supervisor allocate enough time during the supervision session for the puppet processing. As the supervisor and supervisee become more comfortable with the process, it can be adjusted to fit shorter amounts of time.

While there are many types of puppets ranging from marionettes to ventriloquist's dummies (Carter & Mason, 1998), the technique proposed in this chapter focuses on the use of animal hand puppets (puppets that generally fit over the hand and where the fingers and hands are used to move the face, mouth, or body of the puppet). The majority of puppets I work with are animals for several reasons. First, I have found that animals transcend many cultural layers that people cannot. It can be very challenging to find people puppets to represent all races and ethnicities; however, the supervisor can intentionally select core and basic animals with characteristics that resonate with many people across cultures. Second, the use of animal hand puppets offers the supervisee greater freedom to express possible cultural concerns in a nontraditional method. Third, it may be easier and safer for strong and conflicting emotions to be projected onto an animal puppet and then processed.

It is recommended that the supervisor have a variety of puppets available during supervision in order to conduct this process (Figure 5.1); however, the number is not as important as the category of puppets. It is helpful to have at least a few puppets in the following categories (see pictures at the end of the chapter):

Aggressors: These are puppets that show strong, scary emotions and often attach/eat other puppets. Examples: a bear, wolf, bee, spider (Figure 5.2).

1. Magical: These are puppets that have extra powers, relate to superstitions, or are lucky/magical. Examples: rabbit in magician's hat, peacock, three-headed dragon (Figure 5.3).

Figure 5.1

Figure 5.2 Aggressive puppets.

**Figure 5.3** Magical puppets.

2. Nurturers: Puppets that represent love and loving may be placed in the caretaker role, or in need of caring or nurturing. Examples: baby birds in nest, mother armadillo and baby, mother mouse and baby mice (Figure 5.4).
3. Shy: These are puppets that are able to hide in order to stay safe and protected, possibly from aggressor puppets. Examples: dinosaurs in eggs, armadillo that can curl into ball, turtle with shell, snail with shell (Figure 5.5).

**Figure 5.4** Nurturing puppets.

**Figure 5.5** Shy puppets.

Other puppet categories that could be included to help with the processing include aquatic puppets, insect puppets, and generally friendly puppets. It is helpful to have puppets made from different fabrics and textures to appeal to a broader audience. For example, I worked with a supervisee who had sensory integration issues, and who preferred to only work with the smooth-textured puppets such as the ant. The best guideline to use when purchasing a puppet is to choose one that you would be willing to work with yourself. If it does not appeal to you, chances are it will not appeal to your supervisees, students, or clients.

*Modality*   Working with puppets in supervision can occur in individual supervision or group supervision. The technique that is outlined can be easily expanded to include a group interaction and processing response.

### Puppet Processing in Supervision

The steps for puppet processing will now be described. It is helpful for supervisors who use puppet processing to document the key themes that emerge as well as the puppets that are used as the process unfolds. Photos are an ideal way of capturing the staging of the puppets. Steps that are suggested for puppet processing include the following:

1. List 3 to 9 key elements that will be focused on during the processing. These may be people (including the person who is completing this processing), feelings, things, or events.
2. The supervisee then chooses and gathers the puppets that will portray each element. There is no limit to this part of the process. One element may need two or three puppets to adequately express it.

3. The supervisee states which puppet is representing which elements.
4. Puppets are placed physically in the room in such a way as to literally and accurately represent the various elements and display their relationship to the puppets representing the supervisee; for example, a defensive supervisee may choose to place the supervisee and supervisor puppets in opposite corners of a room. Any additional props may be used to help achieve this; for example, placing a puppet on books to portray it looking down on another element (Figure 5.6).
5. The supervisee is asked to step away from the arrangement of puppets and is encouraged to make any adjustments necessary to most accurately portray the elements.
6. The supervisee then steps away from the puppets to a different viewpoint and reflects out loud on the scene as an outsider viewing the elements for the first time. During this step, the supervisor (and other supervisees if supervision occurs in a group format) is listening for affect present in the supervisee's voice, noticing details, and paying attention to any incongruities.
7. The supervisee processes the story from step 6. The supervisee is also asked to process any thoughts or reactions to physically watching the elements symbolized and displayed in the puppets. To facilitate the processing, the supervisee addresses each element by taking each puppet, and touching and manipulating it. The supervisee tries out the abilities of the chosen animal as seen from that element. It is not necessary to actually speak as the puppet. The supervisee can instead speak from the perspective of that puppet in the element to which it

**Figure 5.6** Supervision steps 4 to 6.

was assigned. When used in group supervision, other supervisees can be assigned to the different puppet elements and can share in the processing by expressing what they would feel from that perspective.

8. The supervisee is then offered the freedom to change any puppets in order to resolve or eliminate various elements that are currently present. To do this, the supervisee may bring in different puppets to portray the same elements or to portray new elements. The supervisee discusses what changed in the scene.

9. Processing occurs again (as in Step 6), with the supervisee trying out the new changes. When used in group supervision, other supervisees can be assigned to the different puppet elements and can share in the processing by expressing what they would feel from the changes represented (Figure 5.7).

10. The supervisor then goes through steps 2 to 6 using the same elements identified by the supervisee. By following the same process, the supervisor offers the supervisee a chance to experiment with growth through the selected elements in a safe, less threatening space.

11. The core elements and their representations in each of the stories are processed. The overall experience is processed (Figure 5.8).

*An Example of Puppet Processing* There are two general areas that can be the focus of puppet processing in supervision. The first area focuses on the supervision process and the roles of the supervisee and supervisor in that process. Puppet processing used in this area can foster increased insight, self-awareness, and growth of the supervisee as a developing counselor. The supervisor gains insight and understanding of the supervisee's

**Figure 5.7** Supervision step 9.

**Figure 5.8** Supervision step 11.

development by utilizing puppet processing at various points during the supervision process, such as during the first or second session, at midpoints, and at the close of supervision work with the supervisee. Through the employment of puppet processing, the supervisor and supervisee are also able to assess the actual supervision process itself. As demonstrated in the following example, puppet processing can offer supervisees a safer, less confrontational method of expressing any worries, concerns, hopes, or expectations about the supervisor, counseling, supervision, or themselves.

In the following example, the supervisee was a recent graduate who had been counseling full time for 3 months. The supervisor had noticing that the supervisee had exhibited a pattern of internalizing clients' issues, leading to increased stress. The supervisee was also reporting feeling frustrated with a perceived lack of progress, which was leading to feelings of pressure to do more for the client. The supervisor suggested puppet processing as an opportunity for both the supervisor and supervisee to view these elements in a different light. The puppet processing steps were as follows.

First, key elements identified were the supervisee, the supervisor, pressure to do more, frustration, and stress from internalization of clients' issues. In step 2, the supervisee selected the puppets needed to represent the identified elements. Puppets portraying the elements were the raccoon-in-can (supervisee), the three-headed dragon (supervisor), rabbit-in-hat and spider (pressure to do more), turtle (frustration), and glove puppet with five different animal heads (stress). In steps 4 and 5, the supervisee placed these puppets to physically represent the various key elements. Then, in step 6, the supervisee related the following story about the puppets.

The three-headed dragon supervisor is placed on the armrest looking down on the raccoon-in-can supervisee because the supervisee feels constantly judged by the supervisor. The supervisee feels like mixed messages are received from the supervisor, sometimes positive and supportive, sometimes negative or challenging, and the dragon's three heads represent this. The raccoon-in-can supervisee is over in the corner. In the can with the raccoon supervisee, who has a paw raised for help, are the clients' issues, as represented by different animal heads. The raccoon-in-can supervisee is feeling stressed about having no personal space away from the clients. The can is sitting on top of a turtle representing the supervisee's frustration at how slowly the clients are crawling toward change. Up ahead of and just out of reach of the raccoon-in-can supervisee is a magic rabbit-in-hat symbolizing all of the wonderful, mysterious techniques the supervisee believes are needed in order to make clients change quicker. The black spider crouching on top of the rabbit-in-hat symbolizes the pressure the supervisee feels at needing to do more but being unable to in counseling sessions.

In the following steps (7, 8, and 9), the supervisee and supervisor processed the story by talking about each element and brainstorming possible examples from supervision sessions to further elaborate upon the story. The supervisor then asked the supervisee to change the current puppet story to reflect what the supervisee would like to see. The supervisee changed some of the puppets and told the following story:

Winnie the Pooh is now the supervisor and is holding the raccoon-in-can supervisee, providing complete support, guidance, and an always positive, encouraging message. The raccoon-in-can supervisee has learned the mystical techniques required to become a better counselor, as shown by the magic rabbit-in-hat sitting against the raccoon's can. With these mystical techniques, the supervisee is now able to help the clients, whose issues are no longer in the can with the raccoon, but are instead next to the can and the rabbit. The clients are working on their issues quickly and as busily as bees, as symbolized by the bumblebee resting in front of the clients.

The supervisor and supervisee then processed the story.

In step 10, the supervisor then goes through steps 2 to 6 and, using the same elements as identified by the supervisee, creating an alternate story. The supervisor's story was as follows:

Armadillos now represent both the supervisee and supervisor. The shells of the armadillos represent the internal barriers counselors needed in order to keep clients' issues separate from themselves. The armadillo supervisor was next to and slightly behind the armadillo supervisee, positioned to give support, guidance, and a nurturing nudge when needed to facilitate the supervisee's growth as a counselor. The armadillo supervisee is holding an ant instead of the magic rabbit-in-hat to symbolize that hard and steady work, not mystical techniques, are what is needed in a good counselor. The clients and their issues are still the puppet with many animal heads, and they are still busy as bees, working on their issues. The clients, supervisee, and supervisor are all facing forward as they work on achieving goals in parallel processes.

In the final step, the core elements and their representations in each of the stories are discussed. The overall puppet experience was processed.

The second focus on processing with puppets is the supervisee's counseling work with clients. Puppet processing can help the supervisee develop and gain insight and perspective into clients' stories and issues as well as gain insight and perspective into developing counseling skills. Puppet processing may be particularly helpful in recognizing transference issues present in a session. Because the supervisor also participates in puppet processing, the supervisee is provided with an opportunity to explore the parallel processes that occur in supervision between the supervisor and supervisee, and in counseling between the supervisee and the client.

## Conclusion and Recommendations

Puppet processing is a useful and flexible process that can be incorporated with different theoretical approaches in a supervision session at any point during a supervisee's development. The animal puppets provide external, physical symbols for the safe expression of feelings (Maurer, 1977), conflicts, and the practice of new or challenging skills, resulting in improved decision-making skills and increased self-esteem (Carter & Mason, 1998). The puppets offer a tactile, hands-on approach for supervisees to explore the process of their own intrapersonal and interpersonal development as a counselor. Puppet processing is also useful to encourage divergent thinking skills by increasing creativity (Deacon, 2000) in both the supervisee and supervisor. The elements as portrayed by the puppets allow for an opportunity to restructure and experience core patterns on a visceral level.

Puppet processing offers the supervisor and supervisee a transferable skill. The supervisee in both community and school settings can use puppet processing in counseling sessions to help clients express various elements connected with their issues. The client would receive similar benefits from the process. The supervisor can use puppet processing in group supervision with additional processing leads, as mentioned in the outlined steps. The supervisor can also take puppet processing into trainings and into the classroom for use with students.

The challenges with puppet processing are that some people may not care for puppets or may not feel very creative. However, it is not required to actually speak as if one were the puppet, as in a traditional puppet show. I encourage all of my supervisees to work with the puppet process at least once for the creative exercise and benefits discussed. The puppet process is flexible enough to work with any amount of creativity a person may have because it uses physical, concrete animal puppets to help represent the core elements that are the focus for that session.

The most rewarding part about puppet processing is that it is truly only limited by the extent of one's creativity and imagination. After several years of puppet work in supervision, I continue to be humbled and honored to share in the new story that emerges from puppet processing with my supervisees.

## Using Psychodrama In Counseling Supervision

*Sondra Smith-Adcock and Mark B. Scholl*

In the context of group supervision, the use of activities adopted from psychodrama facilitates participants' creative and spontaneous self-expression. Role-plays and similar here-and-now enactments facilitate increased engagement in the supervision process. As a result, participants feel empowered to experience enhanced self-efficacy, self-esteem, autonomy, self-awareness, and opportunities to enact underdeveloped aspects of themselves (Gladding, 2005). By processing the enactments, participants are able to intentionally integrate new behaviors and personality characteristics into their evolving counselor identities. The use of creative approaches to counseling supervision has been recommended by a number of authors for enhancing the identity development of counselors-in-training (Neswald-McCalip, Sather, Strati, & Dineen, 2003; Newsome, Henderson, & Veach, 2005; Pearson, 2003; Wilkins, 1995; Young & Borders, 1998.

Moreno's (1969, 1975, 1993) psychodrama theory describes a developmental progression culminating in a greater capacity for authentic, intimate relationships. In speaking of the psychodramatic approach, Lipman (2003, p. 6) wrote: "Each time we sociometrically choose a person, place, or thing we are sculpting our identities. We are defining our identities through the roles that we play in any given situation."

In a similar manner to Moreno's theory of ego development, Loganbill, Hardy, and Delworth's (1982) conceptual model of counselor development emphasizes the supervisee's ability to intentionally make conscious choices contributing to his or her growth and development. More specifically, the Loganbill et al. model includes a holistic range of seven sequential developmental issues. In the initial stages, counselors-in-training are more likely to be concerned with developing a sense of competence, their ability to manage emotions, and a sense of autonomy. Next, supervisees are more likely to focus on their capacities for authentic interpersonal relationships with clients and appreciation for diversity. Later on, they become more concerned with issues related to how their identities (e.g., gender, race, religion) influence counseling practices, and with developing a strong sense of purpose in their counseling. Lastly, Loganbill et al. suggested that more advanced supervisees will emphasize issues related to professional ethics.

## Using Psychodrama in Supervision: The Basic Elements and Terminology

The psychodrama-related techniques presented here were developed by two of the authors of the present chapter (Scholl & Smith-Adcock, 2007). We recommend that in applying these techniques, supervisors remain mindful of the developmental sequence proposed by Loganbill et al. (1982). In accordance with their developmental model, an activity designed to promote a sense of competence would be introduced earlier in a supervisee's training than an activity designed to promote more effective management of emotions. We have been using these techniques in our practicum and internship supervision classes for the past 9 years.

*Sociometric Exercises* Sociometric exercises allow individuals to choose where to physically place themselves in order to demonstrate their psychosocial choices. For example, a common warm-up activity requires an individual to stand next to one of four or more pillows best representing how the individual currently feels. These exercises increase participant's self and other awareness, and also emphasize self-responsibility for making social choices. Sociometry gives individuals feedback regarding their patterns, preference, and values (Lipman, 2003). This activity can easily be adapted to ask counselors to stand in areas representing their preferred counseling orientation, preferred counseling role (e.g., supporting, attending, collaborating, etc.), or even their preference for supervisory relationships (e.g., dependent, independent, interdependent, etc.). This sociometric feedback contributes to group cohesion, group vitality, and provides material for further exploration.

*Role Talk* The act of naming an attitude or aspect of oneself (e.g., advice giving) as a role renders that aspect more amenable to change. The idea is to objectify the more specific aspect of the individual so that flexibility and creativity are increased. For example, role talk may occur in the context of a role play, which facilitates isolation and exaggeration of the aspect of the individual. In the words of Blatner (2003, p. 106): "Pinpointing a specific role takes it away from one's general identification with the role and makes it a bit more distant and workable." As a result, the participant is able to be more objective, creative, and flexible.

*Three Stages of Psychodrama*

1. Warm-up: This is the beginning stage of psychodramatic group work, which increases readiness for action and facilitates increased depth during the subsequent *action* stage. The warming-up process promotes group cohesion and a sense of safety. It also allows the director to build a foundation for the action stage by revealing "who" the people are and "what" themes are present in the group's structure (Lipman, 2003, p. 9).

2. Action: The action stage allows the protagonist to enact things in the past, present, or future. Participants work on their identity development while engaged in the past, present, or future. Throughout the duration of this stage, the group members perform and practice new roles and behaviors and, as a result, expand their role repertoires.

3. Sharing: In this stage, the members acknowledge that they are no longer on stage and that they are no longer performing or playing roles. Members once again communicate as in their everyday selves. The sharing phase helps the members to better understand their relationships with one another and to more intentionally and selectively integrate feelings, thoughts, and behaviors from the action stage into their counselor identities.

*The Proper Setting*  In general, the use of psychodrama requires ample space for the group participants to engage in sociometric exercises. Activities sometimes require a space that is free of chairs and tables so that participants are able to move without feeling restricted. Although a stage is not required, it would be helpful to designate a portion of the supervision room (e.g., the front of the room) as the area where the action occurs.

*Materials Needed*  An advantage of psychodrama is that it typically does not require elaborate materials or props. Of course, the materials required can vary a great deal depending on the nature of the activity the supervisor has planned. Most activities can be facilitated with little more than the provision of a few chairs. For example, in one activity described later in this section, five chairs are provided representing five different emotional states from which participants may choose. In other sociometric exercises, we use multicolored objects including pillows, towels, and bean bags to represent a range of subjective choices for participants. Lastly, a number of psychodrama-related approaches may incorporate activities in which participants are asked to draw pictures representing various aspects of themselves. These activities typically require materials such as paper and crayons, markers, or paint.

*Modality*  The use of psychodrama in supervision is best suited for use in a group format. Although some of the techniques could be used with a single supervisee, much of the value of these techniques is based on group dynamics.

## Psychodrama Processing in Supervision

In this section we present a detailed description of a psychodrama-related activity and its application. For this activity we provide a developmental rationale for the activity, describe the activity, and provide an example of our experience applying the technique in our group supervision work. Although we have developed additional activities, a presentation of these activities is beyond the scope of the current section. For additional descriptions of activities we have developed, the reader is referred to Scholl and Smith (2007).

*The Affective Seating Chart*  This activity is based on one used by two psychodrama group counselors (Lipman & Nally-Seif, 2001), who are members of the Psychodrama Training Institute in New York City. Based on the second set of supervisory issues in the Loganbill et al. model, we have used the activity to promote supervisees' awareness of their emotions in counseling sessions, and how they might use these emotions productively. The activity is intended to normalize and facilitate the supervisee's expression of uncomfortable emotions. During the warm-up, five chairs representing five feelings (e.g., anxious, calm, numb, distressed, other) are placed in a circle. Participants are asked to stand by the chair that most closely matches how they are currently feeling. Once all participants have shared, they then return to their original seats. For the action phase, place the five chairs in a row facing the class. Next, facilitate a discussion of the feelings the group members have experienced as supervisors in recent sessions they have conducted. Alternatively, for those without prior counseling experience, you may ask them to consider feelings they have experienced in other helping relationships. Select five prevalent emotional themes, and write them on five sheets of paper. Tape these sheets to the five chairs.

Allow each group member to volunteer to sit in each chair one at a time. Participants may sit in the chairs in any order they desire. For each chair, the volunteer (protagonist) should talk about his or her feelings related to the emotional label in the first person (role talk). After everyone has had an opportunity to volunteer, process the activity by asking everyone to sit in a circle. One at a time, each participant shares what he or she gained from the activity.

I (Scholl) recently introduced this activity to a group of 10 interns. Four prevalent feelings that emerged from the group discussion included *feeling frustrated by my client, feeling annoyed by my client, need to give advice,* and *need to be admired by my client.* These feelings were written on four separate sheets of typing paper, and these sheets were taped to the back of four chairs facing the interns. A fifth chair with a sheet of paper reading "other" was added to permit students to talk about any additional feeling of their choosing. One of the intern participants was a 32-year-old Chinese American woman named Amanda. Prior to this activity, she had been reticent during group discussions. However, when asked to participate in this activity she appeared to welcome the structure and expressed herself openly regarding her frustration in working with one of her internship clients. Although typically she was reserved, on this occasion she was quite emotional as she expressed the irritation she felt toward this client. Expressing these feelings appeared to be cathartic for her, and some of her fellow group members shared similar experiences of frustration with their clients. All 10 participants took a turn sitting in the five chairs and speaking about their emotions in the first person.

Lastly, the 10 supervisees and I sat in a circle and processed what they had gained from the activity. Amanda stated that the activity had allowed her to recognize and speak about her emotions and that she enjoyed finding out that other interns felt similar to the way she did. The processing phase also included a discussion of the importance of understanding one's emotional responses during a session, and an additional discussion of how uncomfortable emotions can be put to positive use in a session.

### Recommendations for Using this Approach in Supervision

Based on our experiences of applying psychodrama-related activities to our supervision work, we have some recommendations for working with supervisees who appear to be uncomfortable with these activities. First, it may be helpful to prepare supervisees for a psychodrama activity by informing them in the previous group meeting. For example, when using the five-chair activity described earlier, a supervisor might ask supervisees to come to the next meeting prepared to discuss two or more uncomfortable emotions they have experienced as counselors, and even provide them with a sample list of feelings to choose from. Second, we recommend that the warm-up phase allow all supervisees to self-disclose and participate in a manner that is comfortable. As previously mentioned, an effective warm-up facilitates a deeper level of exploration during the action stage. Third, participation in an activity should be completely voluntary with no negative consequences for electing not to participate. Even supervisees who do not participate may vicariously experience significant growth. Finally, we believe that it is important to remain flexible in leading the activities. For example, in the activity described earlier (i.e., The Affective Seating Chart), we found that allowing two group members to perform at once enabled hesitant supervisees to overcome feelings of trepidation. In general, we believe that it is especially important to provide a climate of safety and support, and to empathize with supervisees who are reluctant or anxious.

### Recommendations for Training Supervisors to Use the Approach

We recommend that supervisors who plan on using psychodrama-related activities become familiar with Moreno's (1969, 1975, 1993) theory of psychodrama. Blatner (2000) provides a useful overview that discusses both Moreno's theory and some of the basic techniques employed. For supervisors with limited exposure to psychodrama, we also highly recommend participating in psychodrama workshops in order to learn by observing experienced practitioners.

### Conclusion

Our approach to using psychodrama-related techniques in supervision has evolved and developed as a result of our work with supervisees over a long period. In accordance with the Loganbill et al. (1982) model of development, we agree that the techniques or activities should be employed in a manner that supports the supervisees' current developmental concerns. For example, we believe that the activity called The Affective Seating Chart (used to promote emotional awareness) should be introduced to beginning counselors to foster emotional awareness and acceptance, and reduce their anxiety.

Consistent with the spirit and philosophy of Moreno's psychodrama, we recommend that supervisors should feel free to experiment and to modify activities to accommodate their instructional purposes as well as the unique developmental needs of their supervisees. For example, to meet the needs of a particular group, a supervisor may decide to only include two chairs representing two particularly problematic emotions when leading The Affective Seating Chart activity. We have found that our use of these psychodrama-related activities has enabled us to feel more effective as supervision group facilitators. Further, we believe that psychodrama-related techniques contribute to the development of trust and group cohesion by facilitating deeper levels of self-disclosure. Perhaps most importantly, these activities promote spontaneity and flexibility, which opens participants up to their potential for growth and change. We hope that other supervisors will use psychodrama-related activities in their supervision and experience some of the same benefits for themselves and their supervisees.

## Using Bibliotherapy in Counseling Supervision

*Mary Amanda Graham*

Both bibliotherapy and supervision are processes of encouraging individuals to engage in self-discovery and growth (Abdullah, 2002; Bernard & Goodyear, 2004; Pardeck & Pardeck, 1998). Supervision and bibliotherapy relationships are as unique as client and counselor relationships. Bibliotherapy and supervision both focus on the developmental level and needs of the client or supervisee. "Bibliotherapy can be a highly personalized tool because it represents the counselor's unique judgment at so many different junctions of its application" (Riordan, Mullis, & Nuchow, 1996 p. 173). This remains consistent with the supervision process.

The characteristics shared by supervision and bibliotherapy are their unique relationships, goals, objectives, and outcomes toward the growth of the individual. Both relationships are highly individualized based on the needs of the client and supervisee. The implementation of a bibliosupervision model applies a creative tool within the larger context of supervision to assist the supervisee in the development of skills.

### The Graham Model of Bibliosupervision: The Basic Elements and Terminology

Bibliosupervision is a process guided by the supervisor, using fictional children's literature, to support the developmental processes of the supervisee. It is based on Caroline Shrodes' (1949) model of bibliotherapy, which includes a three-step process of identification, catharsis, and insight. The bibliosupervisor assists the supervisee in identifying, analyzing, and relating to the book characters, and storylines as they pertain to counselor development and case conceptualization. The bibliosupervisor also facilitates supervisees' growth processes by assisting them in expressing emotions, cognitions, concerns, and issues, as they relate to counselor development, all done in the safety of the supervision or supervisory setting. The articulation of these emotions, thoughts, and cognitions enables the supervisor to guide the supervisee toward insight, leading to a beneficial dialogue regarding his or her thoughts, feelings, and emotions as they relate to current concerns and issues in counselor development. Together the supervisor and supervisee develop plans of action that will facilitate the supervisees' learning and movement from the status of a novice to that of an expert in the counseling field. The Graham Model of Bibliosupervision (GMB) recommends the use of fictional children's literature to facilitate the growth, development, and working alliance in supervision. Fictional literature provides a wide arena of themes and is easily presented as a nonthreatening intervention. The three stages supervisees experience while participating in the GMB are as follows:

1. Identification: The supervisee is able to identify with characters and storylines presented in the literature that relate to his or her personal development as a counselor.
2. Catharsis: The supervisee becomes meaningfully involved in the story and with the characters in the literature, and is able to process emotions, thoughts, and feelings as they relate to the development of his or her counseling skills and techniques.
3. Insight: After catharsis, the bibliosupervisor is able to facilitate constructive dialogue that aids the supervisee in becoming aware of and working through issues that may arise in his or her developmental processes as a counselor in training. This includes, but is not limited to, case conceptualization regarding client issues, professional development areas, and growth and skill development.

Although the GMB approach recommends the use of children's literature, consistent with bibliotherapy tenets, the supervisor has the option to use any literature he or she deems appropriate. This can include children's literature, adult fiction or nonfiction, and resource material. The media selected must be congruent with the supervisees' development and be applicable to supervisees' growth and skill level (Graham, 2007).

*Modality*   Bibliosupervision can be facilitated in either individual or group supervision. In individual supervision, the supervisor has the opportunity to become more connected to the supervisee by using bibliosupervision. The supervisor can create an individualized learning environment using the techniques that specifically focus on the supervisees' developmental process and client concerns. In individual supervision, the following is a suggested framework for using bibliosupervision:

1. Weekly check-in on current site issues or concerns.
2. Revisit supervisory concerns or issues from the previous session.
3. View and discuss videotape or audiotape.
4. Bibliosupervision experience (flexibly used at any point during the supervisory session that the supervisor deems appropriate).

In group supervision the supervisor has the opportunity to use bibliosupervision to facilitate group discussions on specific counselor developmental issues, clients concerns, and case conceptualization. The bibliosupervision experience can be used to open up dialogue at the beginning of group supervision, to link together reoccurring themes in group supervision, to encourage a deeper level exploration of counselor growth and development, and as a transition into needed discussions that may not arise in a typical group supervision session.

*Bibliosupervision Materials and Framework*

There must be informed consent by the bibliosupervisor and supervisee. This goes beyond the initial informed consent established in any supervision relationship based on the probability that the supervisee will be exploring issues on a deeper, more emotional level in supervision. Because this approach encourages a deep level of exploration and cathartic process, it is important when engaging in bibliosupervision that the supervisee be aware of and agree with the process taking place. The supervisee needs to feel safe and comfortable within the supervision sessions in order to fully benefit from the bibliosupervision experience.

If the bibliosupervision process is thriving, then both the supervisor and supervisee will be able to easily identify growth and change toward professional development. This will be evident through skill development, processing, case conceptualization, and supervisory participation.

Bibliosupervision books should be selected based on thematic match to the developmental process of students undergoing supervision. Before selecting a book to use in supervision, the bibliosupervisor needs to consider books that provide topics or themes focusing on a wide array of developmental issues supervisees can relate to in various stages of development. Books should be evaluated based on themes, subject matter, suitability to supervision, length, appropriate developmental level for supervisee, transferability to supervision, diversity factors, and therapeutic use in supervision.

Below is an example of a 10-week supervision framework using bibliosupervision. Each week a different book is presented based on a specific supervisee and his or her development. Each week the supervisor facilitates the discussion, following the reading of the book. Some sample questions to begin dialogue are included. Questions, reflections, paraphrasing, and guiding will vary depending on the reaction to the book by the supervisee. The bibliosupervisor should consider selecting books that are consistent with and individualized to match the developmental needs of a specific supervisee. Below is an actual series of books one supervisee experienced through bibliosupervision:

**Week 1:**
> **Book:** *Lost in the Woods* by C. Sam and J. Stoick (2004)
> This book is about a young fawn that is left by its mother in the woods. The fawn is confused at first by the mother doe leaving, but learns to trust its instincts. There are several characters in the book that attempt to give the fawn advice.
> **Supervision Themes:** Perspectives, internal reliance and knowledge, trust, questioning, fear, empowerment, change, growth, development

**Guiding Questions (examples used to begin dialogue each week):**

1. What was happening in this story?
2. What themes seem familiar when relating to your counselor training or work with clients?

Following each bibliotherapy experience the supervisor continues the facilitation of dialogue based on themes that arise from the book as well as the guiding questions.

**Week 2:**

**Book:** *Wilfrid Gordon McDonald Partridge* by M. Fox (1985)
This book is about the aging community and losing memory, voice, and empowerment. A small child engages in a relationship with an aging woman and helps her find her voice.
**Supervision Themes:** Listening, validation, talents, acceptance, perspective, connections, change

**Week 3:**

**Book:** *The Giving Tree* by S. Silverstein (1964)
This book is about the relationship between a tree and a boy. It addresses the changing of the relationship as the boy ages and takes from the tree until the tree has nothing left to give. There is a moment of realization for both the tree and the boy.
**Supervision Themes:** Self-care, reliance, change, growth, development, perspective, closure, acceptance, disappointment, perspective, empathy, closure

**Week 4:**

**Book:** *Alexander and the Terrible, Horrible, No Good, Very Bad Day* by J. Viorst
This is a book about a young boy who thinks he is having the worst day ever! Through dialogue he understands that everyone has struggles and bad days from time to time.
**Supervision Themes:** Struggles, emotions, detachment, disappointment, self-care, validation, perspective, control, interventions, change

**Week 5:**

**Book:** *My Mama had a Dancing Heart* by L. Gray (1999)
This book is about the relationship between a mother and her daughter. It addresses relationship changes with the change of seasons.
**Supervision Themes:** Efficacy, trust, closure, strength, reliance, empowerment, career, love, grief, choice

**Week 6:**
>**Book:** *Sneetches* by Dr. Seuss
>This book addresses oppression and differences both internal and external.
>**Supervision Themes:** Comparison, diversity, struggle, social justice, perspective, risk-taking, acceptance

**Week 7:**
>**Book:** *The Old Woman Who Named Things* by C. Rylant (2000)
>This book is about an older woman who will only name nonliving objects based on the fear of losing relationships.
>**Supervision Themes:** Developmental process, closure, attachment, risk-taking, acceptance, change, grief

**Week 8:**
>**Book:** *Harriet, You'll Drive Me Wild* by M. Fox (2003)
>This book is about the many frustrations one may experience when involved in a relationship with another person, specifically a child. The characters have a trying day but in the end learn to appreciate and understand one another's perspectives.
>**Supervision Themes:** Humility, frustration, emotions, failure, coping, risk-taking

**Week 9:**
>**Book:** *Whoever You Are* by M. Fox (2001)
>This book is about honoring differences and diversity and understanding global perspectives.
>**Supervision Themes:** Diversity, social justice, comparisons, change, acceptance, empowerment, uniqueness, communication, families, friendships, relationships, trust

**Week 10:**
>**Book:** *Oh, the Places You'll Go* by Dr. Seuss
>This book is about the journey a person takes to reach his or her goals. There are many challenges and things to think about when taking the journey, but in the end the person taking the journey is left empowered.
>**Supervision Themes:** Empowerment, closure, success, fear, change, moving on, taking risks and steps, excitement, validation, communication, relationships

*Bibliosupervision Processing*

The birth of bibliosupervision came about from my work with supervisees who struggled examining deeper-level supervisory issues. Having only 10 weeks of supervision, I felt that it was my responsibility as a supervisor to create a safe and challenging environment to assist supervisees in examining issues related to counselor development. Having used bibliotherapy in practice with clients, and understanding the impact bibliotherapy had on the growth and development of my clients, I decided to create a model of bibliosupervision.

My first experience using bibliosupervision was with a young man who was resistant to deeper-level dialogue in supervision. His responses in supervision were particularly closed, and when asked, "how are things going at your site or with your clients?" he would respond "great, perfect, no issues." Having been a master's student in training, trained as a counselor supervisor and understanding the developmental levels of supervision, I understood the possibility of this young man masking his areas of concerns and anxieties. I spoke to him about reading a book. He agreed wholeheartedly, and my first bibliosupervision experience with this supervisee was the reading of *Oh, the Places You'll Go* by Dr. Seuss. This was a powerful experience for both of us. When I facilitated the dialogue regarding the book, the supervisee spoke with more depth and intensity than he had in the previous sessions. He spoke about relating to the "waiting place" in the book and how he felt like he was waiting to develop "good" counseling skills, waiting for things in his life to settle down, and waiting for school to be done. This book created a powerful dialogue that led to the examination of his definition of "good" counseling skills, transference, client expectations, wellness, and balance. Each of the supervision sessions following included a book, per the request of the supervisee. Other supervisees who have experienced bibliosupervision have shared their reactions (Graham, 2007):

> "It was useful for reflecting on my experience as a developing counselor—I thought themes discussed provided a deeper understanding of my development and areas of future growth. I found it somewhat less helpful in determining new ways of working with clients and understanding client's perspectives" (p. 51).

> "Being read to lessened my anxiety in supervision and provided a comforting experience. I enjoyed the opportunity to engage with my supervisor around the colorful and creative themes that emerged" (p. 52).

> "The supervisory relationship became more of a human and collaborative relationship. The dialogue regarding the literature provided an opportunity to learn and grow from differing and similar perspectives" (p. 52).

> *"The bibliosupervision process created an environment in which I felt understood, and I was able to discuss themes relevant to counseling and life"*(p. 52).
>
> *"I felt the themes that emerged were mostly directly applicable to my own development as a counselor. In many ways I've felt like a child as a fledgling professional so the simply stated yet powerful messages in the books seemed very appropriate to where I was developmentally"* (p. 53).

### Recommendations for Training Supervisors to Use Bibliosupervision

In order for the bibliosupervision session to be successful in individual or group supervision, it is important that the bibliosupervisor have knowledge of the developmental process of supervision, understand the goals of counselor supervision, and be able to identify and understand current themes facing supervisees. The bibliosupervisor must have an understanding of the developmental aspects of the supervisory process in order to link appropriate literature to the developmental level of the supervisee. It is essential that the bibliosupervisor have a working knowledge of the tenets of bibliotherapy, the written material being used in supervision, and how the selected literature pertains to counselor development and client conceptualization. Bibliosupervision can be integrated within any supervision setting as a tool for developing a strong supervisory working alliance and for the facilitation of skill development for the supervisee.

### Conclusion

It is essential for supervisors to have a variety of techniques available to assist counseling students in the journey of learning, developing, and growing into professional counselors. Bibliosupervision is a creative and nontraditional approach to facilitating the supervision process. Bibliosupervision not only offers a creative approach for supervisors, but also acts as a possible means for developing and maintaining a strong working alliance between the supervisor and supervisee. Bibliosupervision assists in the joining of the supervisor and supervisees in the human condition.

## Using Sandtray-Worldplay In Counseling Supervision

*Elaine Wittmann and Catherine Tucker*

The potential benefits of applying the use of sandplay to the counseling supervision process are evident from my (Wittmann's) recent experience with one of my supervisees. Jane, a clinician with a year of postgraduate experience, presented a difficult case week after week in supervision. The family she was seeing was in crisis, and Jane felt as if she was attempting to put out the wild fires and not getting to the root of the difficulties. As Jane's supervisor, I recognized a parallel process in which I felt frustrated in my attempts to facilitate Jane's development as a counselor.

Sandtrays and figures were in view and available in the room, and clinicians who came for supervision expressed curiosity about this treatment option. I was aware that using the sandtray to gain insights and consider options proved useful for clients, and considered the sandplay process as a useful approach for counselors to present cases that would potentially enhance the supervision process.

In an attempt to help Jane understand her difficult case, she was asked to create the "world of the case" or "put the case in the sand." She chose from miniature figures and placed the dynamics of the case in the sandtray. She grouped family members across the tray, and was asked to "be with this 'World'" she created. Jane had difficulty disconnecting herself from the continuing chaos. I asked Jane to stand and look at the tray in its entirety. She stood and witnessed how she perceived the "World" of this family. When she looked at the sandtray from above, and from various angles, she saw the family in a fresh way with different perspectives and multiple viewpoints. She began to see the alliances, and groupings of conflict. When she was able to observe the family dynamics with these new insights, Jane was able to disengage from the ongoing chaos, and give the family new perspectives to consider.

## Sandtray-Worldplay in Counseling Supervision: The Basic Elements and Terminology

The use of sand as a medium for gaining insights and enhancing the healing process has been recorded across cultures and time. From Tibetan Buddhist and Navajo sand paintings, to divination rituals of the Dogon people of Mali, traditional ceremonies were performed for personal and communal restoration (Baker, 1993; Barnes, 2005; Gold, 1994; Jongeward, 1990; London & Recio 2004; Stevenson, 2006).

H. G. Wells inspired others to consider the richness of children's play as he observed and recorded his own children playing with miniatures and toys in complex scenes on the floor of his home (Wells, 1975). Influenced by Wells' observations and recognition that children "think differently than adults" (Turner, 2005, p. 691), London child psychiatrist and pediatrician Margaret Lowenfeld introduced a box of sand, water, and miniature toys to her playroom in the 1920s. This "Wonder Box," or "The World," evolved into the development of the "World Technique" as a psychotherapeutic tool with children (DeDomenico, 1988; Turner, 2005). Other therapists soon followed and explored the medium of sand and miniatures as assessment tools for applying psychotherapeutic techniques.

In the 1950s, Swiss Jungian analyst Dora Kalff studied with Margaret Lowenfeld, integrated her experience with Eastern philosophy, and developed what is known as "Sandplay." The therapist, silent witness, in the Sandplay process, creates a "free and protected space" or "Temenos" (Turner, 2005, p. 212) whereby the client uses symbols in the sand that derive from an unconscious need to move toward wholeness and healing. The awareness of transference and countertransference between the client and therapist are key healing factors in Sandplay. Ultimately, the goal is for the transference to be made to the sandtray. Archetypes emerge from the cultural experiences, and the collective unconscious as the images are placed in the tray and the story is formed (Turner, 2005; McNally, 2001). Individual sandtray worlds are tracked over time, symbols are interpreted by the therapist, and connections are made between the unconscious and conscious in the move toward individuation.

Drawing on the teachings of Lowenfeld and Kalff and others, Dr. Gisela Schubach DeDomenico described her approach, in the early 1980s, as growing out of her personal "phenomenological, hermeneutic research," and her work with children, adults, families, and couples (DeDomenico, 1988, p. 30). In DeDomenico's Sandtray-Worldplay, the psyche reveals itself as the builder illustrates his or her story in the sand. Objects become real when placed within the sand; they are no longer symbols or represen-tations. These formations are defined by the builder and not interpreted by the therapist. Transference is recognized in Sandtray-Worldplay, but the transfer is with the "World" and not the clinician. The counselor is actively involved in the process as an observer who is also reflecting and jointly experiencing the World of the builder (DeDomenico, 2002b; Rae, 1998).

*The Process of Sandtray-Worldplay*   In Sandtray-Worldplay, the psyche reveals itself and leads the process. The experience is deepened in the tray, and the symbolic becomes concrete. Images can bring powerful insights to consciousness. In Sandtray-Worldplay, the builder and witness move together through four stages: (a) building and observing, (b) experiencing and reflecting, (c) joint experiencing, and (d) photographing. The builder or counselor is simply directed to "put the World in the tray." They are encouraged to "let the figure choose you," and are given time to place the objects in the sand and experience this World they have created. The World becomes concrete and can be touched, experienced, moved, pon-dered, changed, and discussed. The internalized material becomes con-scious. The symbolic becomes alive in the here and now (DeDomenico, 1988, 1992b, 1999a).

The importance of the role of the witness is emphasized in Sandtray-Worldplay. The sandtray process is led by the builder and facilitated by the witness. The witness not only observes the creation of the World in the tray; this empathetic companion must also be fully attentive and be able to hold the outer aspects of the World, while the client holds the inner aspects. The observer takes an active role in the sandtray process by being mindful of her or his own personal responses.

*Sandtray Materials*   Materials needed for sand play methods include sand, sandtrays, water, figures, paper and pencil, and a camera. Generally, sand trays measure 57 × 72 × 7 cm, or approximately 20" × 30" × 3 to 4 in. in depth. This construction allows the builder to encompass the whole World in a glance and contains the space that will be used in the sandtray activity. Trays are constructed of wood or plastic, and the inside sides and bottom are traditionally painted blue. Two trays, one with dry sand and the other with slightly damp sand, allow greater possibilities for the builder. A round tray can be useful to decrease anxiety, bring unity, or leave the builder no place to hide. Deeper, 5-in. trays may be needed for younger children or builders who need to go deeper. Trays are half-filled with sand. Sanitized sand is available in building supply and toy stores, and is appropriate for the sandtray process. Other colors and textures can be used as adjuncts to the play sand, but may not be as amenable to sculpting or shaping. Black, white, garnet, green, coral, and other colors of sand can also elicit different emotions and memories. Water is available to moisten sand, to flow into earthly bodies of water, to cleanse, to flood, etc. An additional tray for water only may be beneficial. (See Figure 5.9 for photograph of sandtray setup).

**Figure 5.9** Wooden and plastic sandtrays hold dry and damp sand. A round sandtray is an alternative. Water and a towel are available. Shelves hold a wide variety of miniatures.

Sandtray miniatures and figures include a wide range of synthetic and natural objects.

They are chosen with intention and include humans and nonhumans, fantasy and reality, natural materials including mineral and vegetation, transportation, and housing to reflect diverse experiences, time periods, ethnicities, and emotions. Figures, usually placed on shelves, or in drawers or cabinets, and behind curtains, are displayed in categories so that the builder has the ability to access and use as the psyche wishes. The figures speak for the builder in a metaphor (Hegeman, 2001; DeDomenico, 2002).

The sandtray process is documented in several ways. Sandtray worlds are documented by the written journey of the movement of the process, the verbalizations of the builder, and with photographs. In the Sandplay model, photographs are not taken in the view of the client, are tracked by the clinician, and are reviewed at the end of the process. In Sandtray-Worldplay, pictures may be taken with the client present and can be given to the client to process between sessions.

### Sandtray-Worldplay Processing in Supervision

As a clinical supervisor, I am challenged to monitor the client care of supervisees as well enhance their professional functioning. I must consider the personal growth of supervisees and find ways to present opportunities for their learning and development (Werstlein, 1994). Using the Discrimination Model (Bernard, 1997), my role involves teaching, skills building, consulting, guiding, monitoring, and evaluating the counselor and following counselor self-awareness.

As a clinician, I use the Sandtray-Worldplay model, and as a supervisor, this model is offered to supervisees. As with Jane, who presented a complex and anxiety-producing case, the counselor is invited to "put the World in the sand." The clinician builds and experiences how he or she perceived the "World" of the clients, the group, the family, the World of the therapeutic issue, the World of the therapy, and the World of the clinician in the therapy. As the clinician moves through stages of Sandtray-Worldplay, he or she is invited to deepen the experience of the World and the figures, and to consider their placement, their perspectives, relationships, and movement. In the same way the clinician holds the space for the client and experiences the World with the client, the supervisor witnesses the clinician's process. Thus, the supervisee's experience can parallel that of the client in many ways.

The supervisor holds the space, experiences the World with the builder (supervisee), and is given a window to observe the process with the clinician. The clinician and supervisor are given opportunities to observe clinical issues in the sand as well as options for treatment for the client, and the role of the therapist. Stages of clinical development can be considered by the supervisor and clinician, and plans for training and skills building can be made as necessary.

This method of case presentation has the capacity to increase clinicians' abilities to perceive dynamics of presented cases, develop skills, and grow as a therapist. Using this method of the sandtray process also gives the supervisor another way to observe clinical issues, and foster the development of the clinician. Sandtray building can help the supervisee develop plans for training and identify areas for skills building. It also provides a training ground for the sandtray techniques and helps to build confidence in its use. The supervisor must be aware of and respond to the needs, abilities, and readiness of the supervisees to use this form of supervision, and must respect and understand the use of metaphors, images, and fantasy.

Clinical issues can present themselves in the sand, emerging both from the client and from the clinician in supervision. When the clinical issues of the client match those of the therapist and/or the issues of the therapist match those of the clinical supervisor, a phenomenon called *parallel process* occurs. Parallel process is a treatment impasse that continues until the issues of the therapist or supervisor can be disentangled from those of the client or supervisee. Sandtray work is often very helpful in both identifying and clearing these parallel issues.

Figure 5.10 illustrates this bidirectional transference and countertransference in the sandtray. The clinician placed the World of the family in the sand and introduced this family who went through a divorce several years before. The presenting problem for the family was the resistance their 7-year-old was expressing to visiting with her father. The builder was asked

**Figure 5.10** Parallel process is represented. Figures on the right represent mother, daughter, and life without the father (presented as the ghost). Figures on the left are father and his new family. The therapist stands in the middle (background) as fairies pull the jewel (the child) back and forth.

to "experience" or to "be with" the figures, get to know this place, and share the associations. In verbal sharing by the counselor, new information was gleaned for the supervisor: the mother's continuing anger at the father and his new family, the child's fear of betraying her mother, the father's powerful domineering stance, and the clinician's allegiance to the mother and anxiety in making contact with the father. The supervisor observed that while the clinician presented the World, she pulled her fingers across the sand nearest to herself. The supervisor wondered aloud about the "counselor figure" and requested that the supervisee explore her thoughts and feelings. The counselor expressed her anxiety in the role, became aware of her physical and emotional responses in the sand, and realized how her own allegiances and resistances may be contributing the lack of movement for the family. By addressing her own issues around conflict, possibilities could be opened for the family, for herself as a counselor, and personally.

A counseling intern placed herself in the sand with a "resistant" adolescent client. In Figure 5.11, the 14-year-old client aimed her arrow at the intern (i.e., a two-headed dragon) as the question was posed by the builder/intern: "How do I work with her hostility?" As the intern experienced the World from the client's position, she understood how the adolescent was attempting to protect herself and ward off continuing danger. The adolescent presented as angry; screaming at the World, including the counselor. The Builder looks at the World of the counselor/dragon in this World and saw her own capacity to "spit fire back and defend self" or to experience the World of the child and "be more open and receptive to the fire (of the client)." The original question was answered with "compassion." The intern

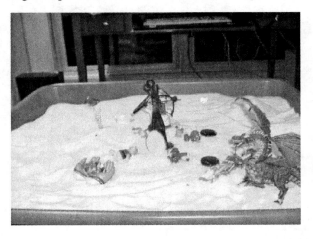

**Figure 5.11** Countertransference issues come alive in the sand. The two-headed dragon (right foreground) sees the child's problematic behavior and the pain behind the behavior.

was able to see the transference of the client on to her environment and her own countertransference.

*Specific Examples of Sandtray-Worldplay Processing*

In this section, I present illustrations of individual and group format applications of the Sandtray-Worldplay approach to supervision. Finally, I present examples illustrating how this approach facilitates supervisee development from the perspective of Stoltenberg and Delworth's (1987) counselor development model.

*Example Illustrating an Individual Format*   A newly licensed clinician expressed frustration as she presented the case of a family with multiple conflicts, turmoil, and pain. Early in treatment, a sandtray representation of the case was created in supervision. Figure 5.12 illustrates the forces that impacted the family: the howling adolescent daughter (wolf) taking center stage, the father who was described as "abusive," mother who did not believe she had any power or control, and the clinician. The builder wrestled with the identification of the primary client and how to proceed with appropriate therapy. Six months later, the counselor, again, presented the family in the sand. The counselor's current frustration seemed to be coming from her perception of a minimum change for the family. This second sandtray [Figure 5.13] gave the counselor a new perspective as she recognized changes. The father was not represented in the World; he was no longer living in the family, the mother had plans to move into a new home, and the daughter still raged. This time, the mother and clinician

**Figure 5.12** Observing treatment over time. First, a howling wolf represents an adolescent daughter.

**Figure 5.13** Six months later, the fence protects and the daughter's pain is recognized.

noticed the adolescent girl, but the fence protected them. They were not afraid to face the child; they were able to see her in her pain. The family was this counselor's client.

*Example Illustrating a Group Format*   I have found applying Sandtray-Worldplay in supervision with groups to be useful as well. In particular, the use of sandplay can assist supervisees who are making the difficult transition from their hectic workday schedule to a group supervision session. With one ongoing supervision group, I offered the sandtray as a beginning silent ritual. Figures were placed in the sandtray, sand was moved, and additions were made during this group check-in. They experienced the World of the group at that moment. They then processed their World verbally and experienced the group as a container, developed group support and cohesiveness, and the supervisor could observe group development in a new way. The participants had the advantage of building confidence with the medium to use with individuals, families, and other groups.

At the start of another ongoing play/sandtray supervision group session, members set individual and group goals in the sandtray. Each member chose a figure for the individual goal, placed the figure in the sand, and was joined by the others. The group could identify with each other: bringing clarity to their work, being grounded, letting go of obstacles, gaining insight, and "filling in the holes in my head." Individual goals were acknowledged and held by the group as a whole. The group goals for each member were then placed in the sand, and "the World of the goals" was processed. With great respect, each member placed a figure in the sand and voiced his or her desire for the group: "Strength from the individual and coming out larger," "learning together as a unit," "experience the organic process and integrate information from each other," "freedom and power in who we each are at the moment of truth as we come together." Figures were moved and honored until the entire group agreed that the World was as it was to be. The group owned this World collectively and became united at this moment. In addition to the identification, clarification, and incorporation of goals, this group experienced an early intimate experience toward group cohesion, and now had a technique they could also use with therapeutic groups, families, classrooms, and administrative groups.

Processing clinical cases in the sand may be accomplished in groups as well. After giving a short review of the case verbally, the same instructions are given to the individual in the group: "Put the World of the client (i.e., family, problem, etc.) into the sand." The group becomes aware of the clinical process, the clinical issues, and development of the case as the individual counselor builds the case in the sand. That is, the presenter is given the opportunity to experience the role of builder and the group as witnesses. In processing sandtray Worlds, group members are also given an opportunity to see the benefits of processing sandtrays in groups.

*Examples Illustrating Supervisee Stage Development* Stoltenberg and Delworth (1987) described three levels of development for the counselor: beginning, intermediate, and advanced. In these levels, the authors considered self-and-other awareness for the counselor, motivation, and autonomy. They identified eight growth areas for counselor, including intervention, skills competence, assessment techniques, interpersonal assessment, client conceptualization, treatment goals and plans, and professional ethics.

Simpson (2000) reported developmental stages of a clinician that paralleled human development. The first-stage—"Entrance into field"—clinicians were described as wide-eyed, naïve, fearful, excited, and self-centered. Considerations for supervision included therapeutic boundaries, and transference/countertransference issues. The second stage was of the "Adolescent" who displayed a "kind of know-it-all" attitude while being overwhelmed at same time. The role of the supervisor is to be "monitoring while encouraging." The third stage of "Maturation" encompasses a sense of mastery while "life continues to humble you." Supervision/consultation considerations include burnout, rest/assimilation, and appreciation of beauty and wisdom.

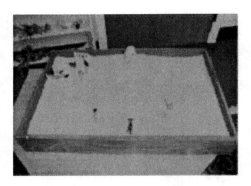

**Figure 5.14** Stages of development for the counselor.

The following illustrations are examples of stages of development for the clinician and how sandtray Worlds reflect that growth. A beginning counselor, an intern working in a school setting, presented a 7-year-old who was "acting out" at home, but not in school. The intern was able to see the boy at school and used a variety of play therapy tools to develop a relationship with the child, but the mother was inconsistent in attending sessions despite transportation offered by the school. The intern spoke with the mother by phone occasionally, but was disappointed by the mother's critical attitude toward her son.

In Figure 5.14, which depicts an early stage of supervisee development, a small deer (the boy) appears in the foreground of the photo with the teacher and counselor to either side as support. A mentor (the bear across from the boy) was described as formidable and an asset to the boy, but uncommunicative with the counselor. The World of the mother was seen in the upper left as a tiny bunny that dug a hole in the sand and was surrounded by a fence. In this enclosure was the father (wrestler), who appeared as controlling and physically abusive to the mother. Younger siblings were included here as well. The supervisee experienced each figure and realized that the mother's hole was so deep that she could not see the World outside the fence. Her son was outside the fence, as was willing assistance, if she could only see outside the fence. The mother was being held in the enclosure by fear of what was inside and outside the fence, and powerlessness. The intern looked at the outside World from the perspective of the bunny and understood. The frustration the intern felt was turned into compassion and a new way of considering the World of the child. He would have to find a new way of reaching the mother.

In the intermediate stage of development, this counselor built on self-awareness and exhibited less dependence on the supervisor as he experienced the case for himself. Figures 5.15 to 5.17 illustrate the journey of a

**Figure 5.15** In the beginning stage, the counselor learns the perspective of the client. The counselor identifies with the character of Robin.

talented builder as he experienced his position as the counselor to a family. It seemed ironic that the clinician identified himself as Robin, junior hero to Batman, possibly identifying his stage of development as an apprentice to a superhero.

In Figure 5.15, the counselor realized that Robin was "standing above the family." Robin, then in Figure 5.16, was moved, and now the clinician was aware that he was standing in the light of the lighthouse, which was identified as therapy. He discovered that he was interfering with the therapeutic process and rethought his role. With these new observations, the counselor joined the family in Figure 5.17 and increases his effectiveness.

At advanced stages, supervisees often focus on their relationships with clients, manage deeper emotions, and make connections to their own life. For example, one master clinician was moved by the situation her 13-year-old client presented. The adolescent was being seen in therapy for issues around her mother's mental illness and the child's removal from the home,

**Figure 5.16** In the intermediate stage, Robin stands above the family in the session.

**Figure 5.17** In the final stage, Robin stands with the family.

but as the builder/clinician presented the case in the sand, she realized that the greater issue was "fitting in" with peers. The girl's clothes were from a thrift store and her less fashionable glasses were purchased by the state. As the counselor experienced the World of the child, she also realized that her World includes her own children, whose desires paralleled those of her 13-year-old client, but she had the financial resources to allow her children to purchase the desired objects.

## Conclusion

As a supervisor applying Sandtray-Worldplay to my work with supervisees, I have repeatedly observed that this approach fosters development in terms of the stages identified by Stoltenberg and Delworth (1987) and Helm Simpson (2000). Further, as supervisees progress through these developmental stages, I have noticed the following changes in their sandplay processes:

- The complexity of the sandtray mirrors the clinician's understanding of the complexities of the case.
- At times, more experienced clinicians presented their cases with more figures in the sandtrays. They seem to be able to "hold" more in terms of metaphor and sandplay "Worlds."
- More mature and advanced supervisees seem to show a deeper understanding of their own journey. Sandtray-Worldplay appears to facilitate a depth of experience that more experienced clinicians seem to accept. Advanced clinicians appear less fearful of presenting their own journey and understanding that we all have a journey.
- With experience, there seems to be a greater honoring and respecting of the client's process.

- Overall, cases presented in the sandtray appeared to accurately and literally reflect the stage of development of the clinician.

After witnessing more than 50 sandtrays in supervision, I have come to the conclusion that the process of Sandtray-Worldplay has enabled me to experience the World of the client, the World of therapy, and the World of the clinician working with the client, which is very different from using the verbal process alone. The process of Sandtray-Worldplay provides the supervisor and supervisee a better understanding of the case, the clinician, the therapy, and himself or herself.

## Summary and Conclusions: Using Expressive Arts in Supervision

In this chapter, skilled counseling supervisors have shared and documented their creative experiences in helping supervisees find insight, growth, and change for themselves and the clients with whom they work. Expressive methods, including Puppet processing, Psychodrama, Bibliosupervision, and Sandtray-Worldplay, have been fully articulated by the supervisors who use them. Furthermore, in this chapter, we have attempted to find and document some of the most creative and innovative approaches to using the expressive arts in supervision—likely those that we do not hear about or consider using regularly. In this regard, this chapter by no means summarizes the full extent to which creative and expressive arts may be used in counseling supervision. The theory and practice of using the creative and expressive arts in supervision is limited only by the imagination of supervisors and the engagement of their supervisees. The development of a working alliance, a desire for growth on the part of both supervisee and supervisor, and the need for change in clients will continue to drive supervisors to develop new and creative ways to approach the complicated and fulfilling task of counseling supervision.

## References

Abdullah, M. H. (2002). Bibliotherapy. *ERIC Digest, 177,* ED470712.

Baker, C. (1993). Navaho sand painting and sandplay. *Journal of Sandplay Therapy.* II (2) 89–103.

Barnes, J. (2005, October 1). Sand mandalas in *New Life Journal.* Thomson Gale.

Bernard, J. M. (1997) *Fundamentals in clinical supervision.* New York: Allyn and Bacon.

Bernard, J. M., & Goodyear, R. K. (2004). *Fundamentals of clinical supervision* (3rd ed.). Boston: Pearson.

Blatner, A. (2000). Psychodrama. In R. J. Corsini and D. Wedding (Eds.), *Current Psychotherapies* (6th ed.) (pp. 560–571). Itaska, Il: Peacock Publishers.

Blatner, A. (2003). "Not mere players": Psychodrama applications in everyday life. In Jacob Gershoni (Ed.), *Psychodrama in the 21st century: Clinical and educational applications* (pp. 103–115). New York, NY: Springer Publishing Company.

Carter, R. B., & Mason, P. S. (1998). The selection and use of puppets in counseling. *Professional School Counseling, 1,* 50–53.

Deacon, S. A. (2000). Using divergent thinking exercises within supervision to enhance therapist creativity. *Journal of Family Psychotherapy, 11*(2), 67–73.

DeDomenico, G. S. (1988). Sand tray world play, Vol. 1–3 in *Sand tray work play: A comprehensive guide to the use of the sand tray in psychotherapeutic and transformational settings.* Oakland, CA: Vision Quest into Symbolic Reality.

DeDomenico, G. S. (1992a). *Introduction to sandtray worldplay: Teaching video #1.* Oakland, CA: Vision Quest into Symbolic Reality.

DeDomenico, G. S. (1992b). *Sandtray worldplay: A psychodynamic technique for indivdiuals, couples, and families.* Oakland, CA: Vision Quest into Symbolic Reality.

DeDomenico, G. S. (1999a). Sandtray—Worldplay within the context of Group Psychotherapy in, Homeyer, L. and Sweeney, D., (Ed.) *The Handbook of Group Play Therapy.* San Francisco: Jossey-Bass Publishers.

DeDomenico, G. S. (1999b). Sandtray—Worldplay Teaching Video #2. *The Sandtray-Worldplay sessions: Methods of journeyer-witness interaction* Oakland, CA.: Vision Quest into Symbolic Reality.

DeDomenico, G. S. (2002a). Group Sandplay on September 11 and 12, 2001: Using Sandtray-Worldplay™ to Work with the Trauma of the Day. *Sandtray Network Journal.* pp. 34–49. Vol. 6 No 1.

DeDomenico, G. S. (2002b). Sandtray-Worldplay: A psychotherapeutic and transformational sandplay technique for individuals, couples, families and groups. *Sandtray Network Journal.* pp. 18–34. Vol. 6 No 2.

Fox, M. (1985). *Wilfrid Gordon McDonald partridge.* California: Kane/Miller Book Publishers.

Fox, M. (2001). *Whoever you are.* Texas: Voyager Books.

Fox, M. (2003). *Harriet you'll drive me wild.* Texas: Voyager Books.

Gladding, S. T. (2005). *Counseling as an art: The creative arts in counseling* (3rd ed.), Alexandria, VA: American Counseling Association.

Gold, P. (1994). *Navajo & Tibetan sacred wisdom: the circle of the spirit.* Rochester, Vermont: Inner Traditions.

Graham, M. A. (2007). The Graham model of bibliosupervisioni: a multiple baseline analysis. Unpublished doctoral dissertation, Oregon State University.

Hegeman, G. (2001) The sandplay collection. Retrieved article from *Sandplay Therapists of America/International Society for Sandplay Therapy* at http://www.sandplay.org/symbols/index.htm.

Helm Simpson, P. (2000). *The making of a therapist: Ssupervision.* www.siteceu.com

James, R. K., & Myer, R. (1987). Puppets: The elementary school counselor's right or left arm. *Elementary School Guidance and Counseling, 21,* 292–299.

Jongeward, D. (1990). *Weaver of worlds: from Navajo apprenticeship to sacred geometry and dreams.* Rochester, Vermont: Destiny Books.

Kalff, D. M. (1980). *Sandplay.* Boston, MA: Sigo Press.

Lipman, L. (2003). The triadic system: Sociometry, psychodrama, and group psychotherapy. In Jacob Gershoni (Ed.), *Psychodrama in the 21st century: Clinical and educational applications* (pp. 3–13). New York, NY: Springer Publishing Company.

Lipman, L., & Nally-Seif, N. (2001). *Telling our stories.* Workshop presentation at the Psychodrama Training Institute, New York City.

Loganbill, C., Hardy, E., & Delworth, U. (1982). Supervision: A conceptual model. *The Counseling Psychologist, 10*(1), 3–42.

London, E., & Recio, B. (2004). *Sacred Rituals: Creating Labyrinths, Sand Paintings, and Other Traditional Arts.* Gloucester, MA: Fair Winds Press.

Maurer, C. G. (1977). Of puppets, feelings, and children. *Elementary School guidance and Counseling, 12,* 26–31.

McNally, S. P. (2001). *Sandplay: a sourcebook for play therapists.* Lincoln, Nebraska: Writers Club Press.

Moreno, J. L. (1969). *Psychodrama: Action therapy and principles of practice.* Beacon, NY: Beacon House.

Moreno, J. L. (1975). *Psychodrama: Foundations of psychotherapy.* Beacon, NY: Beacon House.

Moreno, J. L. (1993). *Who shall survive? Foundations of sociometry, group psychotherapy, and sociodrama.* Roanoke, VA: Royal.

Neswald-McCalip, R., Sather, J., Strati, J. V., & Dineen, J. (2003). Exploring the process of creative supervision: Initial findings regarding the regenerative model. *Journal of Humanistic Counseling, Education and Development, 42*(2), 223–238.

Newsome, D. W., Henderson, D. A., & Veach, L. J. (2005). Using expressive arts in group supervision to enhance awareness and foster cohesion. *Journal of Humanistic Counseling, Education and Development.*

Pardeck, J. T., & Pardeck, J. A. (1998). *Children in foster care and adoption: A guide to bibliotherapy.* Westport (CT): Greenwood Press.

Pearson, Q. M. (2003). Polished rocks: A culminating guided imagery for counselor interns. *Journal of Humanistic Counseling, Education and Development, 42*(1), 116–121.

Rae, R. (1998). Some comparisons of sandtray approaches: a chart developed by Roxanne Rae in *Sandtray Network Journal.* pp. 13–15. Vol. 2 No. 3.

Riordan, R. J., Mullis, F., & Nuchow, L. (1996). Organizing for bibliotherapy: The science in the art. *Individual Psychology, 52*(2), 169–180.

Rylant, C. (2000). *The old woman who named things.* Texas: Voyager Books.

Sams, C., & Stoick, J. (2004). *Lost in the woods: a photographic fantasy.* Michagan: Carl Sams II Publishing.

Scholl, M. B., & Smith-Adcock, S. (2007). Using psychodrama techniques to promote counselor identity development in group supervision. *Journal of Creativity in Mental Health, 2,* 13–33.

Shrodes, C. (1949). Bibliotherapy: A theoretical and clinical experimental study. Unpublished doctoral dissertation. University of California at Berkeley.

Silverstein, S. (1964). *The giving tree.* New York: HarperCollins.

Stevenson, J. (2006) Ceremonial of Hasjelti Dailjis and Mythical Sand Painting of the Navajo Indians. Kessinger Pub.

Turner, B. A. (2005). The handbook of sandplay therapy. Cloverdale, CA: Temenos Press.

Wells, H. G. (1975). *Floor Games.* New York: Arno Press.

Werstlein, P. O. (1994). *Fostering Counselors' Development in Group Supervision in Supervision: exploring the effective components.* ERIC/CASS Counseling Digest Series.

Wilkins, P. (1995). A creative therapies model for the group supervision of counselors. *British Journal of Guidance & Counseling, 23*(2), 245–258.

Young, S. J., & Borders, L. D. (1998). The impact of metaphor on clinical hypothesis formation and perceived supervisor characteristics. *Counselor Education and Supervision, 37*(4), 238–241.

Young, S. J., & Borders, L. D. (1999). The intentional use of metaphor in counseling supervision. *Clinical Supervisor, 18*(1), 137–149.

# CHAPTER 6

# Principles of Best Practices for Clinical Supervisor Training Programs

## L. DIANNE BORDERS

Supervision training opportunities have exploded in recent years. A number of supervision textbooks, edited books, DVDs, online modules, and home study courses are now available. Descriptions of training programs have been published, and supervision workshops and presentations are regularly included at counseling conferences. In addition, an international interdisciplinary conference on clinical supervision is held annually.

Thus, it appears time to assess the status of what we know about effective supervisor training programs. In this chapter, I propose five underlying principles of best practices gleaned from my review of the supervision literature, standards for supervisor training, and some key findings from research on the learning process. These five principles should not be considered exhaustive, and are, of course, influenced by my biases about the conduct of supervision and supervisor training. In addition, readers will note that there is some overlap among the principles (e.g., the core content areas [Principle 1] should be addressed through developmentally appropriate instructional strategies [Principle 3] with both didactic and experiential activities [Principle 2]), although each was emphasized strongly enough in my review that they all seemed to merit individual attention.

## Principle 1

Supervisor training programs should address all the core content areas identified in professional standards and the literature.

Several professional organizations and credential groups have developed standards relevant to clinical supervisor training over the last 20 or so years (e.g., American Association for State Counseling Boards, 2007; American Board of Examiners in Clinical Social Work, 2004; Borders, Bernard, Dye, Fong, Henderson, & Nance, 1991; Dye & Borders, 1990; Falender et al., 2004; National Board for Certified Counselors, 1997). Review of these standards suggests strong consensus regarding the core content areas that need to be included in supervisor training programs. These core topics may be summarized as follows:

- Roles and functions of clinical supervisors (including teaching, counseling, and consultation skills as applied in supervision)
- Models of supervision
- Models of counselor development
- Supervision methods, techniques, interventions, and approaches
- Supervisory relationship dynamics
- Cultural/diversity issues in supervision
- Group supervision (including roles/functions of supervisor, group supervision methods, supervision group dynamics, etc.)
- Ethical, legal, and professional regulatory issues
- Formative and summative feedback methods
- Assessment and evaluation of supervisee competence and developmental growth
- Evaluation of the supervision process
- Supervisor self-assessment
- Administrative supervision skills
- Research on clinical supervision (including all of the aforementioned areas)

For each core topic, the standards suggest covering three areas: theoretical and conceptual knowledge, skills and techniques, and self-awareness. Thus, training programs would necessarily include a range of instructional methods, including readings, opportunities for application and practice, and focus on self-knowledge and self-assessment. Although not always stated explicitly, it is assumed that a specific supervisor training program will give varying emphasis to each core topic area, depending on the supervisors' goals, their background in counseling and supervision, the supervision setting and training program context, and other relevant factors (see following text).

Of existing standards statements, the curriculum guide for supervisor training (Borders et al., 1991), developed under the auspices of the Association for Counselor Education and Supervision (ACES), provides the most explicit framework for the actual design of training programs. For each core area, the guide includes specific learning objectives for developing self-awareness, theoretical and conceptual knowledge, and skills and techniques. These learning objectives suggest *training activities* as well as *competencies* to be evaluated. For example, to achieve the learning objective "Describes the sequential, ongoing nature of counselor development" (Core Content Area: Counselor Development; Theoretical and Conceptual Knowledge), the supervision instructor might outline stages from various developmental models and show video clips of supervision sessions with counselors at various developmental levels. As evidence of this competency, supervisors-in-training might include concrete examples of such growth in their final evaluations of supervisees. Similarly, for the learning objective "Chooses and implements appropriate strategies that enhance the quality of the supervisory relationship" (Core Content Area: Supervisory Relationship; Skills and Techniques), the supervision instructor could include readings and discussion around how various supervision strategies (e.g., Interpersonal Process Recall [IPR], self-disclosure, immediacy) tend to affect the relationship. Later, in supervision of supervision (and/ or in case notes), supervisors-in-training could state their rationale for choosing a strategy relevant to their assessment of and goals for the supervisory relationship and receive feedback on the implementation of that strategy. Learning objectives around cultural issues suggest self-awareness exercises, readings, and demonstrations of awareness, knowledge, and skills during supervision sessions. Research on clinical supervision might be infused into instruction for site or agency supervisors, while at least selected research articles would be critically analyzed in a doctoral-level academic course in clinical supervision.

Getz (1999) described a supervision training and assessment approach based on the ACES curriculum guide (Borders et al., 1991). She referred to the core content areas as competencies. Doctoral students in her supervision course are required to write a summative evaluation that includes, for each competency, goals, action steps, and evidence of goal achievement. The competencies also are integrated into ongoing supervision of supervision sessions using videotapes and peer feedback. In these sessions, for example, students present information about the supervisee (Counselor Development), their focus and role in the supervision session (Models of Supervision), approaches used (Supervision Methods and Techniques), and reactions to the supervisee (Supervisory Relationship). Early in the semester, students also write a supervision informed consent document (Ethical, Legal, and Professional Regulatory Issues) to share with their supervisees.

The ACES curriculum guide (Borders et al., 1991) was intended to be comprehensive and inclusive. Thus, not all of the more than 200 learning objectives may be relevant for any one supervision training program. For example, supervision instructors working with novice supervisors (i.e., those in their first training experiences and who have little or no experience conducting supervision) likely will need to focus primarily on the core content areas of Models of Supervision and Counselor Development so that a framework for thinking about supervision is established. Supervision instructors working with practitioners, such as supervisors in mental health agencies, will need to give more attention to the core content areas of Executive (Administrative) Skills and Ethical, Legal and Professional Regulatory Issues. The core content area Supervisory Relationship includes learning objectives along a range of complexity, subtlety, and professional maturity.

Thus, the ACES curriculum guide (Borders et al., 1991) provides a template for a supervisor instructor's intentional selection of learning goals based on the needs of a particular group of supervisors-in-training. The guide also can serve as a "checklist" for determining if all the core topic areas are being covered at some point in a clinical supervision training program.

## Principle 2

Clinical supervision programs should include both didactic instruction and supervised practice, concurrently and/or sequentially. Experiential activities should involve direct observation of supervision practice with feedback.

Early writers who proposed systematic training in clinical supervision (e.g., Borders & Leddick, 1988; Dye & Borders, 1990; Loganbill & Hardy, 1983; Russell & Petrie, 1994; Stoltenberg & Delworth, 1987; Watkins, 1991) emphasized that training in the theories and concepts of supervision was necessary but insufficient. They urged trainers to include some form of supervised practice as an adjunct and/or follow-up to didactic instruction. Actually, many of these early writers were battling an even more basis issue: that supervision comprised a separate, distinct professional activity from counseling and, thus, specialized training in supervision was necessary for competent, ethical practice. Indeed, there is increasing evidence that *experience as a supervisor alone* does not increase supervisor competence (e.g., Johnson & Stewart, 2008; Lyon, Heppler, Leavitt, & Fisher, 2008; Stevens, Goodyear, & Robertson, 1997; Worthington, 1987). Today, the need for supervisor training is widely accepted, across a number of clinical disciplines (e.g., counseling, psychology, social work, speech-language pathology), although the practice of requiring, even offering, supervisor training in academic programs continues to vary rather substantially across disciplines (Johnson & Stewart, 2008; Lyon et al., 2008; Scott, Ingram, Vitanza,

& Smith, 2000). Anecdotally (based on conference presentations, informal discussions with other counselor educators, etc.), it appears most counselor education doctoral programs offer a two-semester sequence of a didactic course, often including observations and role plays, followed by a semester of supervised supervision of master's-level practicum students. This approach reflects current professional standards and credentialing requirements in the counseling field.

For example, didactic and experiential supervision training is required in accredited doctoral programs (CACREP, 2009). In addition, the American Association for State Counseling Boards (AASCB, 2007) has endorsed an "approved supervisor model" that involves didactic training (graduate course or 30 hr of face-to-face training), 25 hr of supervised supervision, as well as ongoing continuing education in supervision. The requirements for the Approved Clinical Supervisor credential available through the Center for Credentialing and Education (affiliated with the National Board for Certified Counselors [1997]) are similar: a graduate course in clinical supervision or 30 contact hours of workshop training, a minimum of 100 hr of experience providing clinical supervision, and a minimum of 20 hr of supervised supervision. Clearly, both didactic and experiential supervisor training are valued.

In terms of academic training for doctoral students, several combinations and sequences of didactic and experiential training have been recommended (Borders, in press; Russell & Petrie, 1994; Stoltenberg, McNeill, & Delworth, 1998). In addition, descriptions of supervision workshops for practitioners also include didactic and experiential components. The didactic-experiential model, then, appears to be widely accepted and practiced. Empirical investigations of the didactic-experiential approach, though limited, tend to be supportive. Representative reports of academic courses for doctoral students and workshops for practitioners that included at least some empirical evaluation of the training experience are summarized here.

Baker, Exum, and Tyler (2002) compared two small groups of doctoral students on a measure of supervisor development over time. One group ($n$ = 12; experimental group) had completed a course in supervision theory and research and was starting a practicum in supervision. The control group ($n = 7$) had not enrolled in either experience. All participants completed the supervisor development measure at the beginning, middle, and end of the semester. At time 1 (beginning of the semester), there were no significant differences in the experimental and control groups' supervisor development scores, even though the experimental group had completed the didactic supervision course. At times 2 (midsemester) and 3 (end of semester), the experimental group scored significantly higher than the control group. These results suggested that the supervised experience of supervising several master's-level practicum students had a greater impact on doctoral students' self-perceptions of their development as supervisors than did the didactic course alone, which appeared to have little to no influence on their self-perceptions.

Nelson, Oliver, and Capps (2006) conducted focus groups with doctoral students in supervision practicum/internship experiences to explore their perception of the process of becoming a supervisor. One group ($n = 13$) was interviewed over three semesters of their practicum/internship experiences; a second group ($n = 5$) discussed the results from the previous cohort's reports and provided additional comments and observations. The "practicum/internship" training experience was not described, but a reading of the results suggests that both didactic and experiential components were included. Students reported that the combination of academic learning, experiential activities (e.g., role plays, actual supervision with feedback from peers and instructor), and watching (i.e., observing themselves and others) were crucial to their development as supervisors.

In a retrospective study of doctoral students, Lyon et al. (2008) surveyed interns in APA-accredited internship sites across the United States and Canada regarding the extent and quality of their training in supervision. The 233 respondents were primarily from clinical psychology ($n = 151$) and counseling psychology ($n = 67$) programs. More of the counseling psychology interns (73%) than the clinical psychology interns (26%) had completed a supervision course. Respondents reported high frequency of reading assignments and group discussions of readings and cases; teaching methods used less often ("moderate frequency") included individual supervision of supervision and class review of supervision tapes. All teaching methods were rated highly helpful, although the supervision of supervision activities were rated higher than the more didactic teaching methods. Lyon et al. tested the relationship of the reported training activities to interns' self-ratings of supervisor development. Experience as a supervisor (i.e., the total number of hours of providing supervision) did not predict supervisor development levels. Significant predictors were the total number of supervision training activities and the number of hours of supervised supervision. Lyon et al. concluded that "the experience of supervising a trainee, in concert with an opportunity to reflect and consult with a more advanced supervisor, was the best predictor of interns' development of felt supervision competence" (p. 282).

Borders and Fong (1994), however, suggested that experiential training alone is not sufficient to affect counseling doctoral students' felt competence. They followed nine students from two universities who were enrolled in a supervision practicum course. They found no significant differences between pretest and posttest self-reports of cognitive appraisals (difficulty) of their supervision abilities. They also found no significant differences for the students' content of thoughts (e.g., focus on client vs. counselor, focus on counselors' psychological traits vs. the process) nor choices of supervision interventions (multiple-choice measure). The researchers noted several patterns in students' responses that differed from expert raters' responses on the intervention measure. In particular, students tended to choose clinical interventions over educational options, and they avoided addressing relationship issues directly. Borders and Fong cited a number of limitations, such as their sample size and complications with the measures. Nevertheless, results suggested the one-semester experiential-only training experience had little positive impact and seemed to create confusion in the students' conceptualizations about appropriate supervisor roles. Borders and Fong concluded that both didactic and experiential training opportunities were needed to develop doctoral students' supervision confidence, knowledge, and skills.

In a follow-up study, Borders, Rainey, Crutchfield, and Martin (1996) investigated the effectiveness of a supervision course that included both didactic instruction and a brief supervised practicum experience. Didactic instruction (lectures, seminar discussions) was based on the ACES curriculum guide (Borders et al., 1991); the experiential practicum involved supervising one or two first-year master's students in their first counseling practicum (five sessions) with a volunteer undergraduate client. Using multiple pre-post measures of students' cognitions about supervision, the researchers found no significant differences in self-reports of supervisory style and only one difference in supervisory focus; students reported they had emphasized conceptualization skills during their supervision sessions (posttest) more than they had anticipated they would (pretest). At the end of the course, students rated supervision as significantly less difficult and rated themselves as having significantly more skills and resources for coping with the tasks of supervision. Students' conceptualizations (clinical hypothesis formation measure) of their supervisees revealed few significant differences along rated categories (e.g., categories of information sought about the supervisee, elements considered in understanding the supervisee, number of divergent questions asked). There was some indication, however, that the students improved in their divergent thinking. In addition, judges rated students' posttest conceptualizations as significantly clearer and of higher quality. Borders et al. (1996) cited a number of limitations (e.g., sample size, inter-rater reliability). They noted that the supervisors seemed to maintain their pretraining preferences for supervisor style and emphasis, but did report less stress and more confidence about doing supervision following the course.

Others have studied the effects of supervisor training workshops for counseling and/or supervision practitioners. These workshops included both didactic and experiential components, although the experiential methods ranged from role plays only to supervised supervision over some time. In addition, these studies were mostly program evaluations based on participant feedback and/or self-ratings, with few comparison control groups. Although the rigor of these studies was varied, results do suggest that both didactic and experiential activities are needed and valued.

Getz and Agnew (1999) evaluated an extensive training program for supervisors in community agencies, including a 1-day workshop followed by 3 hr of supervised supervision sessions per month for 5 months. The workshop covered many of the core areas in the ACES curriculum guide (Borders et al., 1991), provided instruction in a structured approach to supervision, and included role plays. Evaluation data came from focus group interviews and semantic differential reports. Participants reported the training program gave them credibility as a supervisor and increased confidence, and said they used more direct (e.g., tapes) and experiential approaches (e.g., role plays) in supervision. They thought the supervised supervision was vital and appreciated the structured approach they had learned.

Peace and Sprinthall (1998) provided an extensive supervision in-service training program for experienced school counselors, with a focus on supervising the novice school counselor. During the first semester, supervision theory and practice were covered through a sequence of explaining the rationale for the topic being covered, modeling relevant skills, practicing with peers, and generalizing the learning. Participants were taught a structured approach for supervision "conferences" with supervisees, and were taught how to use a rating scale of supervisor skills consisting of two categories (e.g., direct and indirect behaviors). The second semester training consisted of weekly reviews of recorded supervision sessions, including use of the indirect/direct behaviors rating scale to analyze the conferences. One goal was to increase the use of indirect behaviors (e.g., asks about feelings, accepts or uses supervisee's ideas) over direct behaviors (e.g., giving information, giving direction). A sample of four conferences across the two semesters indicated a "substantial" pre-post increase in the use of indirect behaviors (55% to 74%). Importantly, the conduct of the training also was devised to encourage supervisors' cognitive growth. Peace and Sprinthall reported significant increases on measures of conceptual development and moral judgment. Such cognitive gains are unusual, even over a two-semester time span.

McMahon and Simons (2004) conducted a 4-day training program (20 hr total) for practicing counselors and supervisors in Queensland. Of the experimental ($n =15$) and control group ($n = 42$) participants, most had received less than 1 week of supervision training. Learning objectives were based on the ACES curriculum guide (Borders et al., 1991); experiential activities included case discussions, role plays, and practice supervision sessions. The researchers developed a 30-item questionnaire measuring confidence/self-awareness, theoretical and conceptual knowledge, and skill and techniques in clinical supervision. All participants completed the questionnaire three times: before and after the training program and 6 months later. There were no significant differences between the experimental and control groups at Time 1, but significant differences at Time 2 and Time 3, with the experimental group showing significant gains and the control group showing no changes. The experimental group showed a slight but nonsignificant decline from Time 2 to Time 3, suggesting ongoing supervision or consultation may be prudent to maintain supervisor training gains.

In sum, there is some empirical support for including both didactic and experiential components in supervisor training programs, at least in initial training experiences such as those just reported. Few established outcome measures have been used, but didactic-experiential programs have led to increases in supervisor development (Baker et al., 2002), supervisor confidence (Borders et al., 1996), and cognitive complexity (Peace & Sprinthall, 1998). Based on supervisors' feedback, it appears the value of the didactic component is in providing a framework for understanding supervisor's roles and the functions and goals of supervision. In addition, at least for novices, learning a structure for conducting supervision sessions also seems important. Supervisors consistently gave high ratings to the experiential components of their training, especially actual supervision of counselors with regular observation and feedback from a supervisor/instructor. There is no evidence that a particular sequence of combination of didactic-experiential training is more effective; direct comparisons of different training programs have not been reported. Likely, no one training sequence is appropriate for all training contexts nor all supervisors. In addition, training experiences of supervisor beyond the novice stage have not been studied, although it appears that ongoing supervised supervision is needed. Importantly, experiential activities should be introduced early and often in supervisor training programs, as those who have received supervision of their work are likely to be more open to ongoing supervision and consultation to facilitate ongoing growth of their work (Borders & Usher, 1992; Wheeler & King, 2000).

Suggested sequences of didactic content and supervised experiences (e.g., Borders, in press; Russell & Petrie, 1994; Stoltenberg et al., 1998) have not been tested, but are grounded in developmental models of supervisor development. These models, described next, provide another important principle for constructing supervisor development training programs.

**Principle 3**

Supervisor training programs should reflect a developmental approach in their content and sequencing.

Several models of supervisor development have been proposed (e.g., Alonso, 1983; Hess, 1986, 1987; Rodenhauser, 1995; Stoltenberg & Delworth, 1987; Stoltenberg et al., 1998; Watkins, 1990, 1993). Earlier models (e.g., Alonso, Hess) assumed there was no formal training in supervision; several (e.g., Alonso, Rodenhauser) are specific to psychiatric settings. Thus, the models of Stoltenberg and colleagues and Watkins are more relevant to the focus of this chapter. In addition, Heid (1997) provided an integrative look at relevant models. As will be obvious to the informed supervisor, models of supervisor development parallel models of counselor development in many ways, but in comparison there is much less empirical support for supervisor models (Borders, in press).

*Stoltenberg and colleagues.* Stoltenberg and Delworth (1987) described the first model of supervisor development that was based in an academic setting and which involved both didactic and experiential components. In 1987 (and then again in Stoltenberg et al., 1998), they outlined four levels of supervisor development that are determined by the supervisors' level of counselor development (based on their corresponding model of counselor development) as well as their training and experience in supervision. Level 1 supervisors tend to be anxious, naïve, highly motivated, self-focused, anxious to do the "right" thing, fairly structured, and dependent on their own supervisor. The Level 2 supervisor, overwhelmed by the complexity of supervision, experiences confusion and conflict, and is alternately dependent and independent. The focus shifts from self to the counselor, leading to overidentification with and/or withdrawal from the counselor and to feelings of sympathy or anger. At Level 3, supervisors have genuine interest in supervision and are aware of their strengths and weaknesses in the role. They freely seek consultation as needed. Stoltenberg and Delworth believe the majority of supervisors function at this level. Those who reach the final "integrated" level are both master supervisors and master counselors. They have a wide repertoire of roles and skills, and can work equally well with counselors at a variety of experience levels.

Stoltenberg and Delworth (1987) reported that they tie their supervision training method to the supervisor's developmental level. Pre-Level 1 counseling students are introduced to supervision theory primarily as a way to understand their own development. Techniques are emphasized with Level 1 supervisors through simulations and role plays. Group supervision is recommended for Level 2 supervisors, who need to process their doubts, feelings, and uncertain commitment to supervision. The authors suggested that an academic course on supervision be taken early in the counseling psychology training program, and an experiential class be added just before or during the counseling internship, when the supervisor likely would be doing advanced clinical work as well as providing supervision to novice counselors. In fact, they described good and bad matches based on developmental levels of supervisor and counselor. For example, they suggested that a Level 1 supervisor who is functioning as a Level 2 counselor provides adequate supervision to Level 1 counselors. The integrated supervisor (who also would be an integrated counselor) may be particularly effective in helping Level 2 counselors (and supervisors) work through their confusion and conflict. Supervisors of supervisors need to be functioning at Level 3, Stoltenberg and Delworth indicated.

*Watkins.* Watkins (1990, 1993, 1994) proposed the four-stage Supervisor Complexity Model as well as training and supervision implications for each stage. Novice supervisors experience *role shock* and focus on what they don't know, feel overwhelmed, and are heavily dependent on their own supervisors. Novices need "a clear, strong holding environment" (1994, p. 421) that provides structure, direction, instruction, and modeling. Supervisors in stage 2, *role recovery/transition*, have developed some confidence based on their successes, but are easily shaken by new supervision experiences and supervisee issues. They have limited self-awareness about their impact on counselors and their professional identity as a supervisor. Stage 2 supervisors need a stable "anchor" who can help them ride the ups and downs of confidence, support, and encouragement. In stage 3, *role consolidation*, supervisors are more realistic and settled, more consistently confident, and report more accurate perceptions of self and supervisees. They have a more solid sense of professional identity as a supervisor, including a fairly coherent personal theory of supervision. Stage 3 supervisors are ready to focus on relationship and process issues, including their own values, beliefs, and personal reactions to supervisees, as well as transference, countertransference, and parallel process. When supervisors reach stage 4, *role mastery*, they have a well-integrated, consolidated professional identity as a supervisor, consistently rely on their personal theory of supervision to guide their work, understand their strengths and limitations, and handle unexpected supervisory events effectively. They are best served by a consultant, on an as-needed basis, who challenges them to further refine their beliefs and conceptualizations of supervision.

Watkins' (1990, 1993, 1994) discussions of his model are based on general developmental theories (i.e., Piaget, Erickson, Chickering) as well as models of counselor development (e.g., Hogan, 1964; Loganbill, Hardy, & Delworth, 1982; Stoltenberg, 1981), and also reflect psychoanalytic concepts. He emphasized personality characteristics, such as openness, flexibility, motivation, and nondefensiveness, as influencing how smoothly a supervisor moves along the developmental stages. He asserted that "the most positive supervisor developmental process will result primarily from the interaction of training/supervision in how to be a supervisor, experience in functioning as a supervisor, environmental supports, and constructive personality factors" (1993, p. 70). Later (1995), he asserted that the ability (and willingness) to be self-critical (i.e., reflect on and question one's work on a regular basis) is a key factor—if not *the* key factor—to enhancing supervisor effectiveness.

Watkins' (1990, 1993) model has received some limited empirical support, primarily based on a scale (Psychotherapy Supervisor Development Scale, PSDS) he developed with colleagues (Watkins, Schneider, Haynes, & Nieberding, 1995) to measure key issues in his model. Baker et al. (2002) reported increases in PSDS scores across a semester for 12 doctoral students in a supervision practicum course. Barnes and Moon (2006) conducted a factor analysis that supported the four key areas of supervisor development as reported earlier by Watkins et al.: competence and effectiveness, commitment to supervision and the development of a supervisory identity, self-awareness, and sincerity in the role of supervisor (i.e., being honest in self-evaluations).

Otherwise, there is mostly indirect support of supervisor models from studies of novice supervisors and comparisons of inexperienced and experienced supervisors (see Borders, 1989, for a comprehensive review of early research in this area). Drawing from his experience as a supervisor educator of doctoral students, Ellis (Ellis, 1991; Ellis & Douce, 1994) reported characteristics and critical incidents that reflect developmental assertions about novice supervisors. Similarly, Borders and Fong (1994) found that doctoral students in a supervision practicum tended to use dichotomous thinking and were challenged by relationship dynamics, as would be predicted by the models. Supervisors at more advanced developmental levels (not to be confused with more experience) rarely have been studied.

*Heid.* Rather than propose a stage model, Heid (1997) identified ten "strands" or developmental issues across the levels or stages in existing supervisor development models:

1. Sense of identity as a supervisor.
2. Felt confidence as a supervisor.
3. Degrees of felt autonomy and/or dependence on others.
4. Use of power and authority with supervisees, including the methods and process of supervisee evaluations.
5. Degrees of structure, flexibility, and variety of interventions.
6. Focus on the needs of the supervisees and/or self.
7. Degree of personal investment in supervisee and client success.
8. Emphasis on and use of the supervisory relationship and the process of supervision.

9. Degrees of awareness and appraisal of impact of self on the supervisory relationship and process.
10. Degree of realistic appraisal of competencies and limitations, coupled with an awareness and containment of personal issues and biases and countertransference reactions. (p. 147)

Heid indicated that her Integrated Model of Supervisor Lifespan Development was appropriate for all "experienced supervisors," including those with and without formal training in supervision. She used the ten strands to illustrate the nonlinear nature of development. In line with Hess (1986), Stoltenberg and Delworth (1987), and Borders et al. (1991), she asserted that supervisors may recycle through issues at deeper levels or from other perspectives. (Actually, facilitation of such a "spiraling process" of "progressively more sophisticated levels of awareness and understanding" (Borders et al., 1991, p. 78) would be critical; see *Principle 5* in the following text.) Heid also suggested that supervisors will vary in their continued development along each strand based on factors such as age, gender, ethnicity, culture, professional maturity, and life experience. In fact, she emphasized the intertwining of personal growth and professional development, particularly important life experiences in each (e.g., birth of a child, promotion). Finally, she brought attention to the interaction of the supervisor, counselor, and client, including the ways supervisors are affected by their supervisees and the clients, in addition to the supervisor's reciprocal influences.

Heid (1997) did not offer suggestions for promoting supervisor development along the ten strands, stating only that she hoped they would stimulate "further research and self-reflection that, given sufficient training and external support systems, may prove to be critical to the developmental process of supervisors" (p. 151). Her assertions remind supervisor trainers that developmental models should not be applied rigidly. Supervisors likely will reflect the general characteristics of developmental levels as they progress through their training, but exhibit much individual variation also. In addition, we should heed Heid's reminders that supervisor trainers and/or supervisors of supervision will need to give some attention to the influence of personal life events on a supervisor's development, as well as the impact that particular supervisees and clients have on the supervisor's growth along the ten strands.

In sum, supervisor models strongly suggest a developmental approach to supervisor training. Unfortunately, these models are more descriptive than prescriptive, especially in terms of what content and which experiential activities are the best match for each developmental level. Stoltenberg et al. (1998) suggested some academic training in supervision theory before beginning to supervise, while Watkins' (1990, 1993, 1994) descriptions imply supervisors are supervising during each of his four stages. The view of supervisor growth as developmental recycling (Borders et al., 1991; Hess, 1986; Heid, 1997; Stoltenberg & Delworth, 1987) strongly suggests a sequence of *concurrent* didactic and experiential training, but existing descriptions are either very brief (e.g., Russell & Petrie, 1994; Stoltenberg et al., 1998) or specific to a particular training context (e.g., Borders, in press). It may be that current supervisor instructors need to turn to models of counselor development, as described later, and extrapolate implications of those models in designing supervisor training programs.

## Principle 4

Supervisor training programs should include instruction in a wide range of supervision methods, techniques, and approaches, with an emphasis on the intentional and flexible use of these approaches.

In applying Bandura's (1997) social cognitive theory to supervisor training, Johnson and Stewart (2008) noted that self-efficacy "involves more than the possession of relevant subskills. Rather, it represents the confidence and mastery needed to mobilize energy to use the right skills at the right time in the right way across varying situations" (p. 233). Acquiring a wide repertoire of supervision interventions generates flexibility, which is the first step within Principle 4; gaining the knowledge of when, why, and how to choose among these interventions is the necessary second step to achieve intentional flexibility. A range of supervision skills is promoted in the dominant models of counseling supervision (see following text), so that supervisor training programs should provide opportunities for students to become well grounded in these models early during the training experience.

Bernard's (1979, 1997) discrimination model outlines a matrix of three roles (teacher, counselor, consultant) used to address three focus areas (counseling performance skills, cognitive counseling skills, self-awareness; as labeled by Borders and Brown, 2005). The model does not provide explicit guidance on the selection of role/focus area, but it is clear that a wide range of supervision skills is necessary. Neufeldt (1999) provided examples of behaviors in each of the supervisor roles that illustrate their differential actions and intentions.

Developmental models of counselor supervision (e.g., Blocher, 1983; Loganbill et al., 1982; Stoltenberg et al., 1998) offer the needed framework for choosing the role and focus of supervision, as well as the supervisor skills and approaches that are appropriate for supervisees at various developmental levels. Importantly, counselor developmental level is based on cognitive and psychosocial theories of development and is not equivalent to counselor experience. Thus, the acquisition of counseling skills, conceptualization skills, and greater self-awareness is governed by the counselor's level of cognitive complexity, and encouraging cognitive growth is an underlying yet fundamental goal of developmental models. Such growth is achieved through the appropriate mismatch (i.e., one-half step higher) of supervisor challenges and counselor functioning. The appropriate learning environments for various counselor developmental levels are described in some depth in the models, and there is a rather substantial body of empirical literature supporting the tenets of the models. Of relevance to this discussion is the compelling need to acquire a range of supervision strategies during supervision training programs, including the ability to provide both high structure and low structure, address concrete skills and complex relationship dynamics, *and* the ability "to use the right skills at the right time in the right way" (Johnson & Stewart, 2008, p. 233).

Several studies have indicated that supervisor training results in more flexibility, particularly when expansion of interventions is a goal of the training. In two case studies (Milne & James, 2002; Milne & Westerman, 2001), the efficacy of supervised supervision ("consultancy") to broaden the supervisor's range of behaviors was tested. Both supervisors increased their range of behaviors, particular the use of "guided experiential learning" (e.g., modeling, role play), which was the goal of supervision of supervision. Relatedly, in a thought-listing response to a recorded counseling session, supervisors with more training reported thoughts that suggested they were more flexible, more supportive, less dogmatic, and less critical of the counselor (Stevens et al., 1997).

Additional emphasis on flexibility was found in two systematic reviews of empirical studies of supervision (primarily from the learning disability field; Milne, Aylott, Fitzpatrick, & Ellis, 2008; Milne & James, 2000). Results of both reviews indicated that the use of multiple interventions, methods, and techniques was a pronounced characteristic of effective supervision. Milne and James defined "good supervision" as the balanced use of "symbolic" (e.g., feedback, theorizing), "iconic" (e.g., observing a model), and "enactive" (e.g., role plays) methods.

Although intentionality is a theme in the supervision education literature (e.g., Borders, 2001; Borders & Brown, 2005; need another non-Borders one), few investigators of supervisor training programs have described a specific emphasis on intentionality or measured variables related to intentionality. Such variables would be more cognitive-based, compared to the more behavioral measures of flexibility. Indeed, an implication of the supervisor development models (see Principle 3) is that an underlying, fundamental goal of supervisor training programs is to encourage cognitive growth of supervisors. (Such parallel cognitive goals are more specifically described in developmental models of counselor supervision; for example, see Blocher, 1983.) Higher levels of cognitive complexity are necessary for the intentional flexibility proposed here for supervisors.

The school counseling supervisors who participated in Peace and Sprinthall's (1998) workshop (described earlier) evidenced such cognitive growth. The researchers believed that this growth was the result of the instructor providing different learning environments based on the supervisors' learning needs, with some requiring very high structure, consistent and frequent positive support, multiple practices of skills, and little challenge, while others enjoyed low structure, challenging feedback, and more give-and-take dialogue with the instructor. They also believed weekly reflective journals contributed to the supervisors' growth. Notably, increases in the supervisors' cognitive growth paralleled greater flexibility in their behaviors with their supervisees. Peace and Sprinthall asserted that "there is no viable short-cut" for promoting substantial developmental growth.

A range of supervision methods, techniques, and approaches have been described (e.g., Bernard & Goodyear, 2004; Borders & Brown, 2005), so that the promotion of supervisor flexibility is relatively easy to include in supervision training programs. Methods to encourage intentionality and, even more, underlying cognitive growth of supervisors, are less clear. Current findings from the field of learning theory, described in the following text, may be instructive.

## Principle 5

Supervisor training programs should include instruction in basic principles of learning theory.

Clinical supervision is an educational process (Borders, 2001), which makes it necessary for supervisors to learn how to plan and behave as educators rather than clinicians. One's clinical skills certainly are relevant to the work done in supervision, from the content the supervisor teaches the counselor to the supervisor's perspective on and use of the supervisory relationship. There is wide consensus, however, that supervision is not counseling and should not be for a variety of reasons, such as ethical requirements and the evaluative nature of supervision. Yet most supervisors have vastly more training in clinical processes than educational processes. In making the shift from thinking like a counselor to thinking like a supervisor (Borders, 1992), supervisors must turn their attention from how to construct a client treatment plan to how to create (even craft) the appropriate *learning environment* needed for a counselor to become more competent and effective.

Several supervision writers have referred to the educational nature of supervision (e.g., Borders, 2001; Falender & Shafranske, 2008), but few have provided much explanation of the underlying learning processes and dynamics. Certainly, an educational perspective means that "supervision must be proactive, deliberate, intentional, and goal directed, involving active learning strategies designed to engage a particular supervisee (or group of supervisees)" (Borders, 2001, p. 418). It would be helpful, however, for supervisors to have some understanding of key general processes that greatly affect *how people learn*, whether they are learning math, geography, writing, or counseling.

Bransford, Brown, and Cocking (2000) offered a helpful overview of key learning principles from the perspective of the "science of learning," which views students "as goal-directed agents who actively seek information" (p. 10) by which they can make meaning of their learning and experiences as well as move toward competent performance. It is not possible to provide a complete summary of their work in this chapter. Here, I present three key findings they reported from research on the science of learning, restating them in terms of the clinical supervision context. I will also highlight supervisory interventions from the literature that appear to support these learning principles. Readers may note that several aspects of the first four principles for best practices in supervisor training programs, as noted earlier, are reflected in Bransford et al.'s key findings.

First, counselors come to supervision with preconceptions about how counseling works that may interfere with their learning. Such preconceptions or naïve understandings include equating being a counselor with being a friend to clients, believing counselors "fix" clients, or believing that medication is not helpful or appropriate for any clients. They also may assume that supervisors will tell them the "right" way to do counseling or *the* ethical and legal response to a situation. In addition, they arrive in supervision with conceptions and opinions about persons in authority, safe boundaries in relationships, and their willingness to be known, based on their life experiences and how they have made meaning of these life experiences. Supervisors need to engage in initial and ongoing assessments, then, of counselors' knowledge, skills, and conceptions about counseling, the role of the counselor, as well as supervision and the supervisor. Preconceptions tend to persist, so that ongoing interventions that appropriately challenge them will be needed. Bransford et al.'s (2000) reference to "just manageable difficulties" (p. 24) parallel the one-half step challenges described in developmental models of supervision (e.g., Blocher, 1983; Stoltenberg, 1981). Importantly, Bransford et al. also noted that preconceptions typically are grounded in cultural beliefs, ranging from stereotypes of others to comfort with the active learning strategies they advocated. These cultural beliefs need to be assessed and taken into consideration in designing the supervision environment.

Study of developmental models of supervision (e.g., Blocher, 1983; Loganbill et al., 1982; Stoltenberg, 1981) can help supervisors identify the predictable preconceptions, anxieties, and needs of counselors as well as appropriate learning environments for counselors at various developmental levels. Techniques such as Interpersonal Process Recall (IPR, Kagan, 1980; Kagan & Kagan, 1997) also aim to reveal counselors' thoughts and feelings about clients and the counseling process. Clearly, a safe learning environment is needed if counselors are to reveal their preconceptions and beliefs, including those they themselves suspect are naïve (Bransford et al., 2000). Such a safe, positive, and collaborative environment is emphasized by most supervision writers, who often assert that the supervisory relationship is pivotal to the learning process (see Borders & Brown, 2005).

Second, to help counselors develop competence, supervisors need to help students develop "deep factual knowledge," understand this knowledge within a conceptual framework, and organize their knowledge in ways that allow fluid retrieval and application to new situations. Bransford et al. (2000) cited the growing literature comparing experts and novices in various fields, noting that experts' deep understanding and command of the "facts" "allows them to see patterns, relationships, or discrepancies that are not apparent to novices" (p. 17). Supervisors give attention, then, not only to the "what" but also the "why." They need to ask meaningful questions that encourage reflection, and focus on fewer topics with more depth. Active learning strategies encourage counselors to take control of their own learning, to begin to recognize when they understand and when they need more information. Bransford et al. (2000) noted, however, that "teaching by telling" can be a very effective strategy, especially after students [counselors] first have grappled with issues on their own. In short, supervisors are helping counselors learn how to transfer their learning so they can apply their knowledge to the new and challenging clinical contexts they will encounter over their professional lifespan.

From the supervision literature, use of interventions such as the Socratic method (Overholser, 1991) seem appropriate here, as do some applications of Interpersonal Process Recall (IPR, Kagan, 1980; Kagan & Kagan, 1997). In addition, Milne's (Milne & James, 2002; Milne & Westerman, 2001) application of Kolb's (1984) "experiential learning" model to supervision also reflects aspects of this key finding. In Kolb's model, learners need to cycle through four modes of learning, including reflection, conceptualization, planning, and practical experience, to achieve competence. Neufeldt and colleagues (Neufeldt, 1999; Neufeldt, Karno, & Nelson, 1996) have discussed in detail some strategies to encourage counselor reflection, based on Schön's (1983) ideas for educating reflective practitioners. Indeed, Skovholt and Rønnestad (1992a, 1992b) found that continuous reflection over the professional lifespan was a central process by which novice counselors moved toward becoming expert counselors.

Third, metacognitive approaches to encourage active learning are vital, and such meta-strategies must be specific to the subject area (Bransford et al., 2000). The expert-novice literature again is instructive. Experts actively monitor their work, noting what additional information is required, whether new information is consistent or contradictory, and what analogies may be helpful in solving a new problem. Milne's (Milne & James, 2002; Milne & Westerman, 2001) discussions of Kolb's (1984) experiential learning cycle again seem informative. With the guidance of a supervisor, counselors reflect on their actions so as to become more aware of and intentional in the use of the knowledge base guiding their actions. Supervisors need to give deliberate attention, then, to helping counselors develop such internal dialogues. Modeling their own "thinking aloud" (see Borders & Brown, 2005) in response to a new client or clinical issue is one method for encouraging development of metacognitive skills. In particular, supervisors should model a strategy for "modeling the process of generating alternative approaches ..., evaluating their merits in helping to attain a goal, and monitoring progress toward that goal" (Bransford et al., 2000, p. 19). In addition, supervisors can structure group supervision to encourage counselors to "think aloud" with each other (instead of telling the presenting counselor what they think is going on and what they would do), as a way of providing alternative perspectives and explanations (see Borders, 1991). In fact, in thinking about designing group supervision as a learning environment, Bransford et al. indicated that teachers [supervisors] need to create a classroom community [supervision group] that encourages both *cooperation* in problem-solving and *argumentation* among students [counselors]. Such risk-taking and open discussion encourages cognitive development fundamental to metacognitive skills.

Importantly, such key findings from the science of learning also need to be incorporated into supervisor training programs, on two levels. First, supervisors need to understand how these learning principles affect their work as supervisors as well as how to apply this knowledge in building effective learning environments in individual and group supervision settings. As illustrated earlier, some supervision writers have suggested approaches that are in line with the research on learning, but rarely are supervision approaches presented within that context. Without an understanding of the foundations of learning, supervisors are limited in their ability to modify, adapt, and apply these approaches to the unique needs of each supervisee as well as the novel challenges they will face as supervisors.

Second, supervisor training programs themselves should be grounded in the science of learning and the three key findings. First, supervisor trainers need to continually assess supervisors' preconceptions about counseling and supervision, and create active learning strategies that facilitate supervisors' movement toward a more accurate and complete understanding of the complex nature of the supervision enterprise. Second, supervisor trainers need to focus on helping supervisors build frameworks, based on "deep factual knowledge" of counseling and supervision (the "what"), that provide explanations of "why" and "how" they make choices at the macro level (e.g., conceptualization of the counselor) and the micro level (e.g., the moment-by-moment decision-making in each supervision session) (see also Borders & Brown, 2005). Third, supervisor trainers need to facilitate the development of an active learning environment that encourages open and collaborative discussion. Trainers can both model metacognitive internal monitoring strategies and encourage supervisors to "think aloud" their own strategies that help them think through a supervisory situation, activate relevant factual knowledge, weigh options, predict outcomes, make a plan, and monitor progress.

## Conclusion

Descriptions of supervision training programs have evolved from listings of content of topics to be covered (Principle 1), to descriptions of instructional approaches (Principle 2, including both didactic and experiential components) and descriptions of supervisors' developmental characteristics (Principle 3), to more sophisticated explorations of key educational and learning principles that can inform effective supervision training programs (Principles 4 and 5). Hopefully, this chapter has provided one more link in the evolution toward flexible, intentional, developmental, and empirically based training sequences that produce cognitively expert, behaviorally competent supervisors who have a positive and sustaining impact not only on their supervisees, but also their supervisees' clients. The practice of supervision is truly an art, but an art that should have a solid foundation in the science of supervision practice *and* the science of learning.

## References

Alonso, A. (1983). A developmental theory of psychodynamic supervision. *The Clinical Supervisor, 1*(3), 23–36.

American Association of State Counseling Boards. (2007). *Approved supervisor model*. Retrieved January 21, 2009, from www.aascb.org/associations/7905/files/ AAASCB_Supervision_Model-0607.pdf.

American Board of Examiners in Clinical Social Work. (2004). *Clinical supervision: A practice speciality of clinical social work*. Salem, MA: Author.

Bandura, A. (1997). *Self-efficacy: The exercise of control*. New York: Freeman.

Baker, S. B., Exum, H. A., & Tyler, R. E. (2002). The developmental process of clinical supervisors in training: An investigation of the supervisor complexity model. *Counselor Education and Supervision, 42*, 15–30.

Barnes, K. L., & Moon, S. M. (2006). Factor structure of the Psychotherapy Supervisor Development Scale. *Measurement and Evaluation in Counseling and Development, 39*, 130–140.

Bernard, J. M. (1979). Supervisory training: A discrimination model. *Counselor Education and Supervision, 19*, 60–68.

Bernard, J. M. (1997). The discrimination model. In C. E. Watkins, Jr. (Ed.), *Handbook of psychotherapy supervision* (pp. 310–327). New York: Wiley.

Bernard, J. M., & Goodyear, R. K. (2004). *Fundamentals of clinical supervision* (3rd ed.). Needham Heights, MA: Allyn & Bacon.

Blocher, D. H. (1983). Toward a cognitive developmental approach to counseling supervision. *The Counseling Psychologist, 11*(1), 27–34.

Borders, L. D. (1989). *Training programs for supervisors*. Unpublished manuscript.

Borders, L. D. (1991). A systematic approach to peer group supervision. *Journal of Counseling and Development, 69*, 248–252.

Borders, L. D. (1992). Learning to think like a supervisor. *The Clinical Supervisor, 10*(2), 135–148.

Borders, L. D. (2001). Counseling supervision: A deliberate educational process. In D. C. Locke, J. E. Myers, and E. L. Herr (Eds.), *The handbook of counseling* (pp. 417–432). Thousand Oaks, CA: Sage.

Borders, L. D. (in press). In-house training clinic: An ideal setting for training doctoral students in supervision. In A. K. Mobley and J. E. Myers (Eds.), *Developing and maintaining counselor education laboratories* (2nd ed.). Alexandria, VA: American Counseling Association.

Borders, L. D., Bernard, J. M., Dye, H. A., Fong, M. L., Henderson, P., & Nance, D. W. (1991). Curriculum guide for training counseling supervisors: Rationale, development, and implementation. *Counselor Education and Supervision, 31*, 58–80.

Borders, L. D., & Brown, L. L. (2005). *The new handbook of counseling supervision*. Mahwah, NJ: Lahaska/Lawrence Erlbaum.

Borders, L. D., & Fong, M. L. (1994). Cognitions of supervisors-in-training: An exploratory study. *Counselor Education and Supervision, 33*, 280–293.

Borders, L. D., & Leddick, G. R. (1988). A nationwide survey of supervision training. *Counselor Education and Supervision, 27*, 271–283.

Borders, L. D., Rainey, L. M., Crutchfield, L. B., & Martin, D. (1996). Impact of a counseling supervision course on doctoral students' cognitions. *Counselor Education and Supervision, 35*, 204–217.

Borders, L. D., & Usher, C. H. (1992). Post-degree supervision: Existing and preferred practices. *Journal of Counseling and Development, 70*, 594–599.

Bransford, J. D., Brown, A. L., & Cocking, R. R. (Eds.). (2000). *How people learn: Brain, mind, experience, and school*. Washington, DC: National Academy Press.

CACREP (Council for the Accreditation of Counseling and Related Educational Programs) (2009). *2009 CACREP standards*. Retrieved January 21, 2009, from www.cacrep.org/2009standards.html.

Dye, H. A., & Borders, L. D. (1990). Counseling supervisors: Standards for preparation and practice. *Journal of Counseling and Development, 69*, 27–32.

Ellis, M. V. (1991). Critical incidents in clinical supervision and in supervisor supervision: Assessing supervisory issues. *Journal of Counseling and Development, 38*, 342–349.

Ellis, M. V., & Douce, L. A. (1994). Group supervision of novice clinical supervisors: Eight recurring issues. *Journal of Counseling and Development, 72*, 520–525.

Falender, C. A., Cornish, J. A. E., Goodyear, R., Hatcher, R., Kaslow, N. J., Leventhal, G. et al. (2004). Defining competencies in psychology supervision: A consensus statement. *Journal of Clinical Psychology, 60*, 771–785.

Falender, C. A., & Shafranske, E. P. (2008). Best practices of supervision. In C. A. Falender and E. P. Shafranske (Eds.), *Casebook for clinical supervision: A competency-based approach.* Washington, DC: American Psychological Association.

Getz, H. G. (1999). Assessment of clinical supervisor competencies. *Journal of Counseling and Development, 77*, 491–497.

Getz, H. G., & Agnew, D. (1999). A supervision model for public agency clinicians. *The Clinical Supervisor, 18*(2), 51–61.

Heid, L. (1997). Supervisor development across the professional lifespan. *The Clinical Supervisor, 16*(2), 139–152.

Hess, A. K. (1986). Growth in supervision: Stages of supervisee and supervisor development. *The Clinical Supervisor, 4*(1–2), 51–67.

Hess, A. K. (1987). Psychotherapy supervision: Stages, Buber, and a theory of relationship. *Professional Psychology, 18*, 251–259.

Hogan, R. A. (1964). Issues and approaches in supervision. *Psychotherapy: Theory, Research and Practice, 1*, 139–141.

Johnson, E. A., & Stewart, D. W. (2008). Perceived competence in supervisory roles: A social cognitive analysis. *Training and Education in Professional Psychology, 2*, 229–236.

Kagan, N. (1980). Influencing human interaction – Eighteen years with IPR. In A. K. Hess (Ed.), *Psychotherapy supervision: Theory, research and practice* (pp. 262–283). New York: Wiley.

Kagan (Klein), H., & Kagan, N. I. (1997). Interpersonal process recall: Influencing human interaction. In C. E. Watkins, Jr. (Ed.), *Handbook of psychotherapy supervision* (pp. 296–309). New York: Wiley.

Kolb, D. A. (1984). *Experiential learning: Experience as the source of learning and development.* Englewood Cliffs, NJ: Prentice-Hall.

Loganbill, C., & Hardy, E. (1983). Developing training programs for clinical supervisors. *The Clinical Supervisor, 1*(3), 15–21.

Loganbill, C., Hardy, E., & Delworth, U. (1982). Supervision: A conceptual model. *The Counseling Psychologist, 10*(1), 3–42.

Lyon, R. C., Heppler, A., Leavitt, L., & Fisher, L. (2008). Supervisory training experiences and overall supervisory development in predoctoral interns. *The Clinical Supervisor, 27*, 268–284.

McMahon, M., & Simons, R. (2004). Supervision training for professional counselors: An exploratory study. *Counselor Education and Supervision, 43*, 301–309.

Milne, D., Aylott, H., Fitzpatrick, H., & Ellis, M. V. (2008). How does clinical supervision work? Using a "best evidence synthesis" approach to construct a basic model of supervision. *The Clinical Supervisor, 27*, 170–190.

Milne, D., & James, I. (2000). A systematic review of effective cognitive-behavioural supervision. *British Journal of Clinical Psychology, 39*, 111–127.

Milne, D. L., & James, I. A. (2002). The observed impact of training on competence in clinical supervision. *British Journal of Clinical Psychology, 41*, 55–72.

Milne, D., & Westerman, C. (2001). Evidence-based clinical supervision: Rationale and illustration. *Clinical Psychology and Psychotherapy, 8*, 444–457.

National Board for Certified Counselors: Center for Credentialing Education. (1997). *Approved clinical supervisor*. Retrieved August 13, 2008, from www.cce-global.org/credentials-offered/acs.

Nelson, K. W., Oliver, M., & Capps, F. (2006). Becoming a supervisor: Doctoral student perceptions of the training experience. *Counselor Education and Supervision, 46*, 17–31.

Neufeldt, S. A. (1999). *Supervision strategies for the first practicum* (2nd ed.). Alexandria, VA: American Counseling Association.

Neufeldt, S. A., Karno, M. P., & Nelson, M. L. (1996). A qualitative study of experts' conceptualization of supervisee reflectivity. *Journal of Counseling Psychology, 43*, 3–9.

Overholser, J. C. (1991). The Socratic method as a technique in psychotherapy supervision. *Professional Psychology, 22*, 68–74.

Peace, S. D., & Sprinthall, N. A. (1998). Training school counselors to supervise beginning counselors: Theory, research, and practice. *Professional School Counseling, 1*, 2–8.

Rodenhauser, P. (1995). Experiences and issues in the professional development of psychiatrists supervising psychotherapy. *The Clinical Supervisor, 13*(1), 7–22.

Russell, R. K., & Petrie, T. (1994). Issues in training effective supervisors. *Applied and Preventive Psychology, 3*, 27–42.

Schön, D. A. (1983). *Educating the reflective practitioner*. San Francisco: Jossey-Bass.

Scott, K. J., Ingram, K. M., Vitanza, S. A., and Smith, N. G. (2000). Training in supervision: A survey of current practices. *The Counseling Psychologist, 28*, 403–422.

Skovholt, T. M., & Rønnestad, M. H. (1992a). *The evolving professional self: Stages and themes in therapist and counselor development*. New York: Wiley.

Skovholt, T. M., & Rønnestad, M. H. (1992b). Themes in therapist and counselor development. *Journal of Counseling and Development, 70*, 505–515.

Stevens, D. T., Goodyear, R. K., & Robertson, P. (1997). Supervisor development: An exploratory study in changes in stance and emphasis. *The Clinical Supervisor, 16*(2), 73–88.

Stoltenberg, C. (1981). Approaching supervision from a developmental perspective: the counselor complexity model. *Journal of Counseling Psychology, 28*, 59–65.

Stoltenberg, C. D., & Delworth, U. (1987). *Supervising counselors and therapists: A developmental approach*. San Francisco: Jossey-Bass.

Stoltenberg, C. D., McNeill, B., & Delworth, U. (1998). *IDM supervision: An integrated developmental model for supervising counselors and therapists*. San Francisco: Jossey-Bass.

Watkins, C. E., Jr. (1990). Development of the psychotherapy supervisor. *Psychotherapy, 27*, 553–560.

Watkins, C. E., Jr. (1991). Reflections on the preparation of psychotherapy supervisors. *Journal of Clinical Psychology, 47*, 145–147.

Watkins, C. E., Jr. (1993). Development of the psychotherapy supervisor: Concepts, assumptions, and hypotheses of the supervisor complexity model. *American Journal of Psychotherapy, 47*, 58–74.

Watkins, C. E., Jr. (1994). The supervision of psychotherapy supervisor trainees. *American Journal of Psychotherapy, 48,* 417–431.

Watkins, C. E., Jr. (1995). Researching psychotherapy supervisor development: Four key considerations. *The Clinical Supervisor, 13*(2), 111–118.

Watkins, C. E., Jr., Schneider, L. J., Haynes, J., & Nieberding, R. (1995). Measuring psychotherapy supervisor development: An initial effort at scale development and validation. *The Clinical Supervisor, 13*(1), 77–90.

Wheeler, S., & King. D. (2000). Do counselling supervisors want or need to have their supervision supervised? An exploratory study. *British Journal of Guidance and Counselling, 28,* 279–290.

Worthington, E. L., Jr. (1987). Changes in supervision as counselors and supervisors gain experience: A review. *Professional Psychology, 18,* 189–208.

# CHAPTER 7

# Religion, Spirituality, and Clinical Supervision

## J. SCOTT YOUNG and CRAIG S. CASHWELL

> In the study of the profession to which he had looked forward all his life he found irritation and vacuity as well as serene wisdom; he saw no one clear path to Truth but a thousand paths to a thousand truths far-off and doubtful.

**Sinclair Lewis,** *Arrowsmith*, **1924**

The purpose of this chapter is first to provide readers with a clear understanding of how religion and spirituality are germane to the process of counseling and, by extension, clinical supervision. Second, our purpose is to prepare clinical supervisors to foster supervisee development when working with issues of a religious or spiritual nature. Specifically, the reader will learn that religious conceptualizations are common to the psychological reality of most individuals and, therefore, are worthy of a balanced consideration in counseling endeavors. Furthermore, to assist supervisors in thinking through how best to assist their supervisees with these issues, guidelines are provided upon which clinical supervisors can draw from to conduct supervision sessions. To illuminate these principles, clinical supervisors were interviewed and asked to describe their experiences providing supervision when religion or spirituality was salient to the clinical context. The reflections of these individuals are included to assist the reader in placing the ideas discussed into a real-world frame of reference.

## Introduction

Spirituality and religion are important cultural aspects to most individuals within the United States. Researchers have found that 96% of Americans believe in a "Higher Power," over 90% pray, 69% are members of a religious community, and 43% have attended a service at their church, synagogue, temple, or mosque within the past 7 days (Princeton Religion Research Center, 2000). Although these numbers highlight the salience of religion and spirituality in our culture, they omit those whose personal spirituality does not involve a Higher Power or a religious community, and those whose personal spiritual practice involves practices other than prayer. In short, it is apparent that the United States is replete with people seeking some type of comfort, transcendence, peace, and interconnectedness found in a spiritual life.

The counseling profession has responded to this awareness over the past 15 years. This is evident in the proliferation of textbooks (Cashwell & Young, 2005; Frame, 2002; Kelly, 1995; Miller, 2002) and articles on topics related to the ethical and competent integration of spirituality into the counseling process. Further, the Council for Accreditation of Counseling and Related Education Programs (CACREP), the accrediting body for the counseling profession, has included spirituality as an aspect of client culture that is to be addressed in counselor training in the past two versions of accreditation standards (CACREP, 2001; CACREP, 2009). As further evidence, the Diagnostic and Statistical Manual of the American Psychological Association (DSM-IV-TR; APA, 2000) has now included a V-code for spiritual and religious problems, though the language of this V-code is far from inclusive in terms of the host of spiritual crises, emergencies, and issues that can arise in the therapeutic process. Taken together, these facts suggest that counselors have an interest in the integration of body, mind, and spirit, along with a desire to further understand how to work effectively with clients to integrate the spiritual and psychological realms.

There are many challenges, however, that are inherent in this process. Religiously and spiritually, the United States is notably pluralistic. Although the largest religious group, consisting of just over 76% of the population, self-identifies as Christian (Largest Religious Groups in the United States, n.d.), it is important to be mindful that there is tremendous within-group variance among religious traditions. That is, knowing that someone is Christian or Jewish or Hindu or Buddhist affords only cursory information about the religious and spiritual beliefs, practices, experiences, rituals, and traditions of the individual. As further evidence of the growing religious diversity in the United States, several religious groups have seen dramatic increases in recent history. For example, from 1990 to 2000, New Age spirituality increased by 240%, Hinduism by 237%,

Baha'i by 200%, Buddhism by 170%, Native American Religion by 119%, and Islam by 109% (Largest Religious Groups in the United States, n.d.). The second largest group in the U.S. identifies as nonreligious or secular, comprising 13.2% of the overall population (Largest Religious Groups in the United States, n.d.). In summary, then, not all clients will be interested in a therapeutic approach that integrates spirituality, but most may be.

There has been a substantive shift in recent years of the integration of spirituality and religion into the counseling process. In the early 1990s, researchers (Kelly, 1994; Pate & Bondi, 1992) found that religion and spirituality were discussed in only a small minority of counselor preparation programs. These groundbreaking scholars raised awareness within the profession and encouraged the profession to consider issues related to spiritual and religious development more fully.

More recently, however, counseling professionals report that the integration of spirituality into the counseling process is vital to recognizing the spiritual aspects of the client's culture, as well as how the client's spiritual life supports or hinders the client's overall wellness and growth. For example, one survey of ACA members (Young, Cashwell, & Wiggins-Frame, 2007) found that professional counselors strongly endorsed the existing spirituality competencies to guide clinical practice. Further, although over two-thirds of respondents agreed that the competencies were important, just under 50% of respondents believed they were not capable of practicing in accord with these competencies. The question, as noted by Briggs and Rayle (2005), seems no longer to be "if" but "how" to competently and ethically address client issues related to spirituality and religion.

Similarly, counselor preparation programs seem to recognize the importance of spirituality in the counseling process. A survey of CACREP-accredited programs (Young, Cashwell, & Wiggins-Frame, 2002) found that counselor educators endorsed the spirituality competencies as important. At the same time, and consistent with the responses of practicing counselors, counselor educators indicated a strong need for curricular guidelines and additional training to help them prepare counselors to integrate spirituality and religion into counseling.

Taken together, all of this evidence portrays a clear need within the counseling profession to more adequately prepare counselors to address the spiritual aspects of clients as a component of psychological reality. Although scholars have considered how special coursework on spirituality (Cashwell & Young, 2004; Ingersoll, 1997) and the infusion of spirituality into core courses (Briggs & Rayle, 2005; Burke et al., 1999) might support this aspect of counselor development, the supervision process is an additional vital aspect of training counselors in which to integrate spirituality. Despite this, the appropriate role of religion and spirituality as a topic for clinical supervision has received little attention in the scholarly literature compared to the proliferation of writings on spirituality in counseling (Polanski, 2003). Atten and Mangis (2007) state, "The supervision literature needed to guide supervisors work with clients' faith is scant at best" (p. 291).

Conversations about the integration of spirituality and religion into the counseling process are always challenging. Whenever a counselor and client come together, there are always divergences in belief systems which may be, at times, rigid and inflexible. This occurs even when the two "wear" the same religious or spiritual label (e.g., Jewish, Christian). How much more might we expect divergence, then, when the religious and spiritual traditions of the two differ significantly. The point here, then, is the complexity of spirituality and religion *in dyadic relationships*. When you superimpose a clinical supervisor into this dynamic, the relationship becomes a triadic relationship in which the supervisor's beliefs, values, and attitudes about religion and spirituality enter the process. For example, consider the example of a religiously sensitive supervisee who was working with a religiously committed client but had a supervisor who held a strong belief that religion and spirituality should not be incorporated into "secular" counseling. For the sake of clarity, in discussing the principles below, we focus first on insuring the welfare of the client and secondly on promoting supervisee growth and development.

### Guiding Principles

Supervision exists for the training of the counselor and for the protection of the client (Bernard & Goodyear, 2004). Under the umbrella of this fundamental premise, the content of clinical supervision sessions evolves in numerous directions with a myriad of content. Yet throughout much of the history of the counseling field, the spiritual and religious life of a client was considered either off limits (i.e., not appropriate to discuss as a therapeutic topic) or irrelevant (i.e., does not exist so no need to explore) to the overall psychological well-being of a client. Subsequently, mental health practitioners were generally neither trained nor encouraged to look closely at the spiritual lives of the individuals with whom they worked (Kelly, 1995).

In more recent years, with a move in the field toward wellness models of human development which include spirituality as a central component of optimal functioning (Myers & Sweeney, 2005) and with research evidence that most individuals report holding some spiritual beliefs (Princeton Religion Research Center, 2000), the field appears to have come out of its shared denial about the need to take seriously the spiritual aspects of a clients life. Related to this movement within professional counseling and other mental health fields toward a more direct acknowledgment of the spiritual aspect of normal human functioning, is the role that clinical supervisors may play in assisting counselors-in-training to understand, respect, and at times effectively utilize clients' spiritual perspectives as a component of their healing.

This is no small consideration, given that clinical supervisors, like every other individual, have their own unique religious and spiritual history, along with psychological issues that have formed through their lives. Furthermore, the clinical training and theoretical perspective of the supervisor goes a long way in influencing how he or she will interpret any religious impulse in a client. These realities warrant a discussion as to the decisions that clinical supervisors will make in relation to explorations of clients religious ideas and the influence supervisors will yield when working with supervisees around the spiritual aspects of clients.

As aforementioned, spirituality as an issue related to clinical supervision has received a minimal amount of attention in the literature of counseling and other mental health disciplines, and there is to date no clear consensus as to what is best practice (Bishop, Avila-Juarbe & Thumme, 2003). Therefore, to facilitate this discussion and to bring some order to the conversation, we have outlined a series of guiding principles related to religion and spirituality and clinical supervision practice. The principles were developed from conversations that we have had between us with practicing clinical supervisors and with other counselor educators. Our hope is that these principles will assist in clarifying to supervisors how to proceed when faced with a spiritually or religiously charged client and/or supervisee.

### Principle 1: Protect the Unique Spiritual Perspective of the Client and Recognize That Spirituality Is Highly Individualized

Religion and spirituality are among the most subjective of human experiences, making it difficult to understand using simple concepts or banal expressions. In fact, when we simply try to define spirituality, we discover not its limits, but rather our limits in finding language that is adequate (Kurtz & Ketcham, 1993). It is within this challenging context that clinical supervisors are called upon to support supervisees in recognizing that each person's religious history and spiritual experiences, or lack thereof, are accumulated from a lifetime of stories, practices, and, in many cases, traumas that work together to inform the person's beliefs about and experiences of the spiritual realm. By framing the spiritual impulse as a component of the personal autobiographical narrative which is filled with individual projections, repressions, and identifications, the clinical supervisor can assist the counselor in exploring the psycho-spiritual life of a client, thus gaining a nuanced understanding of how the client thinks, feels, and behaves.

Many counseling students and novice professional counselors express the fear that they might stumble into a difficult conversation for which they can provide no clear resolution if they talk with a client about her or his spiritual life. Counselors-in-training also express the concern that they might disagree with their client about religion and spiritual matters. Further, novice practitioners are afraid they might have to confront a client about some misinterpretation or distortion that exists in the client's thinking about God or religion. To all of these concerns we would state, "So be it. This is as it should be." Why would a counselor be willing to confront clients about other areas of their thinking, feelings or behavior and not be willing to confront them about a spiritual incongruence? In all likelihood, this reluctance reveals much more about the supervisee than about the client.

An integrated multicultural perspective necessarily includes religion as a fundamental component of the individual uniqueness that shapes people's views of themselves and their world (Cashwell, 2009; Fukuyama & Sevig, 1999; Fukuyama, Siahpoush, & Sevig, 2005). Unfortunately, with a few notable exceptions, religious diversity is rarely at the center of discussions of multicultural counseling, suggesting a subtle bias among writers in this area. Yet it is an assumption of ethical practice that counselors *"will not discriminate against a client based on ... religion."* (American Counseling Association, 2005). Given this foundational support of religious diversity by our professional association, it is incumbent upon clinical supervisors to ensure that the spiritual and religious perspectives of the clients under their care are protected.

By modeling for counselors that a client's spiritual views are both important and valid, clinical supervisors are shaping counselors-in-training to think similarly. Often, counselors will celebrate the sexual, racial, and ethnic uniqueness of clients while offering less fervent support for and protection of their rights to hold strong religious views, especially if those views differ from the views of the counselor.

In terms of the practice of clinical supervision, this principle suggests that it is appropriate for a supervisor to directly address any attempts by a counselor to influence the religious orientation of a client if the client has not expressly requested this. Thus, the supervisor watches for evidence that the counselor either strongly identifies with or reacts against the client's spiritual world view, as either extreme may be problematic. As Bernard and Goodyear (2004) suggest, for counselors to hold a true multicultural perspective they must possess or have experienced (a) a pluralistic philosophy, (b) cultural knowledge, (c) consciousness raising, (d) experiential training, (e) contact with minorities, and (f) practicum or internships with minorities. All of these ideas apply to the spiritual and religious realities of a client's life. Therefore, it is incumbent upon the clinical supervisor to support the client in holding a unique religious or spiritual outlook.

There were a number of reflections from clinical supervisors working in both academic and clinical settings who we interviewed that are applicable here. One supervisor said:

> For example, what if a client says, "I am depressed because it is God's will" and the apparent consequence of that stance is that the client's relationships are being damaged? Although I do not believe it is the will of a Higher Power that anyone be depressed and I expect that many supervisees might agree, it is not our place to tell this client he or she is wrong. I might encourage the supervisee to ask the client, "What gifts has God given you?" to begin to reframe the situation, provide at least somewhat of a solution-focus, and work with rather than against the client's belief system.

Another supervisor was asked how he has encouraged a supervisee working with a client struggling with a spiritual/religious issue in counseling. His response reflects the importance he sees in working within the client's worldview:

> … I would have them superimpose where they (supervisee) are with that issue to see if there are any inherent conflicts and how they may be able to minimize those conflicts. Also, based on their conceptualization of the client, how does that inform how they can help the client grow. … that is, I encourage self-exploration for the supervisee, but also challenge the supervisee to conceptualize the client's issue from the client's perspective."

Another supervisor, who has worked as a clinical supervisor for over 10 years, attested that the consequences of failing to follow Principle 1 are:

> Absolutely horrible. If the client is coming from a spiritual perspective and the counselor doesn't get it or understand that, if that is not their orientation, then they will feel like they are two ships passing in the night …

*Principle 2: Promote Counselor Self-Evaluation of Spiritual/Religious Bias*

Counselors-in-training, like all individuals, have a unique religious history that directly informs their views of religion as a whole and of various religious views that a client holds. As Polanski (2003) noted, one of the goals of clinical supervision is to enhance the supervisee's professional functioning, "including personal reflection and values clarification" (p. 131). Several writers have noted that for a counselor to be effective and ethical while addressing issues related to religion or spirituality, the counselor must be aware of his or her own spiritual beliefs (Bishop, Avila-Juarbe, & Thumme, 2003; Polanski, 2003). Through meaningful discussions in the clinical supervision hour, a counselor may recognize when he or she is reacting (either positively or negatively) toward a client's religious impulses. As the supervisor assists the counselor in gaining clarity about his or her own reactions, the counselor is in a much better position to respect the client's religious perspective and to utilize the client's beliefs as a component of treatment when appropriate.

For clinical supervisors, this principle suggests a willingness to directly engage supervisees in conversations about the counselor's religious history, beliefs, and values. This may create anxiety for some supervisors, yet just as religion is a unique component of a client's reality, it is equally true of the supervisee. Anecdotal evidence suggests that clinical supervisors frequently report the challenge of working with the highly religious supervisees who believe it is their responsibility to convert clients to their faith. Directly engaging supervisees in discussion about their spiritual beliefs provides an opportunity to discuss the ethical violation of value imposition. Similarity, counselors who are suspicious of clients' religious commitment can be challenged to open their mind to the reality that individuals who are religiously committed consistently perform better on measures of overall physical and psychological well-being (Cashwell, 2005).

One supervisor, speaking about helping supervisees work with clients with belief systems that are different from their own, emphasized self-awareness by saying, "How do you bridge that gap? I think they can resolve that, but the counselor has to have self-awareness."

Multiple supervisors made statements about the importance of recognizing their boundaries as a supervisor. That is, supporting the supervisee in examining her or his beliefs is acceptable to a point, particularly when it is within the context of a particular client with whom the supervisee is struggling. For example, one supervisor stated:

> I would process with supervisees and hopefully help them to recognize that their spiritual views were negatively impacting their ability to form a significant relationship. Then, I would encourage them to seek out their own counseling to help them clarify their own values and some sense of why they believe what they believe.

Conversely, supervisors may mirror a bias held by many supervisees that spirituality and religion can only be introduced into the counselor or supervisory process if brought up by the "other" (i.e., client or supervisee). One supervisor, herself a highly religious person, may have been speaking to this when she said:

I don't raise spiritual issues on my own. I am more comfortable if they are raised by the client. If I notice a client processing religion, then I encourage the supervisee not to diminish the client's desire to discuss religion.

There appear to be two subtle but clear biases in this approach. First, many hold the bias that it is not possible to introduce topics of spirituality or religion in supervision or counseling without imposing personal values. If the invitations are culturally sensitive, however, it is quite possible to create a milieu in which spirituality and religion can be discussed openly and honestly, in a way such that personal values and beliefs of each person in the relationship are valued, particularly where they diverge. This may provide important modeling for the supervisee. A second bias inherent in the supervisor statement above is that spirituality and religion only have a "place" in the counseling process if the topic is initiated by the client. This goes beyond the first bias, however, by assuming that spirituality and religion only have a place in the therapeutic milieu as manifest content of the client's story. That is, only if the client is overtly talking about his or her religious and spiritual life should this be incorporated into the therapeutic context. Although this is clearly one instance where religion and spirituality might (and in this case, probably *should*) be included, there are others as well. For example:

- Latent content within the client's story (e.g., client's presentation has underlying existential issues of meaning and purpose);
- Spiritual practice as adjunct to counseling (e.g., a client might be encouraged to begin a contemplative practice, such as meditation or centering prayer, that is consistent with his or her belief system);
- The possibility of using psycho-spiritual interventions, such as guided meditations or focusing (Gendlin, 1982; Hinterkopf, 1998), that are consistent with the client's belief system;
- The personhood of the counselor (e.g., discussing how the spiritual beliefs and practices of the supervisee support his or her work as a counselor and how to "recharge" after a difficult session to prepare for the next client); and
- The counseling room as sacred space (e.g., as a counselor, how to create a physical space and an internal space that will best support the client's healing work).

*Principle 3: Encourage Supervisees to Assess Clients' Spiritual Lives and Any Relationship to Their Presenting Issues*

Miller (1999) published a set of competencies developed by members of the Association for Spiritual, Ethical, and Religious Values in Counseling

(ASERVIC) designed to guide counselors in effectively working with spiritual and religious issues in counseling. One of the competencies states, "Counselors can assess the relevance of spiritual and religious issues to the client's counseling concerns." In the context of clinical supervision, supervisees may need assistance in appropriately exploring the role of religion and spirituality in the client's life and how these may relate to presenting concerns.

In some instances, a supervisee might ask questions of a supervisor about the integration of spirituality and religion into counseling work. This provides an opportunity for an in-depth discussion of this integration and affords the supervisor an at least somewhat "open window" for learning about the supervisee's perspectives on religion and spirituality, as well as learning about how the supervisee might think initially about integrating spirituality and religion into his or her work as a counselor.

In our experience, though, these instances are rare and often are prefaced with "Well, I know you are interested in spirituality, so I want to ask you about ..." That is, in many cases, supervisees may only introduce the topic if/when they know you as a supervisor are open and interested in the topic. In the majority of cases, though, it is left up to the supervisor to open this avenue of dialogue.

A supervisee's perspectives on spirituality and religion, and the role of spirituality and religion within the counseling process, can and, we believe, should be assessed in initial supervision sessions. As a supervisor begins to assess the developmental level, theoretical orientation, ego-strength, and interpersonal style of a supervisee, assessment of the spiritual and religious domain can begin as well. We recommend a series of simple questions, offered with the same neutrality with which you assess other aspects of the supervisee. This is not considered a rigid protocol of assessment. The use of subsequent questions depends, to some extent, on the openness of the supervisee to explore the spiritual and religious dimension.

1. How has your theoretical orientation evolved out of your personal and professional experiences?
2. How do you think about the role of clients' religious and spiritual lives in their presentation to you as a counselor?
3. How have your own spiritual and religious experiences influenced your perspectives?
4. How do you think you will assess client religiosity and spirituality?
5. How might you work with what you learn from this assessment of client spirituality?

Initially, these questions are intended to give you some initial perspective on the supervisees' personal experiences with religion and spirituality, how these experiences impact their perspectives on integrating spirituality and religion in the counseling process, and how you might begin to explore specific topics and issues further.

One supervisor, who described himself as a spiritually sensitive counselor, discussed the often found paradox in the supervisory triad and how this impacts his work with supervisees:

> Well, first of all, a supervisee has to have openness to discussing issues of religion and spirituality before he or she can do a good job of assessment. What I mean by this is that I can give a supervisee a set of assessment questions or hand [him or her] an assessment instrument with directions to administer it in the next session. If the supervisee does not buy into this as important, however, [his or her] use of the tool I give them is likely to be so mechanistic that it will not be effective and might, in fact, harm the therapeutic relationship. So, it creates quite a paradox for me as a supervisor when I see a supervisee who is hostile or resistant toward religion and spirituality working with a client where religion and spirituality seem to be important.

From this statement, it seems imperative that there first be a commitment from the supervisee that client religious and spiritual issues are important and need to be assessed further. Even when there is supervisee commitment, supervisees may be unfamiliar with how to conduct such an assessment and need specific direction. A host of quantitative and qualitative assessment recommendations are available in Harper and Gill (2005). One specific assessment that can be introduced in individual, triadic, or group supervision is discussed here. Kelly (1995) provided a conceptual context for assessing religion and spirituality. It is based on two primary dimensions; that of personal significance and problem/issue relevance. That is, the assessment is based on the personal importance of religion and spirituality and the extent to which spirituality and/or religion are related to either the exacerbation or amelioration of the problem. Kelly originally described this nomenclature as a way to assess clients, with direct implications for clinical work. In using this approach in supervision, provide the supervisee with the following handout*:

Assessing Client Spirituality and Religion
Adapted from Kelly (1995)

---

* Adapted from Kelly, E. (1995). Spirituality and religion in counseling and psychotherapy: Diversity in theory and practice (pp. 136–142). Alexandria, Virginia: American Counseling Association.

1. *Religiously committed clients*—clients who have a personal conviction regarding their personal religious beliefs. Because these beliefs are internalized and conscious, they typically are a source of significant influence on attitude, thoughts, and behaviors. Because of the salience of these beliefs, this client likely will be willing to discuss and examine their beliefs and how these beliefs influence his or her presenting issues.

2. *Religiously loyal clients*—clients for whom the cultural aspects of religion, as part of familial and ethnic loyalties, is most salient. Often, traditions and rituals provide norms for beliefs, practices, attitudes, and values. These beliefs, however, are primarily extrinsic and do not necessarily form the value base of the individual. Such a client may need to discuss the culturally and socially oriented behaviors of his or her religion and also consider where her or her personal beliefs, values, and behaviors differ from these.

3. *Spiritually committed clients*—clients who have a strong sense of their personal spirituality while not affiliated with organized religion. There is a strong sense of something beyond the self, of connectedness and openness. Such a client typically is open to exploring personal beliefs and values and how these are related to presenting issues and may, in fact, introduce these topics in the counseling process.

4. *Spiritually/religiously open clients*—clients who do not have a spiritual or religious commitment or a loyalty to a determined religion, yet are open to exploring the spiritual/religious dimensions in looking at their presenting issues and their development and growth. Such clients are not apt to introduce spirituality/religion within a counseling session, but if exposed to these ideas within a non-proselytizing approach, they are likely to explore these issues.

5. *Externally religious clients*—clients who participate in organized religion, but for whom the beliefs and attachments of that religion carry little or no inner conviction related to their religious loyalty or religious commitment. For such a client, the integration of spirituality/religion often has little or no benefit.

6. *Spiritually/religiously tolerant or indifferent clients*—clients who are open generally to spirituality/religion and to the specific spirituality/religion of others, but who are personally indifferent. For such clients, the introduction of spirituality/religion is not warranted and may, in fact, be ethically problematic.

7. *Nonspiritual/nonreligious clients*—clients who consider spirituality/religion, both conceptually and personally, as unreal and unnecessary, if not harmful to understanding reality. To introduce

spirituality/religion into the counseling process with such clients may be harmful and unethical.

8. *Religiously hostile clients*—clients who are personally unreligious and conceptually hostile, in attitude and action, to religions, religious groups, and the influence of religion in society. Often, further assessment of the source of the hostility is warranted, but intended only to clarify the client's perspective to support work on emotional and behavioral challenges while respecting the client's hostility to religion.

After explaining this typology and discussing the general concepts, the supervisor can facilitate a discussion about the types of clients that might be most challenging to the supervisee and why. One point of emphasis within the model is the likelihood that a client within a particular category will be open to exploration of his or her spirituality/religion and the role it plays in the exacerbation or amelioration of the problem. In our experience, these may naturally lead to supervisees exploring where they fit within this typology. In other cases, however, after discussing clients within this context, the supervisor might encourage the supervisee to consider herself or himself within this model, using process questions such as:

1. Where do you fit within Kelly's typology?
2. What are the implications of this for your work as a counselor?
3. Given where you fit within this model, what types of clients might be most challenging for you to work with?

*Principle 4: Be Prepared to Educate Supervisees About
Models of Spiritual/Religious Development*

There are a number of developmental models of spirituality. A full discussion of these models is beyond the scope of this chapter (for additional information on developmental models, see Allport, 1950; Fowler, 1981, 1991; Frame, 2002; Genia, 1995; Washburn, 2003; and Worthington, 1989). The constant among these is that a person's relationship with spirituality and religion is both personal and developmental. Further, developmental models provide a context for understanding differing perspectives without "pathologizing." That is, the spiritual and religious life is a developmental construct that can evolve as the client's thinking and experience evolve. Within this context, counseling is an ideal venue for developmental growth to occur. For our purposes, here, we offer a generic developmental model of spiritual and religious development that can be used to conceptualize clients and supervisees.

*Level 1 (literal and concrete).* A Level 1 client or supervisee simply wants to know what the rules are and to know the consequences of following or disobeying the rules. That is, beliefs tend to be externalized and adherence to the "rules" tends to be rigid. It is at this level that belief systems might be considered dogmatic. Because beliefs tend to be rigid and characterized as "black or white", there is little tolerance for differing beliefs or the people who hold them. As such, Level 1 clients hold expectations that their counselor will work within their belief system and will not make efforts to challenge or change these beliefs (Belaire, Young, & Elder, 2005). By the same token, a Level 1 supervisee will not expect the supervisor ... .

*Level 2 (rebellion and questioning).* The Level 2 client or supervisee is in a psychological space of either rebelling against earlier religious and spiritual teachings and practices or is in a questioning phase. The key characteristic of this developmental level is that the client is "unpacking" early learning and examining it more closely. This may take highly disparate forms, however. For some clients, this can take the form of exploration of different wisdom tradition and often is a time of great openness to different spiritual/religious beliefs, practices, and experiences. Such a client likely would be highly open to the integration of spirituality and religion into the counseling process, as long as the approach was not exclusivist in nature. For others, however, it can be a period of angry rebellion. Using the typology of Kelly (1995) previously discussed, such clients might fit into the category of *"religiously hostile."* In such cases, it might be necessary for the counselor to introduce the construct of spirituality as a distinct construct from religion and be mindful of the fact that the client might not be making the distinction, leading him or her to be hostile toward both religion *and* spirituality. In such cases, the counselor is well-advised to explore without judgment the client's life experiences with religion and spirituality. In most cases, however the integration of spirituality and religion is contraindicated and the supervisee should be discouraged from working within a religious and spiritual framework with the client.

*Level 3 (seeking).* A Level 3 client is clear about some aspects of his or her religious and spiritual life, but not others. Unlike the level one client, the Level 3 client does not feel the need to proselytize beliefs. Commonly, there is an "innerness" to these beliefs that helps the client feel comfortable with these beliefs and not need to proselytize that others "should" believe this way. At the same time, there remains a seeking around certain religious or spiritual beliefs and practices. The integration of spirituality and religion into counseling with level three clients is quite natural and typically requires only the slightest initiative on the part of the counselor. A constructivist framework, although useful with clients at all levels, is particularly effective here as Level 3 clients typically want someone to support them in their exploration and seeking. Often, a Level 3 client will introduce topics of spirituality and religion in discussing personal struggles. With such clients, the supervisee might be encouraged to adopt a nondirective approach to facilitate client exploration.

*Level 4 (peace).* The Level 4 client has gone through the developmental process of internalizing religious and spiritual beliefs. While there may be clarity about beliefs and practices, it is not a dogmatic belief and this client is, by definition, comfortable with people who hold differing beliefs. For this client, counseling might focus on how best to use the belief systems and practices. A supervisee working with a Level 4 client might be encouraged, for example, to process with the client how religion and spirituality can be a source of healing related to presenting issues.

Although the focus in explicating the above model is on clients, it is important to recognize also that supervisors and supervisees can be conceptualized within the same model and that this has implications for the supervisory process. For example, one of us, who would characterize himself as a Level 3 supervisor who champions an appreciation for divergent belief systems, was supervising a Level 2 supervisee who was rebelling against organized religion and was religiously hostile. At the same time, this supervisee professed a desire to work within a pluralist framework and respect the client's belief systems. When working with highly religious clients, however, his disdain, though not overt, was clear to me as a supervisor and probably to clients as well. This played out differently depending on the developmental level of the client. For example, Level 1 clients would often get argumentative and "resistant." In these instances, a Level 3 supervisor was working with a Level 2 supervisee who was working with a Level 1 client. Although a thorough discussion of this supervisory process is beyond the scope of this chapter, it is important to consider the developmental level of all parties involved (supervisor, supervisee, and client) in considering how best to support the supervisee in working with a particular client. Such a conceptualization of development level across supervisor, supervisee, and client can facilitate appropriate and ethical integration of spirituality and religion into the supervision process.

One supervisor highlighted how developmental level impacts the client's experiences of religion and spirituality and how this impacts the supervisory process:

> … I think of a person who is high in cognitive development. If you look at the models and theories of development, people at low levels of cognitive development have no clue about … [the spiritual life]. They want to know what the rules are and want to be sure they live by the rules. As a supervisor, I might recognize that, but I cannot impose that on the client nor should I encourage the supervisee to impose that on the client. I'm not sure [the counselor] would even talk about spirituality. The [counselor] would be talking about religion.

*Principle 5: Consider the Client's Psycho-Spiritual Viewpoint as Potentially Part of the Problem and/or Part of the Solution*

A client's spiritual beliefs can be psychologically stabilizing or destabilizing. This should not be surprising to anyone who has much counseling experience. Clients come to counseling because of the emotional, behavioral, and cognitive incongruence with which they are struggling and religion and spirituality are one aspect of this experience. If clients believe something about their lives based on a religious presupposition, and this belief is causing anxiety, then it is a psychological phenomenon open for discussion in counseling. Supervisees need assurance that their job is not to fix or resolve the religious struggles of a client but rather to help the client explore these struggles.

Exploration of client belief systems in counseling is, in part, a function of the previously described developmental level of the client. That is, there are some clients who are so firmly entrenched in their personal belief system that they will become psychologically reactive to *any* exploration of these belief systems. One function of the supervisor is to help the supervisee consider if and when to introduce an exploration of client beliefs into the counseling process.

If, however, it seems appropriate to support the client in exploring spiritual and religious belief systems, the following questions can be used to explore aspects of the belief system that are helpful and those that are hindering. Does the belief … :

- Build bridges or barriers between people?
- Strengthen or weaken a basic trust/relatedness to the universe?
- Stimulate or hamper the growth of inner freedom and personal responsibility?
- Provide effective or faulty means of helping move from guilt to forgiveness?
- Increase or hamper enjoyment?
- Encourage acceptance or denial of reality?
- Strengthen or weaken self-esteem?

It bears emphasizing here that the principle highlights that a client's psycho-spiritual perspectives should be conceived as potentially *part* of the problem and/or solution. That is, the psycho-spiritual should be integrated within the holistic framework of the person and should *not* be considered solely as either the problem or the solution. One supervisor captured this when he stated that:

> I think that it is a challenge if I have someone who believes that all issues can be solved spiritually, through prayer, meditation, or reading spiritual things. It takes looking at biochemistry, behavior, at the

psychology of what is going on, as well as looking at the spiritual part of things. I will challenge supervisees if they think all issues can be solved with spirituality, because if they are operating in that kind of context, then maybe they need to be a pastor versus being a counselor.

### Principle 6: Encourage the Supervisee to Seek Specialized Consultation

It is common for supervisees to present clients in supervision who come from a faith tradition different from either the supervisee or supervisor or have unique needs relative to spiritual development that extend beyond the scope of competence for either the supervisee or the supervisor. In these instances, it is important to encourage the supervisee to get outside consultation and/or focused study. Faiver, O'Brien, and McNally (1998) coined the term *friendly clergy* to delineate clergy members who have unique authority in churches, temples, or mosques, but who also have training in pastoral care and are cognizant of the interplay between mental health and religion/spirituality. Such members of the clergy are nonjudgmental, caring, and open to the psychotherapeutic process. They may prove invaluable as consultants to supervisees and, in some instances, may also serve as a referral source when the needs of the client cross the boundary from spiritually sensitive counseling to spiritual counseling. One supervisor spoke very clearly to this principle in saying:

> I would have them go and speak to their ... religious leader and address those issues and encourage them to ask the person they are talking to if they would give them other things to read and explore to resolve some of the issues.

### Principle 7: Allow the Supervisee to Struggle

When clients bring religious and spiritual issues to counseling, and particularly when these issues confront a supervisee with his or her own struggles and development, there often is an internal struggle on the supervisee's part. For example, supervisees may present in supervision with some variant of "I believe in diversity, but how can I support a client whose fundamentalist beliefs seem so rigid and dogmatic?" The "easy road" here would be for the supervisor to simply explain spirituality/religion within a developmental context and direct the supervisee. This becomes an example of parallel process. The supervisee is not clear about how to support the client in his or her struggle, and likewise, the supervisor attempts to take away the supervisee's struggle by being didactic and directive.

What the supervisee really needs in these instances, though, is a model and a mirror. The supervisee will benefit from the experience of sitting with a live model of what it means to stay within someone amidst their struggle. By modeling this for the supervisee, he or she will become more conscious of not taking the clients struggle away and, in fact, may see how helpful it is to heighten the struggle to help the client gain emotional and cognitive insight. Depending on the developmental level of the client, this might take the form of:

- Reflecting content, feelings, and meaning to help the client see his or her perspective more clearly
- Offering contrasting perspectives
- Helping the client to examine and own his or her beliefs
- Challenging the client to think about his or her beliefs in sophisticated and critical ways
- Helping the client differentiate the relationship with a Higher Power from a relationship to an institution
- Challenging the client when religious belief is used as an excuse not to take responsibility for his or her life
- Supporting the client in drawing love, encouragement, acceptance, and support from the God of his or her understanding
- Supporting the client in feeling valued and prized by the God of his or her understanding
- Supporting the client in feelings of assurance and peace that God is working in his or her life
- Supporting the client in knowing he or she cannot earn God's favor
- Supporting the client in accepting that he or she is not perfect
- Supporting the client in knowing that he or she is a work in progress and that the relationship with God changes over time

One supervisor captured this principal eloquently when she said:

> … When my supervisee[s] struggle, I try and be supportive of them and let them struggle. Just like with clients, you can't expect growth without first making a mess. Nobody gets to puberty without going through an awkward stage first, and I think that is true of any kind of change or development … you can't do the other [principles] without having the perspective that your supervisee will struggle. If you try and protect your supervisee just like you try to protect your client, none of these things will happen … if supervisees haven't spent time thinking about how spirituality and religion have a bearing on this existence, then you are dead in the water, I think.

### Questions for Consideration in Supervision

Often, supervisors work with supervisees who are providing services to a client who is highly religiously or spiritually oriented, or who holds a belief system that is quite different from the supervisees. If the supervisor does not encourage the supervisee to discuss these issues, this may become an unspoken aspect of the counseling and supervision relationships. To support an initial conversation in supervision about these issues, the following questions may reveal potential issues that will impact the counseling or supervision process.

1. Does the supervisee feel open and accepting of this client?
2. Can the supervisee allow him or herself to experience positive attitudes toward this client?
3. What are the supervisee's opinions and biases with regard to this client's religious or spiritual belief?
4. Does the supervisee harbor a desire to change the client's religious beliefs, practices, or thinking?
5. Can the supervisee identify an impulse within him or herself to argue with or persuade the client into or out of a religious or spiritual perspective?
6. How might the supervisee's personal spiritual/religious history impact his or her ability to extend a nonpossessive love toward this client?
7. What would facilitate the supervisee in increasing his or her compassion for this client?
8. Is the supervisee very different from the client in his or her fundamental approach to life?

## Conclusion

Means for effectively addressing spiritual and religious concerns that arise within the counseling process have received widespread discussion in the professional literature of recent years. The results of recent survey research indicate there is a predilection among counselors and counselor educators to competently support the spiritual development of a client when the individual is so inclined. Although there is some agreement that such issues are important to consider as a component of counseling, how to do so remains less clear. For counselors-in-training and novice practitioners to build their clinical self-efficacy with these issues, effective supervision must both support and challenge supervisees as they work with spiritual domains of clients' lives. We have focused in this chapter on the key principles we believe necessary to maximize the effectiveness of supervision with regard to these issues. Needless to say, the conversation will continue, however at the least, careful reflection on these guidelines will support supervisors in assisting the counselors and clients under their care.

# References

Allport, G. W. (1950). *The individual and his religions: A psychological interpretation*. New York: Macmillan.

Atten, J. D., & Mangis, M. W. (2007). Guest Editors Page. *Journal of Psychology and Christianity, 26(4)*, 291.

American Counseling Association (2005). *ACA Code of Ethics*. Alexandria, VA: Author.

APA (American Psychiatric Association) (2000). *Diagnostic and statistical manual of mental disorders*. Arlington, VA: Author.

Belaire, C., Young, J. S., & Elder, A. (2005). Inclusion of religious behaviors and attitudes in counseling: Expectations of conservative Christians. *Counseling and Values, 49*, 82–94.

Bernard, J. M., & Goodyear, R. K. (2004). *Fundamentals of Clinical Supervision* (3rd ed.). Boston: Allyn & Bacon.

Bishop, D. R., Avila-Juarbe, E., & Thumme, B. (2003). Recognizing spirituality as an important factor in counselor supervision. *Counseling and Values, 48*, 34–46.

Briggs, M. K., & Rayle, A. D. (2005). Incorporating spirituality into core counseling courses: Ideas for classroom application. *Counseling and Values, 50*, 63–75.

Burke, M. T., Hackney, H., Hudson, P., Miranti, J., Watts, G. A., & Epp, L. (1999). Spirituality, religion, and CACREP curriculum standards. *Journal of Counseling and Development, 77*, 251–257.

Cashwell, C. S. (2005). Spirituality and wellness. In J. E. Myers and T. Sweeney (Eds.), *Wellness in Counseling*. Alexandria, VA: American Counseling Association.

Cashwell, C. S. (2009). Spirituality and religion: Unity in diversity. In D. Hays and B. T. Erford (Eds.), *Developing multicultural counseling competency: A systems approach*. Upper Saddle River, NJ: Pearson.

Cashwell, C. S., & Young, J. S. (2004). Spirituality in counselor training: A content analysis of syllabi from introductory spirituality courses. *Counseling and Values, 48*, 96–109.

Cashwell, C. S., & Young, J. S. (Eds.) (2005). *Integrating spirituality and religion into counseling: A guide to competent practice*. Alexandria, VA: American Counseling Association.

CACREP (Council for Accreditation of Counseling and Related Educational Programs) (2001). *2001 Standards*. Alexandria, VA: Author.

CACREP (Council for Accreditation of Counseling and Related Educational Programs) (2009). *2009 Standards*. Alexandria, VA: Author.

Faiver, C. M., O'Brien, E. M., & Mcnally, C. J. (1998). "The friendly clergy": Characteristics and referral. *Counseling and Values, 42*, 217–221.

Fowler, J. W. (1981). *Stages of faith*. New York: Harper Collins.

Fowler, J. W. (1991). Stages of faith consciousness. *New Directions for Child Development, 52*, 27–45.

Frame, M. W. (2002). *Integrating religion and spirituality into counseling: A comprehensive approach*. Pacific Grove, CA: Brooks/Cole.

Fukuyama, M. A., & Sevig, T. D. (1999). *Integrating spirituality into multicultural counseling*. Thousand Oaks, CA: Sage.

Fukuyama, M. A., Siahpoush, F., & Sevig, T. D. (2005). Religion and spirituality in a cultural context. In C. S. Cashwell and J. S. Young (Eds.). *Integrating spirituality and religion into counseling: A guide to competent practice* (pp. 123–142). Alexandria, VA: American Counseling Association.

Gendlin, E. (1982). *Focusing.* New York: Bantam.

Genia, V. (1995). *Counseling and psychotherapy of religious clients: A developmental approach.* Westport, CT: Praeger.

Harper, M. C., & Gill, C. S. (2005). Assessing the client's spiritual domain. In C. S. Cashwell and J. S. Young (Eds.). *Integrating spirituality and religion into counseling: A guide to competent practice* (pp. 31–62): Alexandria, VA: American Counseling Association.

Hinterkopf, E. (1998). Integrating spirituality in counseling: A manual for using the experiential focusing method. Alexandria, VA: American Counseling Association.

Ingersoll, R. E. (1997). Teaching a course on counseling and spirituality. *Counselor Education and Supervision, 36,* 224–232.

Kelly, E. W. (1994). The role of religion and spirituality in counselor education: A national survey. *Counselor Education and Supervision, 33,* 227–237.

Kelly, E. (1995). *Spirituality and religion in counseling and psychotherapy: Diversity in theory and practice.* Alexandria, VA: American Counseling Association.

Kurtz, E., & Ketcham, K. (1993). *The spirituality of imperfection: Storytelling and the search for meaning.* New York: Bantam.

Largest Religious Groups in the United States of America (n.d.). Retrieved April 9, 2007, from http://www.adherents.com/rel_USA.html#religions

Miller, G. (1999). The development of the spiritual focus in counseling and counselor education. *Journal of Counseling and Development, 77,* 498–501.

Miller, G. (2002). *Incorporating spirituality in counseling and psychotherapy: Theory and technique.* Hoboken, NJ: Wiley.

Myers, J. E., & Sweeney, T. J. (2005). *Counseling for wellness: Theory, research, and practice.* Alexandria, VA: American Counseling Association.

Pate, R. H., & Bondi, A. M. (1992). Religious beliefs and practice: An integral aspect of multicultural awareness. *Counselor Education and Supervision, 32,* 108–115.

Polanski, P. (2003). Spirituality in supervision. *Counseling and Values, 47,* 131–141.

Princeton Religion Research Center (2000). Americans remain very religious, but not necessarily in conventional ways. *Emerging Trends, 22*(1), 2–3.

Washburn, M. (2003). Transpersonal dialogue: A new direction. *Journal of Transpersonal Psychology, 35,* 1–19.

Worthington, E. L. (1989). Religious faith across the life span: Implications for counseling and research. *The Counseling Psychologist, 17,* 555–612.

Young, J. S., Cashwell, C. S., & Wiggins-Frame, M. (2002). Spiritual and religious competencies: A national survey of CACREP accredited programs. *Counseling and Values, 47,* 22–33.

Young, J. S., Cashwell, C. S., & Wiggins-Frame, M. (2007). Spirituality and counselor competence: A national survey of ACA members. *Journal of Counseling and Development, 85,* 47–52.

CHAPTER **8**

# The Transtheoretical Model of Change in Clinical Supervision

JOHN R. CULBRETH and CHARLES F. GRESSARD

We start as new counselors, ready to help all those individuals and families that come into our office. We are trained, supervised, graduated, and ready to go. However, the beginning of our counseling careers are often not so easy during those first steps. Take, for example, a new counselor who has been working out of a cognitive behavioral framework since graduate school. This framework will probably work with many clients, but, chances are, the counselor will begin seeing the limitation of this framework when confronted with other types of clients. Seeing this limitation, the counselor may continue trying to assimilate all of his or her clients into the cognitive developmental framework, or, after experiencing a feeling of disequilibrium after failing in this effort, may have to accommodate and expand his or her skill repertoire as well as perception that all clients can be effectively helped from a cognitive behavioral framework. Now this counselor has come to a significant point in his or her professional development. He or she can hold fast with what he or she believes about the adopted theoretical orientation, or consider moving into uncharted theoretical territory that may appear dangerous and confusing. After finally gaining some level of confidence and settling in to his or her work, this new counselor is being challenged with moving in a different direction that is unknown. One way to take care of this is to staff the situation with the supervisor. Surely, he or she will be able to provide guidance and direction on this issue.

As practicing counselors, we tend to use the skill sets we have and try to work with client issues within these skill sets until we realize that the skill set we possess may be inadequate to many of the client issues that we are encountering. When we experience the discomfort of the disequilibrium that goes along with that experience, we then accommodate and begin learning new skill sets. One of the primary vehicles for this accommodation is through clinical supervision. Thus, it is the clinical supervisor's function to promote the concept of on-going change in supervisees. Similar to what we often tell our clients, change represents growth.

Whether supervisors are looking at an increase in skill levels, counselor development, the ability it develops in counseling relationships, or cognitive development, what seems consistent is that counselors need to change in some way in order to increase their efficacy. This seems most evident when looking at developmental stage models, in learning to build relationships, increasing cognitive complexity, learning new skills. Most supervisors and counselor educators can relate stories about how their supervisees needed to make a cognitive shift, or change their thinking, before they could really understand or apply the skills they were working on. No matter what the goal of supervision, it is important that supervisors be able to see that success in supervision can almost always be defined by the extent to which the supervisee makes changes in his or her behaviors.

So what do we know about how humans change? There are several basic models that can help us understand how change occurs and how we can facilitate that process. One of the most obvious places to look for models of change is the realm of human development theories. For example, one of the concepts that can be applied to the process of counselor development, particularly skill development, is Piaget's (1955) processes of assimilation and accommodation. Although Piaget applied his concept to childhood, they can be applied to adult learners as well. In Piaget's model, we develop schemas or constructs of how to perceive the world, and as long as the schemas construct our perception of the world in a way that allows us to understand the world, function effectively, and get our needs met, there is little need for us to change the schemas. And, as long as we maintain our schemas or constructs, we assimilate information from our environment into our schemas. In other words there is no need to change how we view the world. If, however, we find that our schemas are not working well for us, and there is information coming in that is incongruent with the schemas, we face a state of disequilibrium that may force us to change our schemas or, in Piaget's terms, accommodate to what our environment is requiring of us. Note that our cognitive process is such that we probably aren't going to change our schemas or constructs unless the environment or circumstances require it. According to Piaget, we change schemas when we need to. So, from the perspective of Piaget's concepts of assimilation, accommodation, and disequilibrium, it is not difficult to see the process of counselor skill development as a change process that fits well with the transtheoretical model of change.

As is evident in the above example, it is important to understand that human growth and development is a change *process,* and that counselor growth and development can easily be conceptualized in the same way. It follows, then, that if counselor development is in fact a process of making changes, then the transtheoretical model of change (Prochaska, DiClemente, & Norcross, 1992; Prochaska & Norcross, 2001) is probably an important tool for understanding how supervision can be used to help counselors become more effective practitioners and how. In this chapter we will review the original transtheoretical model of change, provide an overview of counselor supervision using the discrimination model (J. Bernard, 1997) and the integrated development model (Stoltenberg, McNeill, & Delworth, 1998), and then apply the transtheoretical model to the clinical supervision environment.

## The Transtheoretical Model

Contrary to the simplified view of this model, that there is a simple, 5 stage process of change that individuals go through in therapy, there are, in fact, three overriding constructs that define the transtheoretical perspective of change in individuals according to Prochaska and Norcross (2003). In an effort to examine commonalities across psychological theories, Prochaska and DiClemente determined that there was a common set of *processes* that people use as they change, either on their own or with the help of a therapist. Also, these change processes occur within a set of change *stages*, or steps, toward change or elimination of unwanted behaviors. Finally, working through stages and processes of change is effective in managing single problems, however, Prochaska and DiClemente proposed that there are different *levels* of change that an individual can address. In other words, each level of change speaks to the depth of change in the person that can be made. Each of these constructs will be briefly discussed as a background for adapting this model to the clinical supervision environment.

### Change Processes

To begin discussing the change process, Prochaska et al. (1992) developed a concise grouping of five primary change processes. Each of these processes involves both an individual experiential level of change and an environmental level of change. Joseph, Breslin, and Skinner (1999) provide an excellent overview of the transtheoretical model components, which we will use as the basis of our discussion of the change processes.

Joseph, Breslin, and Skinner describe *consciousness raising* as an effort to increase a client's awareness of an issue, and has been a fundamental tenet of change throughout the history of therapeutic intervention. Freud referred to this as making the unconscious conscious. Feedback is an experiential, or internal, form of consciousness raising that originates from the individual's own behavior or experience. Education, on the other hand, is a form of consciousness raising that comes from a source external to the client. Whether internally or externally generated, consciousness raising is an effort to help the client "see" information that may result in a change in his or her behaviors, affect, or interrelationship patterns (Joseph et al., 1999).

As a process of change, *catharsis*, typically takes the form of some sort of corrective emotional experience. In essence, this is the purging of negative emotional states through an intense emotional reaction. Often these emotional reactions have been contained or bottled up and not allowed to surface. These perceived negative feelings seek some form of release, often through alternative means such as somatic symptoms, inappropriate or unhealthy relationship patterns, or other negative and unfulfilling behaviors or feelings. Once clients experience the release of the original emotional states, these negative by-products tend to dissipate. A second aspect of catharsis comes from an interaction in the environment, called dramatic relief. When clients have some type of experience where they witness dramatic recreations of events that may be similar to their own lives, this can result in an emotional catharsis. Many times this occurrence is not a planned event, but can used in a therapeutic capacity by clients and therapists (Joseph et al., 1999).

*Choice*, or free will, is another significant aspect of the change process. When clients become more aware of the choices that they have available, they make choices based on all the information provided or acquired, and they understand and accept the anxiety associated with the responsibility of choosing, then this is referred to as self-liberation. Self-liberation is the experiential form of choosing. Social liberation is when more alternatives become available to clients as a result of changes in the external world. These options are often the result of social changes, or adjustments by society, and usually come about through the work of social justice advocates (Joseph et al., 1999).

Two forms of *conditional stimuli* can be involved in the change process. The first, an experiential form, is called counterconditioning. Counterconditioning is when clients modify or change the way that they respond to stimuli in the environment. The environmental, or external, form of managing stimuli is called stimulus control. This is where clients change or modify the environment to reduce the likelihood of the stimulus occurring, thus reducing the occurrence of negative responses to the stimuli (Joseph et al., 1999).

On the opposite side of conditioning is *contingency control*, or managing the consequences of behaviors. Behaviors, emotions, and cognitions are impacted by the consequences that they produce. From an experiential perspective, changing how clients respond to consequences is called re-evaluation. Promoting this behavior provides clients with greater feelings of self-efficacy when they realize that they are no longer governed by unwarranted negative feeling states such as guilt, shame, and inadequacy. When clients change the environmental sources of consequences, they are practicing contingency management. Again, this behavior also promotes client self-efficacy (Joseph et al., 1999).

*Stages of Change*

In an effort to better understand the processes of change, that is, how clients utilize these processes in therapy, five stages to the change process have been developed (Prochaska et al., 1992; Prochaska & Norcross, 2001). Each stage represents a point along a continuum of therapeutic movement for clients. One of the main advantages of this stage model has been an adjustment to how clinicians view client denial and resistance.

When considering clients through this lens of change, denial and resistance are viewed as normal behavior that is expected at certain points, especially the first stage, *precontemplation* (Connors, Donovan, & DiClemente, 2001). This stage is characterized by the client's lack of awareness that there is a problem that needs to be changed. Many clients present for treatment at this stage as a result of pressure for significant family members or friends. Precontemplation clients are often trying to appease these individuals and their concerns. Many times these clients are defensive, resistant to suggestions that their chemical use creates problems in their lives, passive in treatment, and often avoiding changes in behavior.

Once clients begin to consider changing their behavior, they are considered to be in the *contemplation stage* (Connors et al., 2001). This stage marks a significant shift in the thought process of clients. They have begun to honestly examine their usage and are considering making changes. These clients have begun a process of examining the pluses and minuses of their continued use versus discontinuing their use behavior. They may be distressed, trying to understand their behavior, and making attempts to gain control of their behavior. There also may have been unsuccessful attempts to control their use behavior in the past. Different from clients in precontemplation, these clients have the ability to see the possibility of their lives without chemical use. They may not know how to achieve this yet, but it is a possibility in their worldview.

Following the contemplation stage is the *preparation stage* (Connors et al., 2001). This stage is characterized by a commitment to the change process. These clients have learned important lessons from earlier attempts to change their behavior. These clients also have much less ambiguity about making this significant change. They are typically able to see the outcome they desire, understand that they are capable of achieving their goals, and begin to feel comfortable that they can learn additional skills if necessary. Indicative of their attitudinal change, these clients are engaged in the change process and have a strong intent to follow through on their commitment to change. Preparation stage clients also tend to have more environmental and self reevaluation behaviors, and more self-liberation, counterconditioning, and reinforcement management thoughts and attitudes.

The *action stage* begins when clients overtly change their behaviors and their environment in order to address their chosen issues (Connors et al., 2001). This stage is a behavioral manifestation of their commitment to the change process. Clients at this stage may be excited, nervous, and may experience a wide range of emotions dependent upon their successes and their failures in changing. Regardless of outcome, it is important that the client remain focused on moving forward and not fall back into absolute thinking patterns and consider one setback a reason for discontinuing change. Action stage clients are also more willing to follow suggestions from clinicians, including developing strategies and creating activities that support their change efforts. A significant risk at this stage is the possibility of clients determining that they are finished with treatment and ready to move on. Typically, this decision is premature and clients should be dissuaded from this action. Action stage clients are still too new to their changed behaviors and need a longer period of time to move into the next stage.

After a period of time in the action stage, clients will begin to consider themselves in a *maintenance* phase or stage (Connors et al., 2001). This stage is a result of successful efforts to change, and is characterized by clients working to sustain these changes and adapt strategies for new situations and events in their lives as they move forward. A significant focus during this stage is anxiety concerning relapse or slipping back to old behaviors. There may be anxiety associated with various life situations, people, and environments that are cause for concern and increase the risk of relapse. Clients in the maintenance stage will continue to experience temptations to revert to their old behaviors; however, the frequency of these will decrease. Overall, this stage is marked by the clients' efforts to continue doing what works, identifying risks and threats to their changes, and working toward becoming comfortable with new behaviors.

## Levels of Change

The aforementioned processes and stages of change work on problems at five different levels of human functioning (Joseph et al., 1999). The first, and most common level of change is that of symptom relief or situational problems. This level is usually focused on a single, clearly defined problem. The second level of change addresses maladaptive cognitions that may create or exacerbate symptoms or situational issues. Current interpersonal problems, the third level of change, is an examination of clients' interactions with others in their environment. This type of change takes a more systemic view, similar to the fourth level of change, which focuses on family systems conflicts. The final level of change is intrapersonal conflicts or working on change within the individual.

These five levels of change are not considered separate from each other. There are often strong connections between the levels in clients, with changes made at one level resulting in changes at other levels. Also, these levels represent a hierarchy of change depth, which may translate to longer periods of time needed to successfully make the change based on the level of change needed, as well as signifying the possibility of greater resistance with deeper levels of change (Joseph et al., 1999).

*Supervision as a Change Process*   Examining the transtheoretical model of change brings up the question as to what we are looking to accomplish in supervision. In order to apply the transtheoretical model to supervision, it is helpful if we take a look at supervision as a change process. In order to accomplish this task we need to first examine how we define supervision. One of the most popular definitions is provided by Bernard and Goodyear (2004), who define supervision as:

> An intervention provided by a more senior member of a profession to more junior member or members of that same profession. This relationship is evaluative, extends over time, and has the simultaneous purposes of enhancing the professional functioning of the more junior person(s), monitoring the quality of professional services offered to the client, she, he, or they see, and serving as a gatekeeper of those who are to enter the particular profession. (p. 8)

We can see in this definition that the goal of supervision is to enhance professional functioning, monitor service delivery, and perform professional gatekeeping. In order to accomplish these tasks it is implied in this definition that the supervisee must change in order grow professionally, that the supervisee must make changes if the quality of professional services offered to the client is insufficient, and that the supervisee must change or leave the profession if the supervisor does not feel that the supervisee is able to meet the personal and/or professional standards of the gatekeeping supervisor. For all of these goals, it is easy to understand, then, that both the supervisee and the supervisor must be able to work with the process of change. From another point of view, it could be said that there would be no point of even engaging in supervision if either or both of the participants was not committed to engaging in a change process. From this perspective, then, the process of supervision is equivalent to a process of change.

In order to take a look at how the practice of supervision is consistent with a process of change, we can take a look at two prominent supervision models and how the process of change is implied in these models. By taking a look at how important the process of change is to these models, we can begin to see the applicability of the transtheoretical model to supervision, and we will also set the stage for integrating the concepts from these models into a transtheoretical Model of supervision.

There are several models of supervision that have implied the view of supervision as a change process. The most obvious one is Stoltenberg, McNeill, and Delworth's (1998) integrated development model (IDM). This well known model of supervision and counselor development includes three levels: Level 1 is the beginning level in which counselors are anxious and self conscious, dependent on the supervisor, unsure of their skills, and are focused on finding the right answer for the issues they face as a counselor. Level II counselors fluctuate between the dependence of the Level I counseling and a new-found autonomy; they may get discouraged by their inability to have answers for all their clients, and they can express their desire for autonomy by being rebellious with their supervisor. Level II counselors are often described as being in the adolescence of their professional development. Level III counselors are more confident in their abilities, are more flexible in their counseling approaches, are more mature and consistent in their motivation and their ability to focus on the client rather than themselves, and engage in more collaborative and collegial type of supervision. The transtheoretical model can easily be applied to the IDM by viewing the movement from one level to another as a process in which counselors progress through the stages of change in order to move to the next level. Although the process is probably not quite that simple, it is easy to conceptualize how stages of change can fit within one of the more popular supervision models.

The other model is Bernard's (1997) discrimination model. Although Bernard does not use developmental stages to define supervision as a process of change, she outlines three counseling skill areas in which growth takes place; (interventions skills, conceptualization skills, and personalization skills) and defines three roles (teacher, role, and counselor) that supervisors can take to facilitate growth in the appropriate area and at the appropriate time. From the perspective of this model, if you substitute "change" for "growth," you can see that this model can match well with the transtheoretical model. By suggesting that supervisors need to make choices about what role is the most appropriate for counselor growth in a certain area at a certain time, the model implies that a change process is taking place. For example, Bernard's division of roles can be seen as similar in concept to the change processes in the transtheoretical model. Whereas consciousness raising, catharsis, choice, conditional stimuli, and contingency control are important processes for making changes, Bernard's roles can be seen as ways to help these changes occur. Teaching can be seen as perhaps the most appropriate role for facilitating conditional stimuli, and contingency control and the counseling role as the most appropriate for stimulating consciousness-raising and catharsis. Both of these models can be used to help us understand how the transtheoretical model can be applied to the supervision process. In the transtheoretical model described below, we will use both the discrimination model and the IDM to explore how supervisors can apply different supervisor roles to facilitate counselor movement in the stages of change and how counselors' developmental level can affect how they react to supervision at the different stages.

*Transtheoretical Model of Clinical Supervision*    In the following section we will describe how the transtheoretical model can be applied to the change process that occurs in supervision. We will use the stages as the primary template for discussion, integrating aspects of the change processes. We will finish with a discussion of how the levels of change apply to supervisees.

*The Precontemplation Supervisee*    Numerous aspects of this early stage appear similar to characteristics of beginning supervisees, either at the practicum or internship level of training. However, the supervisor viewing his or her work through this transtheoretical lens should not limit this stage to new professionals. Many of these characteristics could also describe a supervisee that is struggling with some level of resistance to supervision, or change, or a supervisee that has been working in the field for many years while not having experienced formalized training in counseling.

The precontemplation stage supervisee may often not realize that there is an issue or problem that needs to be addressed in his or her clinical work. This lack of awareness can result in surprise, or even shock, when the supervisor attempts to address the issue. At this point, the supervisee may respond with the belief that there is not any need to consider doing anything different. Several possible outcomes to this awareness-raising effort by the supervisor may be counselor resistance to changing his or her practice, resistance to trying new skills, resistance to utilizing different approaches based on differences in client problems, or resistance to accommodating variability in client type based on diversity (i.e., the one-size-fits-all approach). From an interaction perspective, the supervisee may become more defensive in posture to the supervisor, which may result in avoiding supervision process discussions. The counselor might generalize this defensive posture to an overall lack of commitment to supervision. Supervision can become viewed as merely an obligation to "endure" as he or she works with clients.

At this stage it is important for the supervisor to create doubt in the counselor's self-assuredness about his or her skills and abilities while maintaining a supportive and open atmosphere for discussion. In preparation for this, understanding some of the possible reactions due to a precontemplation view from the supervisee will facilitate the supervisor's attempt to bring these issues into the discussion. In addition, understanding the dynamics of the precontemplation stage allows the supervisor to prepare more effective awareness and intervention strategies based on specific supervisee personality characteristics. It is also important for the supervisor to review past client outcomes with the supervisee to challenge his or her belief system that successful change is assumed and occurs simply through the clinical effort put forth. Or, conversely, the supervisor may also challenge the supervisee's belief that poor client outcome was merely a function of a lack of readiness to change, or denial, in the client.

From the perspective of Bernard's discrimination model (J. Bernard, 1997), the teaching and counselor role may be more effective at this stage for supervisors than the consultant role. The consultant role works best when the supervisor and the supervisee are in agreement on the goals and process of supervision. This is clearly not the case in the precontemplative stage. The teaching role, in which supervision methods are more instructive, could help precontemplative counselors see that they were using approaches that were not as effective as other approaches. The counselor's inability at this stage to perceive that they were doing something wrong, however, might undermine the teaching role. A combination of the teaching role with a strong emphasis on the counselor role might be the best approach for the precontemplative counselor. In this stage they have to be helped to see that their approaches are not as effective as they could be and to begin to see that a change in approach may be more useful. Because resistance is often so strong in this stage, the counselor role would be consistent with helping the counselors explore, in a supportive environment, how they might not be as effective as they should be and that they might consider some changes in their work as a counselor.

Using the IDM (Stoltenberg et al., 1998), the supervisor would probably want to take the counselor's developmental level into consideration before determining which approach to take with supervisees who are in a precontemplative stage. Counselors in Level 1 will often be anxious and concerned about their performance. They are also looking for "right answers" when it comes to developing their skills. At this level, they are probably open to a more direct approach to raising their consciousness about one of their deficits. Level 2 counselors will probably be more resistant to identifying issues they need to examine. The defensiveness and avoidance mentioned above would be more typical reactions for counselors in this level and would require a more careful and perhaps less direct approach than dealing with counselors in Level I. Supervisees in Level 3 will be more inclined to be open about the need for improvement in their clinical skills and, having a higher level of confidence in their ability to work as counselors, will be able to take in observations from supervisors in a less defensive and more open manner. The number of issues about which they are in the precontemplative stage will be fewer than with Level 1 and Level 2 counselors, so there will probably be less need for thinking about addressing the precontemplative stage when working with Level 3 counselors.

*The Contemplation Supervisee*   When supervisees move into the contemplation stage, they now view their work from a different perspective, not assuming that what they have done is automatically successful. They become more aware that some of their past work may not have helped their clients. However, there is still a significant amount of ambivalence in supervisees toward changing how they work or view their clients. At times, the supervisor may witness a level of concern or distress that results in supervisees trying to exert more control over their clients. This behavior is in direct response to the awareness that clients may not be changing. Rather than accepting a limitation on their abilities, some supervisees may redouble their control efforts. If allowed to progress in this vein too long, the supervisor may have to intervene strongly to protect the client.

As supervisees work through this new awareness of their clinical limitations, it is important for the supervisor to be a source of information and guidance for supervisees. Supervisees will be considering new ways of being as a counselor, and the supervisor can help in clarifying their decision making processes. As this balancing thought process occurs, the supervisor should work to foster professional self-efficacy in supervisees and their decision making capacity. Without doing the work for supervisees, the supervisor can provide guidance to supervisees and facilitate their information gathering and screening as they work toward a decision. The supervisor may have to increase statements of reassurance as supervisees begin to try new approaches and techniques. The creation of an accepting climate for experimentation and the "trying them on for fit" of new skills will go a long way in strengthening the supervisory relationship, as well as creating a strong sense of support for supervisees. Discussing and processing feelings of insecurity, fear, and uncertainty will result in a greater willingness to discuss other more difficult topics, both now and in the future.

From the perspective of Bernard's discrimination model, the teacher role is probably going to be the dominant supervision role for counselors who are working through issues in the contemplative stage. Counselors in this stage will also need a healthy dose of the counselor role to deal with their feelings of insecurity, fear, and uncertainty, and they now need a little more of the consultant role for their experimentation with new skills. The

IDM Level will probably determine how the supervisor combines these roles. Counselors at Level 1 will typically need more of the teacher role; counselors at Level 2 will probably need more of the counselor role and counselors at Level III will probably need more consultant role.

*The Preparation Supervisee*   As supervisees move into the preparation stage, they begin to consider, or are already enacting, some form of change in their counseling stance, view of diversity issues in counseling, or their clinical intervention behaviors. Parallel to this move is an expansion of their client worldview awareness, understanding that clients come to the therapeutic process from a myriad of backgrounds, and bringing a similar number of personal experiences that directly impact the counseling process. The result is a greater awareness of the complexity of the helping process which is contrary to the original, simplified view of helping that was held before. Often, this earlier simplified view is merely a way to manage the greater degree of stress and anxiety associated with the responsibility of this new professional role. However, this coping skill is no longer valid due to the work of the supervisor, resulting in the need for change. Supervisees now begin to make efforts at changing their own understanding of clients, in all of their complexities. As this begins to happen, supervisees learn that they are not in control of the counseling process, and that their clients' problems are not theirs to "fix." And, as this awareness takes hold, supervisees will realize a reduction in ambiguity and feelings of threat from their professional change.

It is important for supervisors working with a preparation stage supervisee to help direct the counselor's focus and plan for change. Supervisors must continue to empower supervisee change with continuing information, skills training, and focus on counselor awareness. Supervisors should make efforts to support the sense of exploration and experimentation that can develop during this stage. Remembering the earlier definition of supervision put forth by Bernard and Goodyear (2004) that included "monitoring the quality of professional services offered to the client," this stage also calls for the supervisor to increase vigilance toward client care. For some supervisees, this point in the change process may be quite tumultuous, while for others it is rather easy. Observing and understanding individual supervisees and how each adjusts to change will help the supervisor manage this period well.

In terms of supervisor role in the discrimination model, it should be fairly clear that, as the counselor commitment to the change process increases, and barring unforeseen difficulties in the supervisee, there is probably less need at this stage for the counseling role with a continued emphasis on the teaching and consultant roles. Both of these roles will support the counselor's desire to explore and experiment. From the developmental perspective, a Level 1 counselor will benefit from the increase in emphasis on these two roles, but they may need more of the counselor role from the supervisor because they may experience an increase in anxiety as they anticipate the implementation of new approaches. They will need a lot of reassurance at this point which, if not provided, could lead to a regression to the defensiveness of the precontemplative stage. Level 2 counselors will probably also experience some anxiety in the preparation stage, but will mostly need some teaching and consultation. Level 3 counselors will need mostly the consultant role from the supervisor, which is the modal role for counselors at this level of professional development.

*The Action Supervisee*    Once a supervisee moves into the action stage, he or she begins to enact the changes in clinical work that have been discussed in supervision. These actions range from efforts to employ new techniques or strategies, adoption of a new stance toward client diversity, to expansion of client/other awareness. The supervisee becomes very motivated to make these changes, often securing outside information, such as research findings and other professional literature, to support these new changes in skills, beliefs, and professional attitudes. The supervision process has now become a much more integral part of the supervisee's clinical life; a necessary component of the change process. Supervisees will try new suggestions from the supervisor, as well as use time in supervision to develop their own approaches and techniques. It is as if the supervisee is now trying on a new clinical wardrobe to check for a good fit, to see if these new ways of thinking and working fit well for him or her.

As discussed in earlier stages, it is even more essential at the action stage that the supervisor supports and empowers the supervisee as new strategies are employed. At this stage, the supervisee has committed to the change process and is moving forward. Reservation or reluctance to change on the part of the supervisor may send a contradictory message to the supervisee, suggesting that change may not be desired. While it is important for the supervisor to always be aware of quality service delivery to the client, it is also important to not quash this new-found clinical and professional enthusiasm.

In addition to monitoring services as the supervisee implements these new interventions or belief systems, it is also important that the supervisor foster an atmosphere of objective outcome evaluation of the counseling process. Making changes simply to change is not a viable clinical approach. Changes should be based in large part on outcome variables that support the change. The supervisee should be encouraged to develop data collection methods to assess outcome. Sources for this informal evaluation include in-session observations, client reports of change or improvement, and outside verification of client changes from friends and family, if available. This provides the supervisee with motivation to continue the change process, as well as support for keeping a critical view of what is effective and what is not.

The primary discrimination model role at this stage will probably be the consultant role, although Level 1 counselors will still need some of the teacher role to insure that their implementation of their new skills are consistent with what was intended. Counselors at Levels 2 and 3 will primarily need the feedback from the supervisor in a consultant role.

*The Maintenance Supervisee*    Once change has been implemented and the supervisee begins to collect evaluation data, he or she has moved into the maintenance stage. This stage represents an on-going evaluation of the changes that have been enacted. New steps or approaches are developed to foster these changes. Also, supervisees will want to examine those clinical situations that have not improved due to the changes adopted in an effort to determine what outside factors may have impacted their work. It is important to note that this is different from the early stance that lack of change is due to the client "not wanting to get better." Rather, at this point the supervisee is expanding his or her clinical worldview to an understanding that some very good interventions may not work due to some client characteristics, and it is important to know this so further changes or adjustments can be made by the counselor that may better meet the needs of that particular client.

Similar to clients taking two steps forward and one step back, it is important for supervisors to convey to supervisees that change is a fluid and recursive process. Supervisors should monitor supervisees as they go through this trial-and-error period in order to support changes that are made and to help supervisees understand that not all changes will work each and every time. Until supervisees have completely integrated the changes, there will be a tendency to revert to old patterns of working and thinking that are familiar and comfortable, especially when presented with a particularly difficult or new client situation. Supervisors should understand that this regression to old patterns is not a form of resistance, but rather a sliding back to a comfortable position or stance. On-going assessment of successful change, and of challenging client situations or new cases, will allow both supervisor and supervisee to address any "slips" to old behavior or thinking as they arise. This will further support the overall integration of these new changes that have been made to become the natural or default position of the supervisee.

The discrimination model role for supervisors when counselors are at the maintenance stage is mostly of a consultant. This would be true for counselors at all three levels. Because of the possibility of regression, which is probably more likely for Level 1 counselors, supervisors for counselors at this level may take on some parts of the counselor role to provide support and to possibly confront signs of regression.

As was hopefully evident in the discussion of these stages of change, supervisee developmental level is not a clear indication of what stage of change a supervisee may be in. Supervisees at any developmental stage can be in any of the stages of change. A key issue for supervisors to consider is how the counselor development level characteristics may or may not impact how supervisory efforts to promote or affect change in the supervisee will be implemented or received. Precontemplation is not the sole domain of the beginning or early stage counselor. Experienced supervisees may struggle with considering a new approach or technique, or may balk at the idea that they are not as a effective with a new client type, similar to beginning supervisees. Supervisors will need to work through the change stages with these supervisees as well. In fact, it is especially important for supervisors to remember this and not assume that their more experienced supervisees won't go through these stages. The result of this assumption may well produce a conflict in the relationship, with the supervisor having unreasonable expectations of the supervisee, or assuming that the supervisee is merely being resistant. As others have noted, another way to consider client (or in this situation, supervisee) resistance is as an indicator that the supervisor is missing something, making inaccurate assumptions, or moving at a pace that is uncomfortable for the supervisee.

*Supervisee Levels of Change*    A significant portion of the supervision process can be classified as working at a situational or symptom relief level of change. For example, supervisees look to the supervisor for guidance on how to use a specific intervention or counseling technique. At this point, the supervisor provides information from a teacher role, helping supervisees understand not only how to use a technique, but also when to use that technique. It may be that a specific supervisee has not tried a particular approach with a specific client type and does not understand the dynamics of how that technique might work. Or, just as possible, a supervisee is not multiculturally competent with a specific type of client, and does not understand the cultural implications of using a particular technique with that client. The supervisor works with the supervisee to address his or her immediate needs as expressed in supervision, as well as identifying additional specific needs to expand the counselor's skill base.

At times during supervision, the supervisor may begin to hear from the supervisee a belief system or perception that may call for an intervention at a different level. While not necessarily considered a maladaptive cognition, as the second level of change is called (Joseph et al., 1999; Prochaska & Norcross, 2003), this may present as some form of faulty logic, past belief system, or incorrect perception of an issue or a client that may be hindering the supervisees' efforts. A particularly good example of this level of change would be multicultural awareness in the supervisee. All counselors come to their work with their past histories and "baggage," if you will. Similar to counselor training programs' efforts to expand trainees' multicultural awareness, knowledge, and skills, the supervisor will have to address these areas as well. When this happens, the supervisor is working on change in supervisee cognitions, beliefs, feelings, and values. The supervisor will help the supervisee view the situation, whatever it may be, from a different perspective, or with a different lens color. At times, this may be a difficult period, similar to the turmoil that can occur as an individual moves through the early stages of multicultural development. It may also be something that the supervisor allows to change at a slower pace, depending on the level of difficulty in adjusting that the supervisee is having. It is important for the supervisor to remember the stages of change that a supervisee goes through during this process and to allow those stages to occur as a natural function of counselor development. Additionally, the supervisor will want to easily move into the counselor role to help the supervisee explore this change process.

There will be supervision situations in which the supervisee is struggling with how he or she is interacting with the client, or, in other words, an interpersonal conflict. Maybe it is a challenging mismatch of client and counselor characteristics, or maybe there are some counter transference issues involved. Regardless, the implications for this situation are significant, with a deterioration in the counseling relationship that may result in the client ending treatment. It is important for the supervisor to address supervisee issues at this level in part as a function of monitoring client care. Helping the supervisee understand how to more positively manage the counseling relationship, using any number of techniques (i.e., immediacy, genuineness), is an important aspect of supervision. The supervisor needs to keep in mind that there may be some level of resistance to this intervention as he or she is made aware of interpersonal conflict. This resistance should be viewed as an indication of the supervisee working at a precontemplation stage with this new information. Hopefully, as the supervisor continues to discuss this issue, the supervisee will become more open to the intervention and begin to move through the change stages to address this problem.

Another level of change that may occur in supervision is systemic learning. Often supervisees, especially those new to the profession, are challenged with looking at client issues beyond the walls of the counseling session. When working with individual clients, it is easy to forget that they are involved in a number of larger systems outside the counseling relationship. Supervisors should be prepared to remind supervisees of this and to help them understand the systemic nature of families, work environments, social networks, and society as a whole. Again, using a multicultural example, supervisees may need to help a client not just adjust and make individual changes, but they may also have to help clients decide about whether to be involved in changes in their families and communities. And, it is very important to remember that work at this level has a number of consequences, both good and bad. A change may occur that is positive, but there may unintended outcomes as well. The supervisor has to remain focused on what is the best outcome for the client, helping supervisees balance between promoting larger scale change versus addressing the needs of the client. A counter transference issue may develop and the supervisor has to be able to clearly see and address this in supervision. Or, conversely, a larger scale change may need to occur and the supervisee may not be able to see it or be willing to address it, in which case the supervisor may need to promote systemic action on the part of the supervisee.

And finally, there is the level of change that involves significant intrapersonal change in supervisees. As we work with clients, we are the tool of client change. It is through the working alliance between counselor and client that clients are able to make progress toward their goals of change. Thus, it stands to reason that this client change process might result in knowledge and awareness that cause intrapersonal change in supervisees. Or, issues in the supervision process might begin to touch deeper, more personal areas of counselors' lives. When making changes at other levels in their professional lives, supervisees may begin to develop a level of dissonance in their personal perceptions, beliefs, and attitudes, resulting in internal stress or dissonance. When this begins to happen, supervisors have to be alert that they do not move into conducting therapy with the supervisee. While this awareness may be very positive, and at times difficult, for the supervisee, a clear boundary needs to be maintained in order to preserve the professional nature of the supervisory relationship. Supervisors can certainly acknowledge these gains and changes in supervisees, and help supervisees integrate new stances or belief systems into their work. However, the clear delineation between supervision and counseling must be maintained. If at any point the supervisor feels that the supervision work is moving, or has moved, into counseling, then a referral must be made for the counselor to work on these issues with a personal counselor of their own. This is not to say that the topic cannot be a part of the supervision conversation. We are merely suggesting that supervisors keep a strong professional boundary in the supervisory relationship, allowing all parties to remain as objective and professional as possible.

## Conclusion

This chapter presented the transtheoretical model of change as a way of viewing the process of counselor growth in the supervision process. This perspective fits well with current models of supervision and provides supervisors with a new perspective on the supervision process. This perspective can also help supervisors work more effectively with the resistance that inevitably accompanies the personal and professional development of counselors. Lastly, viewing supervision as a change process allows supervisors to more effectively apply the variety of current supervision methods and roles.

## References

Bernard, J. (1997). The discrimination model. In C. E. Watkins (Ed.), *Handbook of psychotherapy supervision* (pp. 310–327). New York: John Wiley & Sons.

Bernard, J. M., & Goodyear, R. K. (2004). *Fundamentals of clinical supervision* (3rd ed.). Needham Heights, MA: Allyn and Bacon.

Connors, G. J., Donovan, D. M., & DiClemente, C. C. (2001). *Substance abuse treatment and the stages of change: Selecting and planning interventions.* New York: Guilford Press.

Joseph, J., Breslin, C., & Skinner, H. (Eds.). (1999). *Critical perspectives on the Transtheoretical Model and stages of change.* New York: Guilford Press.

Piaget, J. (1955). *The Child's Construction of Reality.* London: Routledge and Kegan Paul.

Prochaska, J. O., DiClemente, C. C., & Norcross, J. C. (1992). In search of how people change: Applications to addictive behaviors. *American Psychologist, 47*(9), 1102–1114.

Prochaska, J. O., & Norcross, J. C. (2001). Stages of change. *Psychotherapy, 38*(4), 443–449.

Prochaska, J. O., & Norcross, J. C. (2003). *Systems of psychotherapy: A transtheoretical analysis* (5th ed.). Pacific Grove, CA: Thompson/Brooks Cole.

Stoltenberg, C. D., McNeill, B., & Delworth, U. (1998). *IDM supervision: An Integrated Developmental Model for supervising counselors and therapists.* San Francisco: Jossey-Bass.

# CHAPTER 9

# Applications of Narrative Therapy in Supervision

DEBBIE CRAWFORD STURM

Throughout the literature related to supervision, and specifically the development of supervisor identity, the notion of embracing intentionality emerges repeatedly (Borders & Brown, 2005; Bernard & Goodyear, 2004; Clarke, 1991). In other words, as supervisors begin to develop their own identity, the selection of theoretical frameworks, models, and techniques becomes a deliberate process, an extension of who that supervisor wants to become and how he or she wants to be perceived in the supervision relationship. It communicates the supervisor's underlying belief about how people relate to their experience, how they grow, and how they change. Supervisors, through their selection of a theoretical framework, are called to examine their beliefs on how supervisees grow and develop professionally, how their identity as counselor and supervisee is formed, and issues of power and agency. They become intentionally invested in developing their identity as supervisors.

Similarly, new therapists, including those in practicum or internship experiences as well as new graduates, weave their way through a process of developing their identities as counselors and as part of a supervisory relationship. And while supervisors play an integral role in their development process, Carlson and Erickson (2001) believe that for new therapists to gain confidence in their abilities they need to experience personal agency in their work and to experience themselves as having an active role in shaping their lives as therapists. These two factors lead to greater self-awareness. And while this is just one of many reflections on counselor identity development, the notions of intentionality and personal agency lay a partial foundation for the exploration in this chapter.

Specifically, this chapter presents a discussion of narrative therapy and its application in supervision. This chapter also introduces a four-step model blending narrative therapy with interpersonal process recall (IPR), enabling supervisors to intentionally guide supervisees through a narrative approach to this specific in-session supervision technique (Cashwell, 2001; Clarke, 1997). It is designed to facilitate creative thinking about the process involved in IPR and how engaging supervisees' narratives about self, their role as counselor, and their experiences and beliefs about helping impact their interaction with their clients and their developing identities as professional counselors. It is offered primarily to begin guiding supervisor intentionality and facilitate counselor identity development.

## About Narrative Therapy

Narrative therapy, a comparatively new phenomenon in counseling, was originally developed in 1989 by Michael White and David Epston, hailing from Australia and New Zealand, respectively, as a form of family therapy (Besley, 2002). A narrative approach to therapy places an emphasis on language and meaning, deriving its roots in cognitive therapy, but with a postmodern blending of existential meaning. Its very nature and intent is to explore the examined and unexamined truths that govern individuals and allow an opportunity to alter the order and importance of those truths in order to construct a different reality (Besley, 2002). Simply put, by examining the whole story of interactions with the people and systems within which a person lives, the individual is then able to reauthor their story into one that leads to better overall health and functioning.

Narrative therapy is also characterized by the value placed on lived experiences. Monk (1996) described the concept of lived experience as one in which events of the past combine with those in the present and run alongside a person's predicted future experience to create that person's story. By looking at the whole of the lived experience, any one of those three domains can experience change, thereby altering the entire narrative. Furthermore, experiences that do not fit within the current narrative are "pruned" by the individual (p. 45). The narrative experience is not only a process of identifying those parts needing pruning, it is also a process of looking at exceptions to the story, or those parts that need to be nurtured.

Additionally, a key component of a narrative approach is the belief that meaning stems from and is created, or cocreated, through dialogue (Richert, 2003). This is not a finite process. The self is both a process of constantly flowing meaning creation and an ever-evolving narrative—a collection of situation-specific vignettes (p. 193) that can be kept, nourished, discounted, or discarded. And, in terms of supervision, the supervisory relationship, whether it be individual or group supervision, serves as the initial lab within which this occurs with the ultimate hope that supervisees will become proficient in asking themselves curiosity-based questions as the interactions continue. Supervisees, through a curious stance, are invited to explore their "preferred professional self-description" (p. 421) and to deconstruct the meaning of their description. Carlson and Erickson (2001) believe a narrative approach to supervision values the personal nature of a new therapist's hopes, motivations, and desires to be a therapist as well as personal nature of self-knowledge, skills, and lived experience. How new therapists incorporate these into the stories of their lives, personally and professionally, shapes their professional identity and confidence in the therapy relationship.

## Benefits of a Narrative Approach to Supervision

A narrative approach to supervision offers a number of benefits including, but certainly not limited to, its approach to power and agency, its emphasis on lived experience and applicability to a wide range of cultural conditions, techniques such as externalizing the problem that allow supervisees to examine areas of weakness in a safe way, and the process of curious questioning, allowing a safe, accepting line of examination. One of the strengths of narrative therapy is that it offers an approach to exploring not only the *self* in therapy, but narrative therapists also place high value on cultural contexts, power, and knowledge (Besley, 2002; Monk, 1996). McLeod (1996) expanded on that thought by adding that narrative therapy's foundation lies in the notion that people live in cultures and thereby construct their identities from their experience of symbols, meanings, and expectations of that culture. People are seen, then, as being "situated amid a constantly changing web of connections and stories" (Speedy, 2000, p. 366).

A narrative approach provides sensitivity to all forms of oppressions expressed in terms of the dominant narratives in society by first acknowledging that what happens in greater society also plays itself out in the therapeutic and supervisory relationship. By remaining curious about reactions and interactions, narrative supervisors are able to frame examination of sensitive cultural issues as a safe, normal, and natural exploration of lived experiences. Additionally, Semmler and Williams (2000) stated that a narrative approach has additional multicultural strengths, in that it provides a curious and optimistic view of clients, or supervisees, and their ability to handle their problems. In adopting a curiosity-based approach, the supervisor may also model a relationship that can be quite impactful for supervisees who are wounded by internalized racism.

Power is a key issue addressed by narrative supervisors, particularly the relationship construct of power and knowledge (Speedy, 2000). Power is viewed as an always present factor that can be positive and productive, not just responsive or negative. Moreover, power is a socio-political-cultural construct that is negotiated daily in people's lives and is an inescapable component of any relationship or system (Besley, 2002). Narrative supervisors negotiate the power differential by assuming, as mentioned previously, a coauthoring or collaborative role based on a curious stance toward supervisees, empowering supervisees as experts and regarding their views as primary. In supervision, the implicit "expert" power in the supervisory relationship lies within the supervisee, as an "expert" of his or her own experience. The supervisor is far from passive; however, just as with a narrative therapist, the supervisor not only listens and questions with an active curiosity, his or her responses help cocreate the story of the supervisee (Speedy, 2000). This curious, nonknowing stance also helps supervisees uncover inconsistencies, assumptions, and contradictions in their stories. Curiosity, according to Perry and Doan (1994) is an attitude of "not knowing much but always … willing to find out" (p. 122). By maintaining a nonknowing attitude with supervisees, a supervisor is able to remain curious (thereby asking more effective questions), to remain nonjudgmental, and to allow supervisees to be more active, authoritative participants in therapy.

White has coined the phrase "the person is not the problem, the problem is the problem" (Monk, 1996, p. 53) referring to the practice of externalization in narrative therapy. Externalization is a process in which a clear separation between the problem and the person occurs. Once a person has been able to separate from the problem, a new alternative to viewing things can emerge. Externalization also deconstructs cultural paradigms and, by separating problems from people, honors sources of strength and resiliency as defined by the person and his or her cultural experience (Semmler & Williams, 2000). Externalizing the problem also allows the supervisor and supervisee to help deconstruct the narrative, inviting the supervisee to coauthor one that is more fulfilling, powerful, and hopeful (Herman, 1998). This process shifts the balance of power in the supervision relationship from supervisor-as-expert to supervisor as a coauthor and supervisee as the expert in his or her own development.

Speedy (2000) described the nature of the counseling profession as a narrative in and of itself, embodying a tradition of "privileging 'expert' knowledge and of ways of 'constructing' individuals' 'selves' and 'society'" (p. 363). Narrative supervisors are more likely to see themselves as part of a consultative team or committee, working alongside supervisees, rather than as a privileged, knowing expert. Supervisors, therefore, utilizing a narrative approach are engaging in a type of consultative or collaborative relationship.

A few studies exist illustrating the parallel thinking and application of narrative therapy and supervision techniques. According to Speedy (2000), using narrative approaches in supervision would shed "a critical light on the stories we tell ourselves about counseling supervision and on the cultural traditions of these 'common-sense' professional practices" (p. 419). Supervisees, through the curious stance of their supervisor, are invited to explore their "preferred professional self-description" (p. 421) and to deconstruct the meaning of their description. Questions such as "What does that express about you?" "Is there a story behind that?" "What is it?" "If there were no brand names in counseling, how would you describe yourself?" can be used by the supervisor to elicit exploration on the part of the supervisee (Speedy, 2000).

Carlson and Erickson (2001) believe a narrative approach to supervision values the personal nature of a new therapist's hopes, motivations, and desires to be a therapist as well as personal nature of self-knowledge, skills and lived experience. How new therapists incorporate these into the stories of their lives personally and professionally shapes their professional identity and confidence in the therapy relationship. Narrative supervisors often embrace metaphors as a technique. Carlson and Erickson (2001) discussed utilizing a "right of passage" metaphor, encouraging the goal of supervision to become a right of passage from novice to veteran. The supervisor works collaboratively with the supervisee to define and navigate that passage. And rather than creating a dependency on "expert knowledge," supervisees evolve to a point where they recognize the special knowledge they have resurrected or generated.

## Supervision Using IPR

Levitt and Rennie (2004) referred to IPR "intention accessing technique" as a way of guiding supervisees through the process of unlocking the factors influencing their actions, motivations, and identities in the counseling relationship. The parallels between a narrative approach to supervision and IPR's practical applications are many. Richert (2003) states the nature of the therapeutic relationship in narrative therapy must be empathic, collaborative (therapist and client as equals), and active (mutual activity). Likewise, IPR encourages supervisors to take an open, accepting, and nonevaluative role through a process of active exploration with supervisees (Borders & Brown, 2005). In both cases, the therapist must be active in asking questions, making reflections, and suggesting exercises that will enhance client awareness. Additionally, narrative therapists seek "creative, curious, persistent questions" (Besley, 2002, p. 128) to learn about meanings in a person's world and socio–political–cultural assumptions. As mentioned previously, this method holds clients, or in this case, supervisees as the expert of their own experience. Bernard and Goodyear (2004) address the same relationship foundation about IPR, stating that individuals are the best authority on their own experience, both with regard to the dynamics and the interpretation. In each case, the supervisor is seen as a facilitator, a collaborator, an inquirer and a coauthor. As with narrative approaches, IPR naturally leads to the "creation of a dialogue" (Gardner & Turner, 2002, p. 459).

The notion of therapist-elicited questioning is somewhat counter-cultural in the field of counseling (Speedy, 2000), yet the questioning aspect of narrative approaches, while sharing similar parallels to IPR, allows for the introduction of questions that are less reflective than in IPR and more curious. Reflecting again on Monk (1996), curiosity-based questioning offers a way to guard against supervisor expertness and challenge supervisees to go deeper into their experience. While this is not a criticism of IPR, utilizing the narrative-based curiosity focus may in fact add an additional safeguard to the balance of power and its evolution in the supervision relationship.

Again, narrative therapy itself does not specifically address the root causes of problems experienced by the individual; however, the concept of silencing or enforced silence (McLeod, 1996) may be worth remembering in the supervisory relationship. Supervisees may feel, as a result of real or perceived power differentials with clients, the organizations with whom they work, academic expectations, that their true voice should not be expressed. Exploring this as a root of some of their concerns or self-described problems is a possibility. As the supervisor creates questions intended to explore issues of power differential or potential silencing, supervisees learn that the supervision environment is a safe place to explore perceived power differentials in the counseling relationship or at their place of employment or clinical placement.

White and Epston (1990) contend that people's problems occur when their life stories do not align with their lived experiences. Likewise, the reflection process in IPR is designed to help new therapists explore confusion, dissonance, or contradictions in their beliefs about their role and identity of counselor, the execution of techniques, their presence in the counseling relationship, and the ambiguity of applying technique and theory to practice. This lived experience is highly valued and paramount to helping supervisees understand their developmental process.

Another aspect of the narrative approach that fits well is the notion that narrative therapists, whose history derives from family therapy, place a therapeutic value on the presence of an audience in therapy. IPR, similarly, utilizes the present supervisor–supervisee interaction as a vehicle by which to view the there-and-then interaction of the supervisee and client, thereby creating an audience effect. By viewing, stopping, and starting audio- and videotapes, the supervisor and supervisee create an audience for the interaction on the tape. This is equally applicable to group supervision and practicum and internship experiences. Perspectives elicited from multiple viewers are highly valued, explored, and integrated through each of these approaches.

According to Botella and Herrero (2000), the answer to the question "Who am I?" shapes a person's identity at any given moment (p. 410); therefore, the on-going conversation, or the process of creating and cocreating an individual's self-narrative, creates his or her identity. Supervision, as with psychotherapy itself, is a collaborative dialogue, an intentional process designed to transform the developing identity of a therapist (Botella & Herrero, 2000). Intentionally creating meaningful, curious, and reflective conversations is key to facilitating this transformation. Biever (1995) discussed facilitating conversations in therapy and offered several recommendations. Pertinent to this discussion on the supervision relationship, his recommendations include maintaining a not-knowing stance in which the person is assumed to be the expert in their own life; working with the person, not the label; and offering commonplace rather than pathological explanations of difficulties.

Reflecting on a narrative approach to supervision and its similarities to IPR, it appears that several factors emerge suggesting that the marriage of the two would provide for a compatible supervisory relationship. First, both aim to explore intentionality of the counselor, supervisee, and supervisor through an active and collaborative dialogue. Both embrace creative, curious, and persistent questions. Neither is significantly focused on identifying the cause of problems, but examines the root of beliefs that may impede the process and seek to change them to create a more effective interaction. Both accommodate and value an audience and utilize all participants and coauthors in the creation of the narrative. And finally, both narrative approaches and IPR techniques emphasize the lived experience of the participants, stressing the here and now but openly talking about the then and there, with eyes always on the future.

## A Suggested Model of Narrative IPR Supervision

The overarching purpose of blending a narrative approach to supervision with the IPR technique is to help supervisees connect with the story of self that has brought them to the field of counseling and authentically blend that story into the developing narrative of their identity as a counselor. Virtually every counselor in training can describe their motivation for becoming a counselor and the journey that brought them into the room with their first client. But understanding how those personal desires and motivations relate to the counseling process and the process of becoming a counselor takes patient, curious, and reflective discourse to understand. And an environment that accepts that each supervisee's story and discourse will follow its own unique course.

Carlson and Erickson (2001) outlined three steps a supervisor can utilize in guiding a supervisee through a curious questioning process designed to honor supervisees' personal stories and integrate them into their professional identity development. As each of those steps are outlined in the following section, some questions constructed by Parry and Doan (1994) are also provided as examples of how to implement these steps in practice. Questions generated by Carlson and Erickson (2001) are included as well as some generated by this author. Again, as we marry a narrative approach to an IPR process, keep in mind these questions have also been selected to fit into the starting-and-stopping audio/video tape format.

The first step in this three-step process is called *privileging the personal desires and motivations of the new therapist* (Parry & Doan, 1994, p. 209). This step is designed to give new therapists an opportunity to share their sincere desires and motivations for entering the field. While using IPR, it allows the new therapist to reflect on how a particular response or interaction aligns with his or her notion as a developing helper. This step is also useful in the relationship-building phase of the supervisor–supervisee interaction. With so many of the questions centering on the story that brought the supervisee to this point, this step can yield great insight into the hopes, desires, and motivations of the supervisee, as well as allow the supervisor an opportunity to model a curious, accepting stance in the questioning process.

Questions that can be posed as part of relationship building help supervisees tap into the hopes, influences, and beliefs about self that brought them to the field of counseling. Supervisors should ask these with a genuine curiosity about the person with whom they are now forming a relationship, modeling the acceptance and genuineness the supervisor intends to be present throughout the supervisory experience. During this phase, inquiry can include:

- What experiences from your life invited you into this field? (Carlson & Erickson, 2001).
- Could you share your sincere desires and hopes for becoming a therapist? (Carlson & Erickson, 2001).
- What have you been told about yourself and your ability to help others with their problems?
- What do you believe about yourself as a helping person?

During the reviewing, starting, and stopping of video and audio tapes, questions will involve how the supervisees' visions or hopes of themselves as therapists align with the experience of therapy and the relationship with the client. Examples include:

- As you think about that interaction with your client, how did your response align with who you want to be as a therapist?
- As you think about that interaction, how does that fit with your vision of yourself as a therapist?
- How does the process we have seen in this tape fit with your desire to help?
- In what ways is your vision of being a helper exemplified or not exemplified in this portion of the tape?
- If your client were here right now, what would you like to tell him or her about your attempt to help at that moment?

The second step in this process is referred to as *privileging personal knowledge* (Parry & Doan, 1994, p. 212). This step is based on the belief that new therapists have come into the field with a set of beliefs about their knowledge and skills for helping others. More specifically and perhaps even more importantly, they come to the field with a set of beliefs about their ability to use that knowledge and skill to actually execute the skills they will learn in order to help people. They have ideas about what has helped them personally in the past—ways in which they have helped others—and, by the time they reach clinical experiences, an idea how they would like to use theories and skills to be a successful helper.

For many supervisees, the desire to help and the eagerness to see the results of their efforts is high. Often their preconceived notions of what helping will look like or their early attempts to utilize their skills can lead them to question their effectiveness as helpers. Helping supervisees value their beliefs and experiences of helping while still exploring their new role as helper is critical to development of a healthy counselor identity. By reflecting on portions of videotapes, the new therapist is encouraged to reflect on the application of their skills, the impressions they present as a helper, their client's response to them as a therapist, and how that aligns with their beliefs, knowledge, and skills. Examples of questions to ask include:

- What does your own experience of being helped tell you about how to help this person?
- In what ways do you think your client is experiencing your helping qualities?
- Imagine climbing into your client's seat. What would you notice about your attempts to help your client at this point? How would you as client describe you as counselor?

- Let's work on externalizing the problem in this interaction. Can you identify the issue here? Put it out there and name it. What are the influences (people, conditions) of this problem for you?
- If your reaction in that moment was a warning that you had lost your curiosity about the client, how would this interaction change?

This second step also provides an opportunity to utilize the narrative technique of *identifying unique outcomes*, both current and historical. According to White and Epston (1990), it takes only one unique outcome to help change the relationship or interaction pattern. It becomes important for the supervisor to catch the supervisee doing something positive, demonstrating a new or changed approach to the client, or adjusting their approach within session. Questions that address identifying unique outcomes may include:

- I can see you were trying to do something different with your client at that moment. Can you give me an example of something you have done in the past—a specific intervention—that you think may be useful at this time?
- How did you do that? How did you know what to say to that client?
- You had not done that previously with this client. What cues or beliefs about helping were triggered in you at that moment? What differences did you note in the interaction?
- What ways of relating to others have you found most helpful? In what ways does your interaction with this person illustrate that?
- In the past you have said _____, how did you manage not to say it to the client this time?

The third step in this process is called *establishing moral preferences* (Parry & Doan, 1994, p. 214). This step allows supervisees to engage in a personal exploration of their way of being with others and how their way of being affects their client. Supervisees are able to view or hear their interaction with the client and reflect on whether or not their belief about how to be is congruent with their responses and clinical choices. This is also an opportunity to focus on the intentionality of the supervisee. While the first two steps focus on the supervisees' desires and motivations surrounding being a helper and their beliefs about how to help and their effectiveness in moments of helping, this third step integrates the two and brings supervisees to integration of self as counselor. Questions to address this include:

- What are your hopes for how your clients experience themselves when they are with you?
- What is your vision for how you want to be with others in your role as therapist?

- What qualities would you like to have guide you in your relationship with your client?
- How are you making sense of your client's life? Are you hearing what they are telling you or are you making a different sense of it than they are? What do you need to understand about them—experiences and views—that will help you see them through their eyes? What factors do you need to understand about yourself?

While this list is far from comprehensive, it is designed to facilitate creative thinking about the process involved in IPR and how utilizing supervisees' narratives about self, their role as counselors, and their experiences and beliefs about helping impact their interaction with clients and their developing identities as professional counselors. It is offered primarily to begin guiding supervisor intentionality. The use of a narrative approach to IPR is applicable not only with individual supervision, but also with group supervision, such as that in internship and practicum experiences. In the case of group supervision situations, however, it is suggested that during early phase or relationship-building periods, the supervisor take the lead in generating the questions and use a consistent line of questioning with each of the group members until trust and cohesion begins to develop. As the relationship begins to evolve, supervisors will notice the curiosity and intentionality that they model during the questioning process forms a template for continued group process.

## The Fourth Step of the Narrative IPR Model of Supervision

As mentioned previously, the three steps outlined in the narrative application of IPR are not fully comprehensive. They are only part of the story of supervisee identity development. Perhaps one of the most important aspects of using a narrative approach to supervision is not the final product, the altered narrative, but instead the process and experience just prior to the new narrative taking hold. Much like in the counseling relationship, many things happen within a supervisory relationship that go unnoticed. Pauses, hesitations, changing topics, and quick acceptance of feedback with little processing are things common to supervisees. But somewhere in that interaction lies the story, the growing edge. As we invite supervisees to reflect on their experience with the client and with self, it seems equally important to invite them to examine their experience within supervision by adding a reflective, IPR-based component to this model, inviting supervisees to acknowledge experiences in the supervision process itself and revisit them to create alternative endings.

This fourth step is based primarily on research studies conducted and discussed by Levitt and Rennie (2004) using taped sessions with clients and IPR. The use of these taped sessions and IPR with the clients involved in the session revealed some interesting patterns. Rennie (1994) found that clients engaged in two types of storytelling: authentic and inauthentic. An authentic use of storytelling involved the client's use of stories, not for the purpose of detracting from the problem, but because they really wanted to address the problem by using the stories as a means of getting there. An inauthentic use of storytelling in session emerged as a way for clients to avoid directly dealing with problems. Clients managed their level of disclosure, even at the expense of distortion, to protect necessary beliefs or levels of comfort. Through the use of IPR, clients were aware of how they used the story, and were able to reflect not only on the problem but also on the difficulty with dealing directly with the problem.

Similar to Rennie (1994), Levitt (2001a, 2001b) conducted IPR interviews with clients but focused instead on the use of productive and obstructive silences or pauses. Three types of productive pauses were identified: *emotional* (where clients attend to incipient and strong feeling); *expressive* (clients seek labels or symbols to represent their experience within the dialogue); and *reflective* (moments when connections and interpretations are made). Obstructive pauses, on the other hand, were consciously willed at times, particularly when the topic was perceived as dangerous to the client. Obstructive pauses prevent a deepening of awareness. At times avoidance was reported to occur automatically, seemingly without deliberation. Another type of pause includes interactional pauses. These occurred when the client switched from exploring personal issues to think about the experience with the therapist, whether he or she was confused about the therapist's instructions, worried about the therapist's experience or reactions, or protecting the therapeutic alliance.

Reflecting on the conclusions of Levitt and Rennie (2004), a fourth step in the Narrative IPR Model of Supervision is suggested. This step is called *privileging self in supervision* and involves audio or video tape review of supervision sessions in order to help supervisors and supervisees examine the role of story telling, pauses, and silences in the supervision interaction. In doing so, the goal is to enhance awareness of the interactional process and facilitate awareness of communication patterns that enhance or obstruct growth on the part of the supervisee and supervisor. Questions that may be asked include:

- What were you experiencing during that moment of silence? What were you able to learn about yourself or that interaction that allowed you to continue in the way you did?
- When you mentioned the topic of ____, you changed the subject to tell a story about another client. (Stop the tape just before the story begins.) What were you thinking at that moment? Or what do you

wish you had said? (Stopping the tape after the story.) What was the purpose of the story?
- When your peer gave you that feedback, you said thank you and quickly moved to a second question. (Stop the tape before the second question.) What were you experiencing in that moment?
- You seem to take a significant pause when you are asked a question by your peers. Talk about what that experience is like for you and how we can understand what you are experiencing in moments of inquiry.

It has been shown that clients not only will generate meaningful narratives, but also create powerful narratives of avoidance when directly addressing issues that may prove too threatening for themselves or the therapeutic alliance. The same phenomenon is likely in the supervisor–supervisee relationship. By engaging in this fourth step of narrative IPR supervision, both supervisor and supervisee open themselves to the meaning of story telling, pauses, and silences by becoming audience members to their own supervision process. This allows for a natural externalization of the process and a curiosity about the dynamic. Ultimately, this process may allow for an even more effective supervision relationship. And as with all the other steps discussed, this approach to supervision seems to present some curiously interesting possibilities for application in practicum and internship group supervision settings.

## Conclusion

Utilizing narrative therapy offers an array of opportunities for developing supervisors, particularly those who are seeking a more collaborative relationship with their supervisees and may prefer a more equal balance of power. In addition, its multicultural implications are significant. Narrative therapy, as introduced by White and Epson (1990), drew upon the work of Foucault who observed that, with the growth of capitalism, the human experience has become more and more defined by cultural definitions. That same notion of culture defining development is paralleled in the development of a therapist whose culture is defined in terms of professional, educational, theoretical or organizational expectations. And intertwined with all the cultural definitions, each supervisee brings to the table a set of personal hopes, motivations, and aspirations.

A substantial portion of this discussion on narrative therapy and IPR focused on the application of questioning. Monk (1996) cautioned that there is a tendency in narrative therapy to focus too heavily on asking the right questions resulting in potential failure to give enough energy to the therapeutic relationship. Thereby, the questions above should be seen as a tool for fostering the relationship, with the relationship always being at the forefront. Additionally, when using a narrative form of IPR in group supervision, such as a practicum or internship course, it can be beneficial to encourage students in the group to generate questions for the IPR process. Given the value of the lived experience in a narrative approach, peers of the supervisee may create questions that can closely touch the experience of the supervisee. And allowing students to become more integral parts of the process, thereby increasing their agency, helps foster the strength of their perceived role and identity in the supervision process. In the end, supervisors will create a stronger supervision team.

Very little research has been conducted on using a narrative approach to supervision. No empirical studies have been conducted at the time of this writing. And none have explored the notion of putting a narrative lens on an established supervision process. This is an area that offers much potential for future research and an opportunity to coauthor the development of future counseling professionals. Additionally, the work conducted by Levitt (2001a, 2001b) and Rennie (1994) provides interesting applications for counselor education, particularly for creative and meaningful new ways of structuring supervision during the clinical phase of counselor training. Providing students an opportunity to reflect on the role of silence, pauses, and their unique manner of storying creates not only a more powerful supervision process, but a greater awareness of how these aspects play out in the counselor and client relationship.

Herman (1998), who reported on his personal experience of being supervised by a supervisor employing a narrative approach, expressed hopefulness in the progress of his own narrative as it continued to develop through supervision. He simply stated, "I know the author well" (p. 104). It is exactly that sense of agency and ownership that the process of employing a narrative approach to supervision suggests is possible. And the net result is a supervisee who truly owns the process of becoming a therapist.

## References

Besley, A. C. (2002). Foucault and the turn to narrative therapy. *British Journal of Guidance and Counselling, 30*(2), 125–143.

Bernard, J. M., & Goodyear, R. K. (2004). *Fundamentals of clinical supervision* (3rd ed.). Boston: Pearson Allyn and Bacon.

Biever, J. L. (1995). Stories and solutions in psychotherapy with adolescents. *Adolescence, 30*(118), 491–499.

Borders, L. D., & Brown, L. L. (2005). *The new handbook of counseling supervision* (2nd ed.). Mahwah, NJ: Lawrence Erlbaum Assoc.

Botella, L., & Herrero, O. (2000). A relational constructivist approach to narrative therapy. *European Journal of Psychotherapy, Counselling & Health, 3*(3), 407–418.

Carlson, T. D., & Erickson, M. J. (2001). Honoring and privileging personal experience and knowledge: Ideas for a narrative therapy approach to the training and supervision of new therapists. *Contemporary Family Therapy, 23*(2), 199–220.

Cashwell, C. S. (2001). IPR: Recalling thoughts and feelings in supervision. *Reading for Child and Youth Care Workers, 33*, 1–4. (Retrieved on 9/18/2006 from http://www.cyc-net.org/cyc-online/cycol-1001-supervision.html)

Clarke, P. (1991) Interpersonal process recall in supervision. In G. Shipton, *Supervision of psychotherapy and counselling.* Buckingham, UK: Open University Press.

Gardner, C., & Turner, N. (2002). Spaces for voices: A narrative of teaching outside our disciplines. *Teaching in Higher Education, 7*(4), 457–471.

Herman, K. C. (1998). Composing and revising a counselor's narrative. *Counseling and Values, 42*(2) 101–105.

Levitt, H. (2001a). Clients' experiences of obstructive silence: Integrating conscious reports and analytic theories. *Journal of Contemporary Psychotherapy, 31*(4) 221–244.

Levitt, H. (2001b). The sounds of silence in psychotherapy: Clients' experiences of pausing. *Psychotherapy Research 11*(3), 295–309.

Levitt, H., & Rennie, D. (2004). Narrative activity: Clients' and therapists' intentions in the process of narration. In L. Angus, & J. McLeod, *The handbook of narrative and psychotherapy: Practice, theory, and research.* Thousand Oaks, CA: Sage.

McLeod, J. (1996). The emerging narrative approach to counseling and psychotherapy. *British Journal of Guidance and Counselling, 24*(2), 173–184.

Parry, A., & Doan, R. (1994). *Story re-visions: Narrative therapy in the post-modern world.* New York: Guilford Press.

Rennie, D. L. (1994). Storytelling psychotherapy: The client's subjective experience. *Psychotherapy, 31*, 234–243.

Richert, A. J. (2003). Living stories, telling stories, changing stories: Experiential use of the relationship in narrative therapy. *Journal of Psychotherapy Integration, 13*(2), 186–210.

Semmler, P. L., & Williams, C. B. (2000). Narrative therapy: A storied context for multicultural counseling. *Journal of Multicultural Counseling and Development, 28*(1), 51–62.

Speedy, J. (2000). Consulting with gargoyles: Applying narrative ideas and practices in counseling supervision. *European Journal of Psychotherapy, Counselling & Health, 3*(3), 419–431.

White, M., & Epston, D. (1990). *Narrative means to therapeutic ends.* New York: Morton.

CHAPTER **10**

# On Becoming an Emotionally Intelligent Counseling Supervisor

JOSEPH B. COOPER and KOK-MUN NG

Emotions have long been the province of counseling and psychotherapy. From Freud through Perls to the current models of attachment theory (Pistole & Watkins, 1995) and emotionally focused therapy (Johnson, 2004), emotional exploration and processing skills have been central to these psychotherapeutic models. However, the case is quit different when it comes to counseling supervision which has been primarily perceived as a supportive, educative, and learning collaboration between two or more individuals (Bernard & Goodyear, 2004). Though the covert and overt emotional experiences of the supervisory dyad have been perceived to be important in the formation of the supervisory working alliance (Bordin, 1983) and anxiety has been singled out to be a common emotional experience among supervisees (James, Allen, & Collerton, 2004; Ronnestad & Skovholt, 2003), only few supervision models factor in a significant role of emotion (e.g., Holloway, 1995; Ronnestad & Skovholt, 2003; Schuman & Fulop, 1989).

Emotions represent a complex system of cognitive and behavioral responses that serve to orient individuals to the specific issues that are important and in need of attention, and aid them in the grounding of new learning. They also serve to promote the development and maintenance of the empathic bond between participants in a relationship (Siegel, 2007). As such, we believe emotional awareness and regulation play a key role in counseling supervision by providing supervisors and supervisees access to adaptive information they can use to navigate through the often difficult terrain of the supervisory process. It is our belief that effective counseling supervisors are emotionally intelligent individuals who use their emotional intelligence to create a supervision environment that fosters supervisee personal and professional growth that ultimately benefits clients. In this chapter we will (a) review the literature on the roles and functions of emotions in general and counseling supervision in particular, (b) examine the current research on emotional intelligence and explicate its implications for counseling supervision, and (c) delineate some characteristics of an emotionally intelligent supervisor. We will also propose research directions for increasing greater understanding of emotional intelligence in the theory and practice of counseling supervision.

## Emotions: Definition and Functions

What are emotions and why do we have them? Do they serve a purpose, or are they evolutionary relics that we simply have not been able to shed? It is important to address these questions about the purpose and function of emotion, because by doing so, we believe this will highlight the crucial role emotions play in human relationships as well as to encourage thoughtful reflection about how emotional intelligence is critical to enhancing the quality of supervision. Broadly, emotions can be regarded as behavior controlled by distinct brain systems shaped by natural selection and seen as constructed from cues, whether the cues are interpersonal, environmental, or intrapsychic (Matthews, Zeidner, & Roberts, 2002). From a neurobiological perspective, the emotional system is hypothesized to be a mechanism for computing the affective significance of stimuli (LeDoux, 1989). From a psychological perspective, emotions are related to information processing mechanisms for self-regulation (Matthews et al., 2002) and are subjective experiences embedded in the outcome of appraisal, or the awareness of situational meaning structure (Frijda, 1988).

Emotion researchers are generally in accord on the functions of emotions, assigning them to four broad, and sometimes overlapping, areas of purpose: (a) Emotions serve an adaptive and survival function, (b) emotions provide the organism with a value system for the appraisal of meaning, (c) emotions perform an organizing and integrating function, and (d) emotions carry out a social-commutative function. The following will provide a brief overview of each of these functions.

Drawing on the theories of Darwin, proponents of evolutionary psychology view emotions as the product of natural selection whose purpose is to ensure the survival of the species (Gross, 1999). How do emotions contribute to our adaption and survival? Siegel (1999) proposes that emotions are adaptive because they represent a value system for the appraisal of meaning, which allows the organism to determine if external or internal stimuli are useful, neutral, or harmful. In turn, this emotional processing prepares the brain and the rest of the body for action. Emotions tell us *to do* something. Siegel contends that emotions serve an adaptive and survival function by alerting one to stimulus that can be potentially dangerous, and encouraging proximity to stimuli that are deemed to be safe.

Johnson (2004) and Compi (1999) also regard emotions as adaptive. However, they further understand emotions as a higher level information processing system that integrates physiological responses, meaning schemes, and action tendencies to provide feedback about the environment and the personal significance of events. Emotions provide all incoming stimuli with meaning and motivational direction, and function to create state-dependent memory regarding such stimuli. Within the brain, emotions link various systems together to form a state of mind. Indeed, Damasio (1999) has proposed that feeling is the original pathway by which human consciousness came into being. As humans encounter objects in the environment, these experiences are encoded in the form of feelings that represent the effect the object has on the human body state. From this, humans accord meaning and value to external objects, which is then translated into specific responses aimed at keeping us alive and healthy.

Another function of emotions is to aid in social communication. This social-functional model understands the expression of emotion as a form of social communication. From this perspective, emotions signal and orient one to socially relevant information that is considered to be of potential use for understanding how to engage successfully in interactions with others (Keltner & Kring, 1998). Emotions convey important information about people's thoughts, intentions, and social encounters. Because of this, paying close attention to other's emotion allows a person to perceive and experience elements of another person's mind (Siegel, 1999). This is not a new concept. The ability to experience and relate to another individual's emotional and cognitive state has also been referred to as mirroring (Kohut, 1971), reflective function (Knox, 2003), and empathy (Rogers, 1951), to name a few. Salovey and Mayer (1990) have proposed that empathy may be a central characteristic of emotional intelligence, because emotional appraisal and expression appear to be related to empathy. Obviously, this function of emotion has important implications for counseling supervisors and their capacity to develop a cohesive supervisory working alliance with their supervisees (Carifio & Hess, 1987).

## Emotions in Counseling and Supervision

### Emotions in Counseling

Emotions and emotion-related processes lie at the heart of counseling and psychotherapy. Though counseling theories and models tend to emphasize different aspects of emotional functioning, counselors and therapists have long concerned themselves with working with emotional experiences of their clients (Greenberg & Safran, 1989). The role of emotion in counseling and psychotherapy has been recognized as vital to the process of therapeutic change (Greenberg & Pascual-Leone, 2006).

The ability to accurately perceive clients' emotions, especially those that provide adaptive information, is of particular importance because therapeutic empathy requires counselors to be able to recognize both the quality and intensity of clients' emotional experience (Machado, Beutler, & Green, 1999). Also, counselors' ability to facilitate the identification of emotions and emotional awareness within clients enhances client learning and contributes to client change (Greenberg & Pascual-Leone, 2006). Greenberg and Safran (1989) suggested that for the purpose of intervention, there are at least four broad categories of emotional expressions which need to be distinguished: (a) adaptive primary emotion, (b) secondary emotion, (c) instrumental emotion, and (d) maladaptive primary emotion. The emphasis given to emotion identification and processing skills and other related techniques (e.g., reflection of feeling, personalization of feeling, and immediacy) in counselor training that are considered fundamental components of the therapeutic interview (Young, 2005) further underscores the importance of emotion in counseling.

Counselors' emotions and emotional well-being have been recognized as critical factors in the formation of the therapeutic alliance that has been deemed as one of the primary tools in counseling (Reilly, 2000). Researchers have found that counselor trainees experienced falling silent and emotionally withdrawing from the session in reaction to strong client affect as well as to their own strong affect (Melton, Nofzinger-Collins, Wynne, & Susman, 2005). Melton et al. recommended that counseling trainees be taught emotion management skills in order to prevent their emotional reactions from impeding their performance. On the one hand, counselors' emotional reactions can impede the counseling process; on the other hand, these emotions serve to provide functional information to the counseling process. Authors have argued that therapists' emotional responses in session provide relevant information, and better therapy will result if therapists remain sensitive to this information and utilize it in the process of planning and implementing therapy (Kimerling, Zeiss, & Zeiss, 2000).

*Emotion in Supervision*

Though there is extensive writing and research on the role of emotion in the counseling process, the relevance of emotion to the supervisory process has received much less attention (Follette & Batten, 2000). In this section we review the existing literature on emotion and counseling supervision.

Though there are many theories and models of supervision in counseling and related disciplines, "most tend to focus on methods rather than on the process of supervision" (Roberts, Winek, & Mulgrew, 1999, p. 291). With the exception of models based on experiential psychotherapies, existing supervision models do not include emotion-related variables as major theoretical components and practice focus. Even with the experiential supervision models, the focus is on the part of the therapist with respect to client change rather than emotion expressed within supervision (Follette & Batten, 2000; Greenberg & Safran, 1988).

In Gestalt therapy supervision, emotions can aid the supervisor in determining interventions and aid the trainee in understanding the client's dynamics. With awareness and present-centeredness, supervisors can use their own emotional reactions as the basis for appropriately chosen and effective interventions to help trainees learn how to recognize, understand, and express emotion. This, in turn, aids them to make genuine contact with clients in a manner that facilitates therapeutic work (Yonteff, 1997).

Wetchler (1998; 1999) adapted the principles of Emotionally Focused Therapy to the supervisory context. In this model, emotions in supervision are used to help identify repetitive therapist/client sequences and improve attachment with the trainee's client. Wetchler contends that therapists may become stuck in therapy by exhibiting secondary emotions through anger or frustration with a client. In this model, supervision can aid trainees in identifying and accessing their primary emotions toward their clients, which in turn will increase their bonding level, and subsequently their ability to hypothesize and intervene more effectively.

Cognitive-behavioral therapists have recently begun to discuss the role of emotion in the supervision context. Reilly (2000) stated that the role of cognitive therapy supervisors includes helping "trainees learn to identify their own automatic thoughts and emotions and teach them how to use this information productively in therapy" (p. 343). With the development of new approaches to treatment within the paradigm of cognitive-behavioral therapies that concern with acceptance, validation, and behavioral change (e.g., Functional Analytical Psychotherapy, Acceptance and Commitment Therapy, and Dialectical Behavioral Therapy) and have emotions occupying a central focus, Follette and Batten (2000) asserted that "training process should also address the student therapist's development with regard to emotion in therapy" (p. 306). Follette and Batten further argued that supervisors' willingness to be emotionally present and express their emotions in response to their students' struggle and pain as vulnerable healer can have a much more powerful influence on their students than lengthy, intellectualized discussions of the role of emotion in supervision.

Several studies have explored the emotional experiences of trainees within supervision. Schmidt (1979) examined the most common emotive reactions trainees experience towards their clients; anger, boredom, guilt, and anxiety. These emotional reactions could be a red flag indicating to supervisors that their trainees may be having difficulty with their clients. The function of supervisors is to help their trainees identify these emotive reactions, which, in Schmidt's model, are used to highlight the associated self-statements that interfere with the trainees' ability to do effective interventions. Supervisees' negative emotional reactions may also be related to supervisors' behavior. Gray, Ladany, Walker, and Ancis (2001) reported that supervisees attributed counterproductive events in supervision (i.e., hindering, unhelpful, or harmful events in relation to supervisees' growth as therapists) to their supervisors' dismissing their thoughts and feelings. These negative events weakened the supervisory working alliance.

In line with Ronnestad and Skovholt's (2003) study, James, Allen, and Collerton (2004) discovered the most frequent emotion experienced during supervision sessions by trainees was anxiety. James et al. suggested that movement from lower to higher levels of trainee competence often creates a degree of discomfort/and or anxiety. James et al. further recommended that supervisors graduate the learning steps, such that the level of anxiety is never so high as to become overwhelming, yet it increases in sufficient measure to foster learning.

Wester, Vogel, and Archer (2004) found that male supervisees with higher restricted emotionality responded to their lack of power within the supervisory relationship by using a turning-against-self psychological defense, and they reported lower levels of counseling self-efficacy. Supervisors are advised to be knowledgeable about gender role issues and understand how they impact male supervisees' emotional well-being and responses in supervision. Supervisors are further advised to be cognizant of countertransference feelings related to gender role issues in order to avoid letting these feelings impact their ability to understand the gender role-related experiences of their supervisees.

The supervision literature is beginning to discuss and document the role of emotion in supervision. Supervisees' emotional experiences in supervision impact their experiences and learning. Emotions play a very important role in supervision as they relate to supervisees' learning and growth and providing effective treatment to clients. These emotions include, but are not limited to (a) clients' emotions being discussed in supervision, (b) supervisees' emotional responses to their clients and the therapeutic process,

(c) supervisees' emotional responses to their supervisors and the supervisory process, and (d) supervisors' emotional responses to their supervisees and the supervisory process. Given such vital and extensive role emotions play in counseling and supervision, the absence of a theoretical framework in the counseling supervision literature to aid supervisors in understanding, managing, and utilizing emotions is surprising. We believe that the theory of emotional intelligence provides the heuristic to address the need.

## Emotional Intelligence and Supervision

Emotional intelligence (EI) may be viewed as a collection of emotional abilities that constitutes a form of intelligence that is different from either cognitive intelligence or IQ (Bechara, Tranel, & Damasio, 2000). Though EI has only received limited attention in the counseling literature, it has gained much interest from researchers and practitioners across disciplines since it was formally introduced in 1990 by Salovey and Mayer. The concept was popularized and received national attention in the mid 90s when Goleman (1995) published a book titled *Emotional Intelligence*. Since then, subsequent authors have also proposed their own models of EI, resulting in a number of different and sometimes conflicting conceptualizations of the construct (Tett, Fox, & Wang, 2005). However, for the purpose of this chapter, we will follow the definition put forth by Mayer and Salovey (1997) who first formulated a theory-based model of EI.

Essentially, Mayer and Salovey (1997) believed that emotions could be integrated into reasoning, and that the ability to do this facilitated adaptation and efficacy. They first defined EI as a set of interrelated skills used to monitor one's own and other's feelings and emotions, to discriminate among them, and to use this information to guide one's thinking and actions. They later revised their definition of EI by proposing the *regulation of emotion* as an additional skill, thus creating the current four-factor model of EI: *perceiving emotions, utilizing emotions, understanding emotions, and managing emotions.* According to these authors, EI represents:

> The ability to perceive accurately, appraise, and express emotion; the ability to access and/or generate feelings when they facilitate thought; the ability to understand emotions and emotional knowledge; and the ability to regulate emotions to promote emotional and intellectual growth. (p. 10)

It is important to note that the four branches of EI are organized in a hierarchical manner, with perception of emotions at the bottom and regulation of emotions at the top. The order of the branches represents the extent to which the ability is integrated within an individual's overall personality.

Within each branch there is a developmental progression of skills from the more basic to the more sophisticated (Mayer, Salovey, & Caruso, 2004).

In the first branch, EI represents the ability to accurately identify emotions in self and others. To be emotionally intelligent requires the ability to perceive the various ebb and flow of emotions one experiences on a daily basis and to accurately name those emotions. Although counselors are trained to perceive and work with clients' emotional states, they may find it difficult at times to correctly identify their own as well as their clients' emotional states. Individuals with higher EI are expected to be better at identifying emotions in self and in others. To be emotionally intelligent means to be emotionally self and other aware. Such awareness relates to empathy. In counseling training, trainees are taught to listen and follow verbal and nonverbal emotional cues of clients, and accurately identify and reflect them back to clients in attempt to aid clients in gaining awareness and processing the emotional information. Reflection of feeling is an example of a counseling skill related to this EI branch.

The second branch of EI is the ability to assimilate emotions in thought. This EI skill includes, (a) the ability to generate emotions that facilitate judgment, memory, and decision making, (b) the ability to use emotions to prioritize thinking or redirect attention to important events, and (c) the ability to utilize different emotions to encourage different ways one can approach problem solving. In essence, this branch represents the ability to use emotions to enhance our intelligence and help us make important decisions. For instance, a supervisor may perceive his supervisee as experiencing anxiety about a certain client, and this awareness of the supervisee's emotional reaction offers the supervisor important information on how to proceed in a way to maximize the supervisee's learning experience. With this awareness, the supervisor might decide that it would be best to focus on creating a safe environment by asking the supervisee to pause and take in few deep breaths and reflect on his anxiety before moving on to discussing specific interventions or conceptualization skills. This intervention would likely help to reduce the supervisee's anxiety level so that it will not interfere with his or her learning. Compare this to a supervisee who is feeling excited about his or her work with a client. All things being equal, emotionally intelligent supervisors would probably intervene much differently with the anxious supervisee than they would with the excited supervisee. Immediacy, compliments, and the miracle questions are counseling skills that exemplify this EI domain.

Being in tune with one's emotion does not imply blindly following one's emotional reactions, or "gut" feelings. However, we want to stress that to be emotionally intelligent means integrating both thinking and feeling to help make informed decisions. Thoughtful reflection on emotional cues aids us in determining if these feelings and their associated desires reflect our values of what is healthy and worthwhile.

The third branch, *understanding and analyzing emotions*, represents (a) the ability to differentiate and label complex feelings and emotions; (b) the ability to understand the causes of emotions; and (c) the ability to understand the relationships among emotions. In addition to accurately identifying emotions, this branch concerns the ability to correctly discriminate between the various *shades* of emotions. For instance, as my supervisee discusses a difficult case with me, is she experiencing anger or mild frustration? Is she feeling hopeless about this case, or is she feeling worried about the outcome? Or, is she experiencing all these emotions? How do I understand what may be causing these feelings? To be an emotionally intelligent supervisor requires one to pick up on the fine nuances of emotions and to correctly discriminate between them. We don't want to confuse rage with irritation or grief with despair, for instance. By doing so, we can model to our supervisees this ability to differentiate emotions, and they in turn can begin to use this skill in their own work with clients. Personalizing meaning and problem, reframing, interpretation, and advanced empathy are counseling skills reflecting ability in this EI domain.

Finally, the fourth branch of EI is *managing emotions*. This essentially includes the ability to stay open to our emotional experience and to regulate and alter the affective reactions of self and others. To pause and reflect upon our emotional experiences without blindly acting them out is one of the defining traits of being human. From infancy we learn to regulate our emotions. Babies will engage in thumb sucking behaviors in order to self-soothe, and adults, for example, will take deep breaths to help calm themselves in the face of anxiety (Greenberg, 2002). Yet, it is important to stress that this EI skill does not mean emotional suppression. We cannot control when and what emotions will arise, but we can control and regulate how we respond to those emotions (Malan & Coughlin Della Selva, 2006). Supervisors may not be able to control the experience of angry feelings in response to a supervisee, but they can regulate how they respond to those feelings. They may count to 10, use coping self-talk, or verbally express to the supervisee their feelings and reaction. Supervisors with higher levels of EI are able to access their inner resources and utilize appropriate techniques to regulate their emotions for the betterment of the supervisory relationship. Relaxation and mindfulness are skills that exemplify those in this EI domain.

The fourth EI branch also includes the ability to regulate emotion in others. Siegel (1999) has proposed that our understanding of emotions should take into account a more interpersonally oriented explanation of the genesis of emotion. According to Siegel, we need to begin thinking of emotion not so much as existing only within the individual, but that emotions are also created in a relationship between people. Siegel writes that "Emotion also reflects the essential way in which the mind emerges from the interface between neurophysiological processes and interpersonal relationships" (p. 131). Thus, in relationship, we can help regulate the emotions of others, which of course has long been the affair of psychotherapeutic work. And we unconsciously engage in such emotion-regulating activities with others on a regular basis. We may place a hand on a friend's shoulder to gesture concern as he or she discusses a difficult day; we may soften our voice and speak in soothing tones to a coworker who is upset; we may alter our body position toward someone who is angry, providing him or her with a safer "space" that is less threatening; and we may verbally reassure someone experiencing shame and guilt. Reflect back to our prior example of the supervisee who was experiencing anxiety about a client. The supervisor who recognized the supervisee's anxiety used EI skills to help regulate the anxiety by offering supportive and affirming empathic responses. Also note that this example illustrates the typical hierarchical sequence of the four branches of EI. The supervisor used the first branch of EI to accurately identify that the supervisee was indeed experiencing anxiety. With this identification of emotion, the supervisor was able to use the second branch of EI to facilitate making a judgment concerning how to proceed with the supervisee. In the third branch, the supervisor used EI skills to aid in better understanding the possible cause and consequence of the anxiety, and based on this information, was able to use EI skills in the final branch to help regulate the supervisee's anxiety to manageable levels.

*Trait Versus Ability EI*

As we noted earlier, since the publication of Salovey and Mayer's (1990) initial paper on EI, there have been several differing conceptualizations of EI in the literature (e.g., Bar-On, 2000; Goleman, 1995). Tett et al. (2005) divided these differing conceptualizations into two general categories: (a) *ability EI* and (b) *trait EI*. As an ability, EI represents a set of cognitive skills assessed via maximal performance measures in recognizing emotional information and using this information to carry out abstract reasoning and direct response strategies. Trait EI, or emotional self-efficacy, is a personality *trait* that encompasses emotion-related self-perceptions and dispositions, and is measured by self-report inventories (Petrides & Furnham, 2001). Trait EI refers to "a constellation of *behavioral dispositions* and *self-perceptions* concerning one's ability to recognize, process, and utilize emotion-laden information" (Petrides, Furnham, & Frederickson, 2004, p. 278). In other words, trait EI measures the *extent to which* one believes EI skills exist; whereas ability EI actually measures how well one uses those EI skills.

It is important to make this distinction between ability and trait EI, because many of the EI studies in the literature have only assessed for trait

EI, or individuals' *perception* of their proficiency in using EI. Although more research needs to be done on ability EI, what has been done has found trait EI to be predictive of such constructs as counselor empathy and the strength and quality of professional and interpersonal relationships (Brackett, Warner, & Bosco, 2005; Lopez et al., 2004; Schutte et al., 2001). Thus, a person's belief that he or she does have strong EI skills, or emotional self-efficacy will bear a positive impact on the quality and strength of that person's interpersonal relationships. This has important implications for the supervisory relationship.

*Emotional Intelligence in Personal and Professional Relationships*

Because empirical and theoretical literature on the role and function of EI in counseling supervision is limited, findings on the impact of EI in other types of relationships provide important points of reference for counseling supervisors to understand the potential utility of EI in counseling supervision. A number of studies have explored the effects of EI on both personal and professional relationships; and overall, these studies have found EI to be predictive of both the quality and strength of those relationships (Brackett, Mayer, & Warner, 2004; Lopez et al., 2004; Wong & Law, 2002). For example, in a series of studies that explored the influence of EI on interpersonal relationships, Schutte et al. (2001) found trait EI to be positively associated with such qualities as empathic concern, the ability to self-monitor, and marital satisfaction. Participants with higher EI scores desired more inclusion and more affection in their relationships, showed more cooperative responses toward their partners, and gave the highest satisfaction rating to their partners who were adept at recognizing and managing emotions in self *and* others.

Similar to the research findings on EI and interpersonal relationships, investigations into the influence of EI on professional relationships (e.g., manager/subordinate relationships) have also found a positive association. Several studies have found self-report EI to be predictive of conflict resolution skills among supervisors and staff, subordinate job performance, management effectiveness, and overall team cohesiveness (Jordan & Troth, 2002; Rahim et al., 2002; Rapisarda, 2002). Jordan and Troth (2002) found that employees' EI, specifically the ability to deal with emotions and the discussion and control of emotions, was positively related to the use of a collaborative conflict resolution style. Similarly, Rahim et al. (2002) found that the EI of the supervisors, specifically their self-awareness, self-regulation, empathy, and social skills, were positively associated with their subordinates' use of problem-solving strategies. These studies indicated that EI, specifically the management of emotions and self-awareness factors, can enhance the effective use of problem-solving and conflict resolution skills within professional relationships, and that managers' EI can have a positive impact on their subordinates' ability to effectively solve problems.

*EI in Counseling Research*

To date, limited research exists on EI and counseling and related fields. Existing findings support the relationship between EI and counseling skills self-efficacy. Martin, Easton, Wilson Takemoto, and Sullivan (2004) found that EI scores predicted counselor self-efficacy and differentiated noncounselors from both counseling students and professional counselors. In Phase II of their study, Easton, Martin, and Wilson (2008) reported findings that corroborated those in Phase I. They further found that two EI factors (i.e., *identifying own emotions* and *identifying other's emotions*) correlated significantly with most of the scales in the counseling self-efficacy measure. In a recent study that examined the relationship between counseling students' empathy and their level of EI, researchers found that EI explained a significant proportion of the variance in counselor empathy (Miville, Carlozzi, Gushue, Schara, & Ueda, 2006).

Because of the important role emotion plays in relationships, as well as the significance of the supervisory working alliance in contributing toward supervision effectiveness and satisfaction (Wheeler, 2002), Cooper and Ng (2008) investigated the relationships between supervisor and supervisee trait EI and perceived supervisory working alliance among 64 master's-level, community-setting, internship-supervisory dyads. They found that supervisees and supervisors with higher levels of trait EI tended to report higher levels of the supervisory working alliance. Their findings further revealed that the predictive strength of supervisor trait EI on the working alliance was much stronger for supervisors than for supervisees. Perhaps, more advanced practitioners (viz., supervisors) are (a) more self-aware of their emotional efficacy and are able to use their emotional skills to facilitate the development and maintenance of the working alliance, and/or (b) supervisors were able to use their advanced training and experience in supervision to help them foster working alliance with their supervisees, thus, leading to a stronger working alliance. Though preliminary, these findings suggest EI plays an important role in the development and maintenance of the working alliance in supervision.

## Application of EI to the Supervisory Process

*Identification of Emotions in Self and Others*

As discussed earlier in the chapter, one of the core components of EI is the identification of emotion in self and other. Counseling supervisors can use this skill to: (a) identify their own internal emotional responses to our supervisees, and (b) to help supervisees identify the emotions they experience in relationship to either their clients or their experience of the supervision process. What can supervisors gain by becoming aware of their emotional responses towards their supervisees? First, their emotional responses potentially provide them with important information regarding the state of their working alliance with their supervisees. Second, through parallel process, supervisors could be experiencing some of the feelings their supervisees experience toward their clients or their supervision sessions. Either way, paying attention to emotions can provide insights into important areas that may need further exploration and clarification. The following case example illustrates the process.

*Supervisor:* I have noticed a recurring feeling I keep experiencing throughout our session together today, and would like to share it with you, and I also would be interested in your take on this. (Use of relational immediacy in collaborative invitation and alliance building.)

*Trainee:* Sure, what is it?

*Supervisor:* As you were talking about this case, I noticed feeling distant and disconnected; it is subtle, but there. (Identifying the emotions.)

*Trainee:* Mmm ... you mean with me right now?

*Supervisor:* Well, yes with you, but also with the client's case you have been sharing as well.

*Trainee:* That is interesting, because I feel that way with this client sometimes in our sessions. Honestly, I get bored. She goes on and on, and I don't know what to do with her anymore.

*Supervisor:* So you are experiencing some of the same feelings with your client that we are now experiencing in our session together. I think it is important to look at this, because we don't want to continue this pattern; here or with your client. What do you think this feeling is trying to tell you? (Exploring how emotions provide important information about relationships.)

*Trainee:* Well, really, to be honest, it means that we are not connecting at all with each other—I mean with my client, and I guess with you today, too.

*Supervisor:* Right, I agree with you. What do you think this disconnect with your client is about?

*Trainee:* I guess in some ways it is how we avoid exploring what is hard to talk about ... . I think sometimes with my client we avoid dealing with the real issues, and so I just let her go on and on. But it's not helpful.

In this vignette, the supervisor, by paying close attention to her feelings (bored and disconnected) within the supervision session, was able to use this EI skill to form an intervention with her supervisee. However, when using this EI skill, it is important for the supervisor to first reflect upon the identified emotion and make an effort to understand the possible meaning of the emotion before intervening with supervisees. Supervisors need to make sure that the emotion does not stem from their blind spots or unresolved issues, and that it truly reflects the dynamic of the supervisory relationship. Care should be taken when addressing the topic with supervisees to avoid rupturing the supervisory working alliance.

## Using EI to Facilitate the Emotional Bond

One of the supervisor's primary tasks in early supervision is to establish a strong supervisory relationship with supervisees (Patton and Kivlighan, 1997). Bordin (1983) operationalized the supervisory relationship as the mutual agreement of the goals and tasks of supervision as well as the emotional bond (i.e., the mutual feeling of liking, caring, and trusting) between the supervisor and the supervisee. The case example below illustrates how EI skills can be used to strengthen the emotional bond with a supervisee who is displaying a number of "resistant" behaviors: missing supervision sessions, coming late to sessions, and arguing with the supervisor over interventions and theory.

*Supervisor:* I'd like to do something different today and focus on our relationship for some of the session. Is that ok with you?

*Trainee:* Sure.

*Supervisor:* I was thinking that in order to help me be most helpful to you, I would really like some feedback about how you have experienced our work together so far.

*Trainee:* Mmm ... it's been ok, pretty good, I guess. (Trainee gives vague response and frowns.)

*Supervisor:* You think it's "pretty good." I noticed when you said "pretty good," you frowned. Can you recall what your feeling was just then? (Use immediacy and confrontation skills to focus on nonverbal and associated feeling.)

*Trainee:* Mmm ... a little irritation I guess.

*Supervisor:* Ok. Could you tell me more about that feeling?

*Trainee:* Well, it's just ... sometimes I feel like you expect me to be perfect, and I get frustrated when you tell me what I ought to do with a client ... like I can't make any mistakes or don't have ideas of my own. (Trainee does not name any specific feelings, but offers thoughts associated with feelings of irritation about supervision.)

*Supervisor:* So you're feeling pressured from me to be a perfect counselor, and also feeling dismissed when I give you ideas to try or offer intervention suggestions. I understand, and personally have felt some tension, both within me and between us. (Personalizing supervisee's emotional experience. Self disclosing and naming the implied feelings.)

*Trainee:* Oh, yeah, I agree ... and you have definitely irritated me a few times! (Supervisee smiles.)

*Supervisor:* (Choosing to strengthen the alliance.) You feel irritated when you experience me pressuring you to perform and dismissing you. I want to assure you that it's never my intent to cause to dismiss you. So my question now is: What would you like to be different about how we work together?

Here the supervisor explored the supervisee's feelings toward him (the supervisor) and his approach to the supervisee within supervision sessions. Once some of the feelings were identified and expressed, the supervisor used this emotional awareness to explore the nature of their misalliance and how they both could begin to repair the rupture in their relationship.

*Using EI Skills to Understand, Analyze, Assimilate, and Regulate Emotion in Self*

In the following example, the supervisee is having difficulty with a client who has been fairly inactive in therapy and has been missing some sessions as well. The supervisor begins to help the supervisee explore her feelings about the client (*identification, understanding, and regulation of emotions*) and then begins to look at how these feelings may be affecting the therapy relationship with her client. Finally, the supervisor uses the EI skill of *assimilating emotions into thought* to help the trainee begin to identify how she might intervene in new and different ways.

*Supervisee:* (Discussing her client.) I don't know, she seems to close up on me and has not done any of the homework I've given her, and she has missed the last session. I don't know what to do about it.

*Supervisor:* Right. Help me understand the feeling you have toward your client.

*Supervisee:* I feel like she needs to appreciate all the effort I am putting into helping her! (Supervisee confuses a thought for her feelings.)

*Supervisor:* Yes, you want her to appreciate your efforts to help, and when you say this to yourself—"she does not appreciate all the hard work I am doing—What do you feel toward her? (Supervisor reframed her initial statement as a thought, and continued mild pressure for her to identify the feelings.)

*Supervisee:* (pause) Mmm ... good question ... . I am not sure what I am feeling right now ...

*Supervisor:* Ok, let's try this. If you pay attention right now to your body— what do you notice physically as you think about your client and this issue you are having with her? (Helping trainee to develop awareness of how feelings have a physical counterpart, which aids in the identification and regulation of emotion.)

*Supervisee:* I feel tense, uptight.

*Supervisor:* If you were to give it a name, how might you name the emotion that is related to this physical experience?

*Supervisee:* Mm … I'd say nervousness and irritation. And, well … to be honest, I am also frustrated with her. It makes me angry that I feel like I am working harder than she is. I feel like I am wasting my time with her. (Here our trainee continues to differentiate her feelings, specifically anger and frustration from her anxiety, which aids in the regulation of emotion. She also seems to blame her client for causing her emotional reactions.)

*Supervisor:* Exactly, so in addition to the anxiety, you are also feeling quite angry toward your client. You don't want to work harder than she does. Let's take a moment to explore how these feelings have been affecting your work with her and how you can use these emotional responses to help you understand yourself and your client. (Affirming supervisee, naming specific feelings, and collaborative invitation to explore.)

*Supervisee:* (Pause) I would say I have been more curt and impatient, and tend to problem-solve with her. Give her suggestions and homework, stuff like that. I have noticed that when giving her advice she tends to shut down on me. Mm … I think she's probably not ready for my suggestions.

*Supervisor:* Right. What else might be happening?

*Supervisee:* Mm … wow, I think I've jumped the gun. What she needs from me is not advice.

*Supervisor:* Here are a couple things I'd like to suggest you to work on this week. First, consider what you can do when you notice yourself feeling tense, uptight, and irritated with your client. Second, consider what might be happening to your client? Is she really not ready to hear your suggestions or problem-solving? Then, think about what needs to happen so your relationship with your client can be different.

In this vignette, the supervisor helped the trainee to become aware of her feelings about her client and used this to explore how these feelings were in turn affecting her work. Through this process a number of important EI skills were used: *The identification of emotions* (anxiety and anger), *understanding, analyzing, and regulation of emotion* (differentiating shades of emotions, specifically anxiety from anger), and finally the supervisor began to use the skill of *assimilating emotions into thought* by encouraging her to explore how these feelings have affected her work with this client, and how she can use this awareness to examine how she might intervene differently next time.

## An Emotionally Intelligent Supervisor

Overall, research findings support the important role emotions play in supervision and counseling. In counseling, emotions bond the client and counselor in a therapeutic alliance. The counselor's ability to facilitate the identification of emotions and emotional awareness within the client enhances learning and contributes to client change (Carter, 2003; Heesacker & Bradley, 1997). Based on findings regarding EI in both professional and personal relationships, counseling supervisors can begin to conceptualize how they can use EI to accomplish two broad goals with their supervisees. First, they can help their supervisees identify and develop a greater awareness of emotions and emotional cues both within themselves and in their clients. With this awareness, supervisors can help their trainees use this information to enhance the quality of the services they render to their clients. Second, supervisors can use EI to aid in their own work with their supervisees; for instance, fostering the development of a sound supervisory working alliance, managing and repairing ruptures in the alliance as they occur, and assisting in determining the types of interventions to use to promote the development of supervisees' clinical skills and professional dispositions.

Based on current theoretical understanding and empirical research on emotions and EI in human relationship functioning in general, and in counseling, psychotherapy, and counseling training in particular, we posit that the theory of EI provides a heuristic to conceptualize the role and functions of emotions, as well as to organize and utilize the emotional experiences of the therapeutic triad (i.e., supervisors, supervisees, and clients) to promote growth and healing for members of the triad. As such, based on Mayer and Salovey's (1990) EI model, we offer the following hypotheses on the relationships between EI and supervision as starting points to begin the discourse in the counseling supervision literature. Supervisors with higher levels of EI have:

1. Higher levels of knowledge about the role and functions of emotions in human functioning (e.g., thoughts and behavior) in general, and in the context of supervision in particular.
2. Higher levels of skill in identifying emotions in themselves, their supervisees, and their supervisees' clients.
3. Greater ability to generate necessary emotions to facilitate their thought processes and behavior, as well as those of their supervisees, in order to achieve higher levels of supervisory working alliance and better supervision outcomes.

4. Higher levels of skill in utilizing emotional information in the context of supervision to promote supervisees learning about themselves as well as how to foster effective therapeutic working alliances with their clients.
5. More skill at managing their own and their supervisees' emotions in the context of supervision, thereby bringing about better supervision outcomes.
6. Greater levels of psychological well-being.
7. More skill at teaching and role-modeling to their supervisees how to assist their clients gain EI skills in order to achieve greater emotionally well-being.

In conclusion, what we have attempted in this chapter is to begin a conversation on emotions and EI in relation to counseling supervision because such discussion has been curiously missing in the counseling supervision literature. The field is wide open, though leadership and supervision literature in other disciplines have begun examining the role of EI in their work in recent decades. We recommend that supervision theorists and researchers further explore the role of emotion and the theory of EI in supervision. Future research should investigate personal characteristics and supervision skills of supervisors who have high levels of EI. Studies should also explore if interactive effect between supervisor and supervisee EI exists in relation to supervisory processes and outcomes. Future work should examine if what we have delineated above regarding EI in the context of supervision can be supported empirically. Studies should also investigate how cultural and diversity factors interact with EI in the context of supervision. Because extant EI studies in counseling on trait EI relied on self-report measures, future studies should also determine if ability EI is a better predictor of supervisory processes and outcomes than trait EI.

## References

Bar-On, R. (2000). Emotional and social intelligences: Insights from the emotional quotient inventory. In R. Bar-On and J. D. Parker (Eds.), *The handbook of emotional intelligence* (pp. 363–388). San-Francisco, CA: Jossey-Bass.

Bechara, A., Tranel, D., & Damasio, A. R. (2000). Poor judgment in spite of high intellect: Neurological evidence for emotional intelligence. In R. Bar-On and J. D. A. Parker (Eds.), *The handbook of emotional intelligence* (pp. 192–214). San Francisco, CA: Jossey-Bass.

Bernard, J. M., & Goodyear, R. K. (2004). *Fundamentals of clinical supervision.* Boston, MA: Pearson Education, Inc.

Bordin, E. S. (1983). A working alliance based model of supervision. *The Counseling Psychologist, 11*(1), 35–41.

Brackett, M. A., Mayer, J. D., & Warner, R. M. (2004). Emotional intelligence and its relation to everyday behavior. *Personality and Individual Differences, 36*, 1387–1402.

Brackett, M. A., Warner, R. M., & Bosco, J. S. (2005). Emotional intelligence and relationship quality among couples. *Personal Relationships, 12*, 197–212.

Carifio, M. S., & Hess, A. K. (1987). Who is the ideal supervisor? *Professional Psychology: Research and Practice, 18*, 244–250.

Carter, S. (2003). The nature of feelings and emotion-based learning within psychotherapy and counseling: Neuroscience is putting the heart back into emotion. *European Journal of Psychotherapy, Counselling, and Health, 6*(3), 25–241.

Compi, L. (1999). Affects as central organizing and integrating factors: A new psychosocial/biological model of the psyche. *British Journal of Psychiatry, 159*, 97–105.

Cooper, J. B., & Ng, K. M. (2008). Trait emotional intelligence and perceived supervisory working alliance of counseling trainees and their supervisors in agency settings. *Manuscript under review.*

Damasio, A. R. (1999). *The feeling of what happens: Body and emotion in the making of consciousness* (1st ed.). New York: Harcourt Brace.

Easton, C., Martin, W. E., & Wilson, S. (2008). Emotional intelligence and implications for counseling self-efficacy: Phase II. *Counselor Education and Supervision, 47*, 218–232.

Follette, V. M., & Batten, S. V. (2000). The role of emotion in psychotherapy supervision: A contextual behavioral analysis. *Cognitive and Behavioral practice, 7*, 306–312.

Frijda, N. H. (1988). The laws of emotion. *American Psychologist, 43*(5), 349–358.

Goleman, D. (1995). *Emotional Intelligence.* New York: Bantam.

Gray, L. A., Ladany, N., Walker, J. A., & Ancis, J. R. (2001). Psychotherapy trainees' experience of counterproductive events in supervision. *Journal of Counseling Psychology, 48*, 371–383.

Greenberg, L. S. (2002). *Emotion focused therapy: Coaching clients to work through their feelings.* Washington, DC: American Psychological Association.

Greenberg, L. S., & Pascual-Leone, A. (2006). Emotion in psychotherapy: A practice friendly review. *Journal of Clinical Psychology: In Session, 62*(5), 611–630.

Greenberg, L. S., & Safran, J. D. (1988). Training in experiential therapy. *Journal of Consulting and Clinical Psychology, 56*, 696–702.

Greenberg, L. S., & Safran, J. D. (1989). Emotion in psychotherapy. *American Psychologist, 44*, 19–29.

Gross, J. J. (1999). Emotion and emotion regulation. In L. A. Pervin. and O. P. John. (Eds.), *Handbook of Personality: Theory and Research* (pp. 525–552). New York: Guilford Press.

Heesacker, M., & Bradley, M. M. (1997). Beyond feelings: Psychotherapy and emotion. *The Counseling Psychologist, 25*(2), 201–219.

Holloway, E. L. (1995). *Clinical supervision: A systems approach.* Thousand Oaks, CA: Sage.

James, I. A., Allen, K., & Collerton, D. (2004). A post-hoc analysis of emotions in supervision: A new methodology for examine process features. *Behavioral and Cognitive Psychotherapy, 32*, 507–513.

Johnson, S. M. (2004). *The practice of emotionally focused couple therapy.* New York: Brunner-Routledge.

Jordan, J. J., & Troth, A. C. (2002). Emotional intelligence and conflict resolution: Implications for human resource development. *Advances in Developing Human Resources, 41,* 62–79.

Keltner, D., & Kring, A. M. (1998). Emotion, social function, and psychopathology. *Review of General Psychology, 2,* 320–342.

Kimerling, R. E., Zeiss, A. M., & Zeiss, R. A. (2000). Therapist emotional responses to patients: Building a learning-based language. *Cognitive and Behavioral practice, 7*(3), 312–321.

Knox, J. M. (2003). *Archetype, attachment, analysis.* New York: Brunner-Routledge.

Kohut, H. (1971). *The analysis of the self.* New York: International Universities Press.

LeDoux, J. (1989). Cognitive-emotional interactions in the brain. *Cognition and Emotion, 3,* 267–289.

Lopez, P. N., Brackett, M. A., Nezlek, J. B., Schutz, A., Sellin, I., & Salovey, P. (2004). Emotional intelligence and social interaction. *Personality and Social Psychology Bulletin, 30*(8), 1018–1034.

Machado, P. P., Beutler, L. E., & Green, R. G. (1999). Emotion recognition in psychotherapy: Impact of therapist level of experience and emotional awareness. *Journal of Clinical Psychology, 55,* 39–57.

Malan, D., & Coughlin Della Selva, P. (2006). *Lives transformed: A revolutionary method of dynamic psychotherapy.* London: Karnac.

Martin, W. E., Easton, C., Wilson, S., Takemoto, M., & Sullivan, S. (2004). Salience of emotional intelligence as a core characteristic of being a counselor. *Counselor Education and Supervision, 44*(1), 17–30.

Matthews, G., Zeidner, M., & Roberts, R. D. (2002). *Emotional intelligence: Science & myth.* Cambridge, MA: The MIT Press.

Mayer, J. D., & Salovey, P. (1997). What is emotional intelligence? In P. Salovey and D. Sluyter (Eds.), *Emotional development and emotional intelligence: Implications for educators* (pp. 3–31). New York: Basic Books.

Mayer, J. D., Salovey, P., & Caruso, D. R. (2004). Emotional intelligence: Theory, findings, and implications. *Psychological Inquiry, 15*(3), 197–215.

Melton, J. L., Nofzinger-Collins, D., Wynne, M. E., & Susman, M. (2005). Exploring the affective inner experiences of therapists in training: The qualitative interaction between session experience and session content. *Counselor Education and Supervision, 45,* 82–96.

Miville, M. L., Carlozzi, A. F., Gushue, G. V., Schara, S. L., & Ueda, M. (2006). Mental health counselor qualities for a diverse clientele: Linking empathy, universal-diverse orientation, and emotional intelligence. *Journal of Mental Health Counseling, 28*(2), 151–165.

Patton, M. J., & Kivlighan, D. M. (1997). Relevance of the supervisory alliance to the counseling alliance and to treatment adherence in counselor training. *Journal of Counseling Psychology, 44,* 108–115.

Petrides, K. V., & Furnham, A. (2001). Trait emotional intelligence: Psychometric investigation with reference to established trait taxonomies. *European Journal of Personality, 15,* 425–448.

Petrides, K. V., Furnham, A., & Frederickson, N. (2004). Emotional intelligence. *The Psychologist, 17*(10), 574–577.

Pistole, M. C., & Watkins, C. E. (1995). Attachment theory, counseling process, and supervision. *Counseling Psychologist, 23*(3), 457–478.

Rahim, M. A., Psenicka, C., Polychroniou, P., Zhao, J. H., Yu, C. S., & Chan, K. A. (2002). A model of emotional intelligence and conflict management strategies: A study in seven countries. *The International Journal of Organizational Analysis, 10*(4), 302–326.

Rapisarda, B. A. (2002). The impact of emotional intelligence on work team cohesiveness and performance. *The International Journal of Organizational Analysis, 10*(4), 363–379.

Reilly, C. E. (2000). The role of emotion in cognitive therapy, cognitive therapists, and supervision. *Cognitive and Behavioral Practice, 7,* 343–345.

Roberts, T. W., Winek, J., & Mulgrew, J. (1999). A systems/dialectical model of supervision: A symbolic process. *Contemporary Family Therapy, 21,* 291–302.

Rogers, C. R. (1951). *Client-centered therapy.* Boston, MA: The Riverside Press.

Ronnestad, M. H., & Skovholt, T. M. (2003). The journal of the counselor and therapist: Research findings and perspectives on professional development. *Journal of Career Development, 30,* 5–44.

Salovey, P., & Mayer, J. D. (1990). Emotional intelligence. *Imagination, cognition, and personality, 9*(3), 185–211.

Schmidt, J. P. (1979). Psychotherapy supervision: A cognitive-behavioral model. *Professional Psychology, 10*(3), 278–284.

Schuman, E. P., & Fulop, G. (1989). Experiential group supervision. *Group Analysis, 22*(4), 387–396.

Schutte, N. S., Malouff, J. M., Bobik, C., Coston, T. D., Greeson, C., Jedlicka, C. et al. (2001). Emotional Intelligence and interpersonal relations. *The Journal of Social Psychology, 14*(4), 523–536.

Siegel, D. J. (1999). *The developing mind: How relationships and the brain interact to shape who we are.* New York: Guilford Press.

Siegel, D. J. (2007). *The Mindful Brain: Reflection and attunement in the cultivation of well-being.* New York: W. W. Norton.

Tett, R. P., Fox, K. E., & Wang, A. (2005). Development and validation of a self-report measure of emotional intelligence as a multidimensional trait domain. *Personality and Social Psychology Bulletin, 31*(7), 859–888.

Wester, S. R., Vogel, D. L., & Archer, J. (2004). Male restricted emotionality and counseling supervision. *Journal of Counseling and Development, 82,* 91–98.

Wetchler, J. L. (1998). The role of primary emotion in family therapy supervision. *Journal of Systemic Therapies, 17*(3), 71–80.

Wetchler, J. L. (1999). Integrating primary emotion into family therapy supervision. *Journal of Family Psychotherapy, 10*(4), 71–76.

Wheeler, S. (2002). A review of supervisor training in the U.K. In I. Flemming and L. Steen (Eds.), *Supervision and Clinical Psychology* (pp. 15–35). New York: Brunner-Routledge.

Wong, C. S., & Law, K. (2002). Development of an emotional intelligence instrument and an investigation of its relationship with leader and follower performance and attitudes. *Leadership Quarterly, 13,* 1–32.

Yonteff, G. (1997). Supervision from a gestalt perspective. In J. C. E. Watkins (Ed.), *Handbook of psychotherapy supervision* (pp. 147–163). New York: Wiley.

Young, M. E. (2005). *Learning the art of helping: Building blocks and techniques* (3rd ed.). Upper Saddle River, NJ: Pearson Education.

# Index